GLOBAL
ENVIRONMENTAL
POLITICS

DILEMMAS IN WORLD POLITICS

Series Editor

George A. Lopez, University of Notre Dame

Dilemmas in World Politics offers teachers and students of international relations a series of quality books on critical issues, trends, and regions in international politics. Each text examines a "real world" dilemma and is structured to cover the historical, theoretical, practical, and projected dimensions of its subject.

GLOBAL ENVIRONMENTAL POLITICS

Third Edition

Gareth Porter,
Janet Welsh Brown,
and Pamela S. Chasek

Westview Press
A Member of the Perseus Books Group

Dilemmas in World Politics

Copyright © 2000 by Westview Press, A Member of the Perseus Books Group

Published in 2000 in the United States of America by Westview Press, 5500 Central Avenue, Boulder, Colorado 80301-2877, and in the United Kingdom by Westview Press, 12 Hid's Copse Road, Cumnor Hill, Oxford OX2 9JJ

Visit us on the World Wide Web at www.westviewpress.com

Library of Congress Cataloging-in-Publication Data
Porter, Gareth, 1942–
    Global environmental politics/by Gareth Porter, Janet Welsh Brown, Pamela S. Chasek.—
3rd ed.
        p. cm—(Dilemmas in world politics)
    Includes bibliographical references and index.
    ISBN 0-8133-6845-6
    1. Environmental policy. I. Brown, Janet Welsh. II. Chasek, Pamela S., 1961-
III.Title. IV. Series

GE170 P67 2000
363-7'056—dc21   00-040805

The paper used in this publication meets the requirements of the American National Standard for Permanence of Paper for Printed Library Materials Z39.48-1984.

10   9   8   7   6   5   4   3

Contents

□　□　□

Illustrations

□   □   □

Acknowledgments

This book has been made possible by the inspiration, encouragement, and assistance of many colleagues. The series editor, George Lopez, had the clarity of mind to think of including a book on this topic in the series.

In addition to all of our colleagues who were thanked in earlier editions of this book, we are grateful to the following colleagues for their insights and documentation: Stas Burgiel, Chad Carpenter, Aaron Cosbey, Adam Vai Delaney, Charlotte de Fontaubert, Felix Dodds, Peter Haas, Calestous Juma, Jonathan Krueger, Rachel Kyte, Jag Maini, Bill Mankin, Richard Parker, David Schorr, Jim Sniffen, Andrey Vasilyev, Durwood Zaelke, and the staff of the *Earth Negotiations Bulletin*.

Finally, Pamela Chasek would like to thank in particular her husband, "Kimo," and her sons, Sam and Kai, for having had to put up with the distractions that have accompanied this project over the past two years.

Gareth Porter
Janet Welsh Brown
Pamela Chasek

Acronyms

ACP	Africa, the Caribbean, and the Pacific
AGBM	Ad Hoc Group on the Berlin Mandate
AID	Agency for International Development (U.S.)
AOSIS	Alliance of Small Island States
APEC	Asia-Pacific Economic Cooperation
ASOC	Antarctic and Southern Oceans Coalition
ATCPs	Antarctic Treaty Consultative Parties
BCSD	Business Council on Sustainable Development
CAFE	Corporate Average Fuel Economy standards (U.S.)
CANZ	Canada, Australia, and New Zealand
CBD	Convention on Biological Diversity
CCAD	Central American Commission on Environment and Development
CCAMLR	Convention on the Conservation of Antarctic Marine Living Resources
CDM	Clean Development Mechanism
CFCs	chlorofluorocarbons
CI	Conservation International
CITES	Convention on International Trade in Endangered Species
COFI	Committee on Fisheries (FAO)
COICA	Coordinadora de Organizaciones Indigenas de la Cuenca Amazonica (Coordinating Council of Indigenous Organizations of the Amazon Basin)
COP	conference of the parties
CRAMRA	Convention on the Regulation of Antarctic Mineral Resources Activities
CSD	Commission on Sustainable Development
CTE	Committee on Trade and Environment (of the World Trade Organization)
EC	European Community
ECE	Economic Commission for Europe

ECLAC	Economic Commission for Latin America and the Caribbean
ECOSOC	Economic and Social Council (UN)
EDF	Environmental Defense
EEB	European Environmental Bureau
EEC	European Economic Community
EEZs	exclusive economic zones
ENRIN	Environment and Natural Resources Information Networking
EPA	Environmental Protection Agency (U.S.)
ETMs	environmental trade measures
EU	European Union
FAO	Food and Agriculture Organization (UN)
FCCC	Framework Convention on Climate Change
FIELD	Foundation for International Environmental Law and Development
FOE	Friends of the Earth (U.S.)
FOEI	Friends of the Earth International
FRG	Federal Republic of Germany
FSC	Forest Stewardship Council
G-7	Group of Seven
G-77	Group of 77
GATT	General Agreement on Tariffs and Trade
GCIP	Global Climate Information Project
GDP	gross domestic product
GEF	Global Environment Facility
GHG	greenhouse gases
GMOs	genetically modified organisms
GNP	gross national product
GRID	Global Resource Information Database
GWP	gross world product
HCFCs	hydrochlorofluorocarbons
HFCs	hydrofluorocarbons
HIPC	Heavily Indebted Poor Countries
IADB	Inter-American Development Bank
IAEA	International Atomic Energy Agency
IBA	Industrial Biotechnology Association
ICC	International Chamber of Commerce
ICREAs	international commodity-related environmental agreements
ICS	International Chamber of Shipping
ICTSD	International Centre for Trade and Sustainable Development

IDB	Inter-American Development Bank
IFF	Intergovernmental Forum on Forests (UN)
IFIs	international financial institutions
IGOs	international governmental organizations
IIED	International Institute for Environment and Development
IISD	International Institute for Sustainable Development
ILO	International Labor Organization
IMF	International Monetary Fund
IMO	International Maritime Organization
IMOF	Interim Multilateral (Ozone) Fund
INC	Intergovernmental Negotiating Committee
INGO	international nongovernmental organizations
IOs	international organizations
IPCC	Intergovernmental Panel on Climate Change
IPF	Intergovernmental Panel on Forests (UN)
IPM	integrated pest management
IPR	intellectual property rights
ISO	International Organization for Standardization
ITTA	International Tropical Timber Agreement
ITTO	International Tropical Timber Organization
IUCN	International Union for the Conservation of Nature
IWC	International Whaling Commission
JI	joint implementation
JUSCANZ	Japan, United States, Canada, Australia, and New Zealand
KENGO	Kenya Environmental Non-Governmental Organization
LMOs	living modified organisms
LRTAP	(Convention on) Long-Range Transboundary Air Pollution
MAI	Multilateral Agreement on Investment
MARPOL	International Convention for the Prevention of Pollution from Ships
MDBs	multilateral development banks
MEAs	multilateral environmental agreements
MMPA	Marine Mammal Protection Act (U.S.)
MOP	Meeting of the Parties
NAFO	Northwest Atlantic Fisheries Organization
NAFTA	North American Free Trade Agreement
NAM	Nonaligned Movement
NASA	National Aeronautics and Space Administration (U.S.)

NATO	North Atlantic Treaty Organization
NEPA	National Environmental Policy Act of 1969 (U.S.)
NGOs	nongovernmental organizations
NIEO	New International Economic Order
NOAA	National Oceanic and Atmospheric Administration (U.S.)
NRDC	Natural Resources Defense Council
NWF	National Wildlife Federation
OAS	Organization of American States
OAU	Organization of African Unity
ODA	official development assistance
ODS	ozone-depleting substances
OECD	Organization for Economic Cooperation and Development
OPEC	Organization of Petroleum Exporting Countries
ORNL	Oak Ridge National Laboratory
PACD	Plan of Action to Combat Desertification
PIC	prior informed consent
POPs	persistent organic pollutants
ppb	parts per billion
PPMs	processes and production methods
PrepComs	Preparatory Committee meetings of United Nations conferences
PVC	polyvinyl chloride
QELROs	quantified emission limitation and reduction objectives
RMP	Revised Management Procedure
SAR	Second Assessment Report (IPCC)
SEED	Sustainable Energy and Environment Division (UNDP)
SICA	System for the Central American Integration
SIDS	Small Island Developing States
SPREP	South Pacific Regional Environment Programme
TAED	Transatlantic Environment Dialogue
TBT	Agreement on Technical Barriers to Trade (GATT)
tce	tons of coal equivalent
TEDs	turtle excluder devices
TFAP	Tropical Forest Action Plan
TRAFFIC	Trade Records Analysis of Flora and Fauna in Commerce
TRIPs	Agreement on Trade-Related Aspects of Intellectual Property Rights
UNCED	United Nations Conference on Environment and Development

UNCLOS	United Nations Convention on the Law of the Sea
UNCSD	United Nations Commission on Sustainable Development
UNCTAD	United Nations Council on Trade and Development
UNDP	United Nations Development Programme
UNEP	United Nations Environment Programme
UNFPA	United Nations Population Fund
UNGA	United Nations General Assembly
UNGASS	United Nations General Assembly Special Session
UNICEF	United Nations Children's Fund
USDE	Unit for Sustainable Development and Environment
VOCs	volatile organic compounds
WALHI	Wahana Lingkungan Hidup (the Indonesian Environmental Forum)
WBCSD	World Business Council on Sustainable Development
WEDO	Women's Environment and Development Organization
WHO	World Health Organization
WICE	World Industry Council for the Environment
WMO	World Meteorological Organization
WRI	World Resources Institute
WTO	World Trade Organization
WWF	World Wildlife Fund (U.S.) or Worldwide Fund for Nature (international)

ONE

□ □ □

The Emergence of Global Environmental Politics

Until the 1980s, global environmental problems were regarded by major powers as minor issues that were marginal to their national interests and to international politics. But because of the rise of environmental movements in the industrialized countries and the appearance of well-publicized global environmental threats that could affect profoundly the welfare of all humankind—such as the depletion of the ozone layer, global temperature increases, and depletion of the world's fisheries—global environmental issues have assumed a new status in world politics. These issues are no longer viewed as merely scientific and technical issues but as intertwined with central issues in world politics: the international system of resource production and use, the liberalization of world trade, North-South relations, and even international conflict and internal social and political stability.

Growing international concern about the global environment is no historical accident. It is a belated response to the fact that the major components of the biosphere, including the atmosphere, the oceans, soil cover, the climate system, and the range of animal and plant species, have all been altered by the intensity of human exploitation of the earth's resources in the twentieth century. The by-products of economic growth—the burning of fossil fuels; the release of ozone-destroying chemicals; emissions of sulfur and nitrogen oxides; the production of toxic chemicals and other wastes and their introduction into the air, water, and soil; and the elimination of forest cover, among others—cause cumulative stresses on the physical environment that threaten human health and economic well-being. The costs of these activities to future generations will be much higher in both developing and highly industrialized countries than they are to the world's current population.

1

In the past two decades, scientific understanding of global environmental issues has increased enormously. The realization that environmental threats can have serious socioeconomic and human costs and that they cannot be solved by the unilateral decisions of states has given impetus in recent years to increased international cooperation to halt or reverse environmental degradation. That realization has also unleashed a new political force, a global environmental movement that undertakes increasingly effective transnational action on various issues. But in each case some states, and certain economic interests, have opposed strong international actions to reduce or eliminate activities that threaten the global environment.

The result is an intensifying struggle over global environmental issues. As global negotiations multiply on issues affecting a wide range of interests around the world, the stakes for all the participants in the struggle have continued to grow. As an introduction to global environmental politics, this chapter highlights the economic and environmental trends underlying the emergence of environmental politics as a major issue area, defines the scope of the issue area, and outlines some of its major characteristics. The chapter also traces some of the major intellectual currents and political developments that have contributed to the evolution of global environmental politics, including the 1992 United Nations Conference on Environment and Development (UNCED).

GLOBAL MACROTRENDS

The rise of global environmental politics can be understood only within the context of the major changes in the global environment resulting from the explosive growth of economic activity and population in the latter half of the twentieth century. Global economic, demographic, and environmental macrotrends do not reveal the differences between rich and poor countries or between social strata within countries. But these macrotrends do describe the gross physical changes driving global environmental politics.

It is not the total world population per se but total population multiplied by per capita consumption that is the measure of total potential stress on the global environment. The per capita gross world product (GWP)—the total of goods and services produced and consumed per person throughout the world—has been growing faster than world population for decades. Consumption of natural resources by modern industrial economies remains very high, in the range of 45 to 85 metric tons per person annually when all materials (including soil erosion, mining wastes, and other ancillary materials) are counted. It currently requires about 300 kilograms of natural resources to generate $100 of income in the world's most advanced economies. Given the size of these economies, this represents a truly massive scale of environmental alteration.[1]

The cumulative effect of resource-intensive production that is commonplace in developed countries is serious environmental harm. Specifically, this type of production often requires moving or processing large quantities of primary natural resources that do not end up being used in the final product. For example, fabricating automobiles and other metal-intensive products in Japan requires mining and processing a yearly per capita equivalent of about 14 metric tons of ore and minerals. Growing the food required to feed a single U.S. resident causes about 15 metric tons of soil erosion annually. In Germany, producing the energy used in a year requires removing and replacing more than 29 metric tons of coal overburden for each German citizen, quite apart from the fuel itself or the pollution caused by its combustion. These hidden material flows from mining, earth moving, erosion, and other sources, which together account for as much as 75 percent of the total materials that industrial economies use, are easy to ignore because they do not enter the economy as commodities bought and thus are not accounted for in a nation's gross domestic product. But they are quite important in terms of the total environmental impact of industrial activities, since they represent a truly massive scale of environmental alteration.[2]

But while environmental problems have been the starting point for many critiques of consumption in the West, globally, the growing gulf in consumption levels within and between countries is equally if not more alarming. Although the world has gone through a consumption explosion in recent decades with spending growing sixfold since 1950, the fruits have not been shared fairly. The world's richest countries make up only a fifth of global population but account for 45 percent of all meat consumption, 58 percent of total energy use, 84 percent of paper use, and 87 percent of vehicle ownership.[3] At the other end of the spectrum, the poorest fifth of the world's population—more than 1 billion people—still lack food, shelter, housing, water, sanitation, and access to electricity. Given these extremes, many consumption priorities appear consistently skewed in favor of private affluence and public squalor; for example, basic health care and nutrition for all would cost about $13 billion a year, whereas more than $17 billion is spent on pet food in Europe and the United States alone.[4]

Population growth worldwide also has a major impact on the environment. Global population doubled between 1950 and 1987 (from 2.5 billion to 5 billion) and reached the 6 billion mark in October 1999. The world population grew at 1.33 percent per year between 1995 and 2000, which is significantly less than the peak growth rate of 2.04 percent in 1965–1970 and less than the rate of 1.46 percent in 1990–1995. Projections of future population growth depend on assumptions about fertility trends, which will be affected strongly by actions undertaken in the coming years. If high-quality family planning information and services are readily available to all families who want them, however, world population could stabilize at as low as 7.3 billion around 2050, according to the United Nations Population Fund (UNFPA). However, without proper education and services, the population in 2050 could be as high as 10.7 billion. (See Figure 1.1.) Whereas the most significant increases to date in consumption have occurred in the most highly industrialized, richer countries, most of the population growth (97 percent in 1998) has been in the poorer, developing countries, with the fastest growth rates in the poorest countries.[5]

Population growth and consumption patterns contribute to environmental degradation at the global and national levels by increasing the stress on natural resources and vital support services, such as the ozone and climate systems. The increased numbers of people and their needs for refrigeration, transportation, and manufactured goods will have far-reaching implications for **climate change** and ozone depletion. And high

FIGURE 1.1   World Population Size: Past Estimates and Medium-, High-, and Low-Fertility Variants, 1950–2050

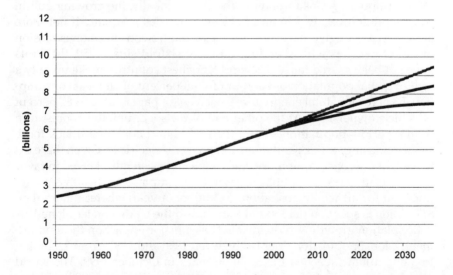

SOURCE: Population Division of the Department of Economic and Social Affairs of the United Nations Secretariat, *World Population Estimates and Projections: The 1998 Revision,* Briefing Packet, New York, 1998, mimeo: Figure 1.1.

population growth rates will have pronounced impacts on the natural resource bases of developing countries, especially with regard to agricultural land, forests, and fisheries.

Developing countries, with 80 percent of the world population, consume about one-third of the world's energy, a share that is expected to grow to about 40 percent by 2010 if present trends continue.[6] Current growth in world energy consumption in developing countries is driven by rapid industrial expansion and infrastructure improvement, high population growth and urbanization, and rising incomes that enable families to purchase energy-consuming appliances and cars.[7] If present trends in energy and fossil fuel consumption continue, by 2010 global energy consumption and carbon dioxide emissions will rise by almost 50 percent above 1993 levels.[8] (See Figure 1.2.) There is general agreement that further increases in energy efficiency in production processes will need to be combined with shifts in consumption patterns toward goods and services hat are inherently less energy- and resource-intensive if greenhouse gas emissions are to be stabilized.

FIGURE 1.2   Past and Projected Trends in Energy Demand, 1970–2010

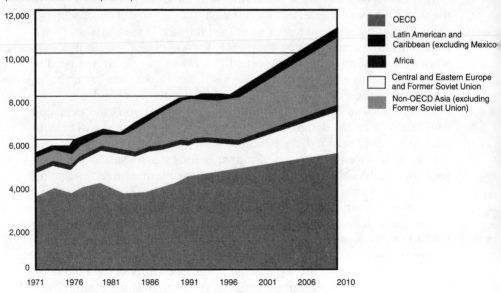

(million metric tons of oil equivalent)

Legend:
- OECD
- Latin American and Caribbean (excluding Mexico)
- Africa
- Central and Eastern Europe and Former Soviet Union
- Non-OECD Asia (excluding Former Soviet Union)

SOURCE: Reprinted with permission from the World Resources Institute, *World Resources 1998–99* (New York: Oxford University Press, 1998).

In some parts of the world the conversion of land to agricultural uses appears to have been positively correlated with population growth rates, even controlling for other factors such as agricultural trade and yield increases.[9] And as land becomes increasingly scarce, farmers are forced to turn to intensive agriculture, with dramatically higher levels of irrigation and chemicals, contributing to soil erosion, salinization, deteriorating water quality, and, in some cases, desertification. Population pressures on land, which result in increased migration of farmers to forested areas in search of cultivable land, is one of the major causes of tropical deforestation.[10]

Overall, the convergence of population growth, rising demand for lumber and fuelwood, and the conversion of forests to agriculture are putting increasing pressure on the world's forests. Deforestation, in turn, has led to the loss of the earth's **biodiversity** (variety of living things), encompassing both the mass extinction of species and the loss of genetic diversity within species, which is taking place at a historically unprecedented rate. Scientists began warning in the 1980s that one-fourth or even one-half of the earth's species could be lost over a few decades, largely because of the destruction of tropical forests, which hold an estimated 50 to 90 percent of all species. That would constitute the sixth great "spasm of extinction" in the earth's history; natural evolution took millions of years to recover from the five previous such episodes.[11]

The earth's biodiversity is not confined to the tropical forests. Many of the world's major fisheries are overfished or on the edge of collapse. Since the waters and biological resources of the high seas belong to no nation, it is perhaps not surprising that overfishing has become a serious problem. Sixty percent of the world's important fish stocks are "in urgent need of management" to rehabilitate them or keep them from being overfished, according to the Food and Agriculture Organization of the United Nations.[12] Staples such as tuna, swordfish, Atlantic salmon, and even cod could soon be on the danger list. The industries they support will be crippled. And inefficient fishing practices waste a high percentage of each year's catch. Twenty-seven million metric tons of "by-catch" (unintentionally caught fish, seabirds, sea turtles, marine mammals, and other ocean life) die every year as they are carelessly swept up and discarded by commercial fishing operations.

In addition to overfishing, the marine environment is under siege from land-based sources of marine pollution, which is believed to account for nearly 80 percent of the total pollution of the oceans. The major land-based pollutants are synthetic organic compounds; excess sedimentation from mining, deforestation, or agriculture; biological contaminants in sewage; and excessive nutrients from fertilizers and sewage.

The world's freshwater resources are also under serious stress. Global water consumption rose sixfold between 1900 and 1995—more than double the rate of population growth—and continues to grow rapidly as agricultural, industrial and domestic demand increases.[13] (See Figure 1.3.) A 1997 United Nations assessment of freshwater resources found that one-third of the world's population lives in countries experiencing moderate to high water stress.[14] The global water situation is expected to get considerably worse over the next 30 years without major improvements in the way water is allocated and used. The UN projects that the share of the world's population in countries undergoing moderate or high water stress could rise to two-thirds by 2025.[15] Population growth and socioeconomic development are driving the rapid increase in water demand, particularly in the industrial and household sectors. Agriculture still dominates water use, but its share is expected to decline.

Environmental quality in urban areas is also a major problem. The world's urban population is currently growing at four times the rate of the rural population.[16] Between 1990 and 2025, the number of people living in

FIGURE 1.3   Estimated Annual World Water Use, Total and by Sector, 1900–2000

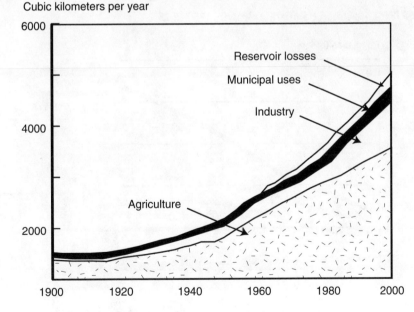

SOURCE: Sandra Postel, "Facing Water Scarcity," in Lester R. Brown et al., *State of the World, 1993* (New York: W.W. Norton, 1993), p. 23.

urban areas is projected to double to more than 5 billion; this would mean that almost two-thirds of the world's population will be living in towns and cities, implying both heavier pollution of water and air and a higher rate of consumption of natural resources. An estimated 90 percent of the increase will occur in developing countries.[17] (See Figure 1.4.) The current pace and scale of urbanization often strain the capacity of local and national governments to provide even the most basic services to urban residents. An estimated 25 to 50 percent of urban dwellers in developing countries live in impoverished slums and squatter settlements, with little or no access to fresh water, sanitation, or refuse collection.[18] In such situations, both environmental quality and human health and well-being are at risk.

These major changes in the global environment, which have resulted from intense economic development, population growth, and inefficient production and consumption patterns in the latter half of the twentieth century, are the forces that shape global environmental politics. Thus, with this as a backdrop, it is time to look at the issues and politics that revolve around natural resources and the environment.

FIGURE 1.4   Urban Population Growth, 1950–2025

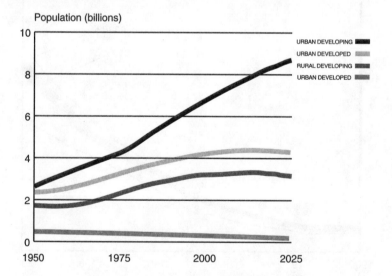

SOURCE: Reprinted with permission from the World Resources Institute, *World Resources 1998–99* (New York: Oxford University Press, 1998).

AN INTRODUCTION TO GLOBAL
ENVIRONMENTAL POLITICS

The scope of the issue area of global environmental politics is defined by two dimensions of any international environmental problem: the environmental consequences of the economic activity in question and the states and nonstate actors involved in the issue. If the consequences are global, or if the actors in the issue transcend a single region, we consider it a global environmental issue.[19]

There are many ways of looking at global environmental issues. Oran Young, for example, groups international environmental problems into four broad clusters: commons, shared natural resources, transboundary externalities, and linked issues.[20] The **commons** are the natural resources and vital life-support services that belong to all humankind rather than to any one country. These include Antarctica, the high seas, deep seabed minerals, the stratospheric ozone layer, the global climate system, and outer space. They may be geographically limited, as in the case of Antarctica, or global in scope, such as the ozone layer or the climate system. Shared natural resources are physical or biological systems that extend into or across the jurisdiction of two or more states. These include nonrenewable resources, such as pools of oil beneath the surface, renewable resources such as migratory species of animals, or complex ecosystems that transcend national boundaries, such as regional seas or river basins.

Young's concept of transboundary externalities refers to activities that occur wholly within the jurisdiction of individual states that produce results affecting the welfare of those residing in other jurisdictions.[21] Transboundary externalities include the consequences of environmental accidents such as Chernobyl and the loss of biological diversity caused by the destruction of tropical forests, measured in the potential for the development of new drugs. Linked issues refer to cases where efforts to deal with environmental concerns have unintended consequences affecting other regimes and vice versa. The most controversial of this type of issue is the link between efforts to protect the environment and to promote economic development within countries or trade between countries. For example, does the protection of the stratospheric ozone layer or the global climate system require developing countries to forgo the use of products or resources such as fossil fuels that have played key roles in the development of industrialized societies?[22]

All sectors of the international community are involved in addressing these clusters of global environmental issues. There are multilateral agreements aimed at reducing environmental threats. The policies and actions of various international institutions affecting the environment are an integral part of the issue area. The development-assistance agencies of large donor countries, United Nations agencies such as the United Nations Environment Programme (UNEP) and the Food and Agriculture Organization, multilateral financial institutions such as the World Bank and International Monetary Fund (IMF), and even the World Trade Organization (WTO) and the **General Agreement on Tariffs and Trade** (GATT) make decisions that have impacts on the environment. These institutions are the targets of lobbying and pressure by both states and nonstate actors, including nongovernmental organizations (NGOs) and multinational actors.

States have different combinations of internal economic and political forces that influence their policies toward environmental issues. The actual costs and risks of environmental degradation, moreover, are never distributed equally among all states, so some are less motivated than others to participate in international efforts to reduce environmental threats. Nor do states have the same perceptions of equitable solutions to environmental issues. Yet despite these disparate interests, states must strive for consensus, at least among those states that significantly contribute to and are significantly affected by a given environmental problem.

One of the distinctive features of global environmental politics is the importance of veto power. In every global environmental issue there is one state or a group of states whose cooperation is so essential to a successful agreement for coping with the problem that it has the potential to block strong international action. When such states oppose such an agreement or try to weaken it they become **veto** or **blocking states** and form **veto coalitions.**

On the issue of a whaling moratorium, for example, four states, led by Japan, accounted for three-fourths of the whaling catch worldwide, so they could make or break a global regime to save the whales. Similarly, the "Miami" group (consisting of Argentina, Australia, Canada, Chile, the United States, and Uruguay), as major grain exporters, blocked consensus on a Biosafety Protocol under the Convention on Biological Diversity in February 1999 for fear that the proposed provisions on trade in genetically modified crops would be too stringent and would hamper grain exports.[23] The role of veto coalitions is central to the dynamics of bargaining and negotiation in global environmental politics.

Because of the importance of veto power, even economically powerful states cannot count on being able to impose a global environmental agreement on much less powerful states if the latter are both strongly opposed to it and critical to the agreement's success. For example, the highly industrialized countries could not pressure Brazil, Indonesia, Malaysia, and other tropical forest countries to accept any binding agreement on the world's forests during the 1992 Earth Summit. Moreover, weaker states can use their veto power to demand compensation and other forms of favorable treatment in global environmental negotiations.

A second characteristic of global environmental politics is that the political dynamics of issues often reflect the roles of state actors in international trade in a particular product. The issue of international hazardous waste trading, for instance, is defined by the relationship between industrialized countries that are exporting the waste and developing countries that are potential importers. The issue of international trade in endangered species is defined by the roles of the developing countries that export illegal wildlife products and the major economies that import them. On tropical deforestation, trade relations between tropical timber exporters and consuming nations are critical to the dynamics of the issue.

In each of these issues, the roles and relative bargaining influences tend to be defined by a country's position in international trade in the product. In some cases, it is the producing-exporting countries that have the veto power; in others, it is the importing countries. In one case, tropical deforestation, both producers and importers have roughly equal veto power, and with few exceptions neither major exporting states nor major importing states have had any interest in limiting their trade in tropical timber.

But industrialized states and developing states do not have equal veto power over the outcomes of global environmental regimes. Although some developing states may have the ability to either prevent an agreement from being reached or to bargain for special treatment on some environmental issues, the major economic powers have the ability to wield veto power on most of the regimes they negotiate. Their wider veto power is related to the combination of their important economic role in production and consumption as well as their ability to deny funding for a regime if they oppose it.

A third characteristic of global environmental politics is that economic power can affect the positions of states and even the outcome of bargaining on international agreements in some circumstances, whereas military power does not constitute a useful asset for influencing such outcomes. The ability of a country to give or withhold economic benefits such as access to markets or economic assistance can persuade states dependent on those benefits to go along with that power's policy, provided that those benefits are more important than the issue at stake in the negotiations. Thus Japan and the Republic of Korea have accepted international agreements on drift-netting and whaling because they feared the loss of fishing benefits from the United States. And Japan succeeded in ensuring the support of some small nonwhaling nations for its prowhaling position by offering assistance to their fishing industries.

Military power has not had any impact on the outcome of negotiations on global environmental issues. Global environmental politics do not give rise to a **hegemonic power** in the traditional sense of a state with the ability to use military power to coerce other states into accepting the hegemon's position. There is no positive correlation between dominant military power and leadership on global environmental issues, and there may be a negative correlation between the two in that high levels of military spending divert financial resources from environmental issues. Moreover, it is almost universally accepted that global environmental threats can be successfully addressed only through the active cooperation of the key actors. Using military force to enforce an environmental agreement would be an impractical option even if it were politically acceptable.

The fourth characteristic of the politics surrounding global environmental issues is that the outcomes of multilateral bargaining processes usually result in cooperation to curb environmental threats, despite the obstacles of veto power and sovereignty. The overarching international political system within which global environmental issues are negotiated is a decentralized system in which sovereign states are free to act on their own definition of national interest. But during the past two decades ever larger numbers of states have been able to reach agreement to address global environmental problems, sometimes giving up significant freedom of action in the process. The ways in which sovereign states with divergent interests are able to act collectively is one of the major themes of this book.

The fifth characteristic of environmental politics is the importance of public opinion and nonprofit NGOs, especially environmental NGOs, which are both national and international in scope. Environmental issues, like human rights issues, have mobilized the active political interest of large numbers of citizens in key countries, inducing shifts in policy that helped turn the tide in a number of environmental issues. Public opinion, channeled through electoral politics and NGOs, has had a substantial, if not decisive, influence on the outcomes of global bargaining on whaling, Antarctic minerals, ozone depletion, and climate change. Public opinion has not played comparable roles in the security and economic issue areas, which tend to be much more heavily dominated by bureaucratic or economic elites.

INTERNATIONAL REGIMES
IN ENVIRONMENTAL POLITICS

The Concept of International Regimes

Understanding the nature of global environmental politics entails recognition of the importance of **international regimes.** The concept of international regime has been defined in two very different ways. According to the first definition, it is a set of norms, rules, or decisionmaking procedures, whether implicit or explicit, that produces some convergence in the actors' expectations in a particular issue area. In this broad definition, it may be applied to a wide range of international arrangements, from the coordination of monetary relations to superpower security relations. This way of conceiving regimes has been strongly criticized for including arrangements that are merely agreements to disagree and have no predictability or stability.[24] Although a set of norms or rules governing international behavior may exist in some issue areas in the absence of a formal international agreement, it is difficult to identify norms or rules in the global environmental area that are not defined by an explicit agreement.

The second definition of regime—and the one used in this book—is a system of norms and rules that are specified by a multilateral agreement among the relevant states to regulate national actions on a specific issue or set of interrelated issues. Thus, there are regimes for whaling, climate change, protection of endangered species, and the prevention of ozone depletion, to name a few. Regimes are always created and operated through the mechanism of multilateral negotiations. Negotiations take place when states consider the status quo unacceptable. Quite often states anticipate high costs, even crisis, if existing trends continue. Although it is in every state's interest to reach agreement on how to manage the problem, it is also in its interest to give up as little and gain as much as possible. Nevertheless, the expected value of the outcome to each state, and hence the total value of the outcome, must be positive, or there would be no incentive to engage in negotiations or to accept the outcome. In multilateral negotiations, all states must win (or be better off than with no agreement) or they will not come to agreement.[25]

Most regimes take the form of a binding agreement or legal instrument. On global environmental problems, the most common kind of legal instrument is the **convention,** which may contain all the binding obligations expected to be negotiated or may be followed by a more detailed legal instrument elaborating on its norms and rules. Because the members of international regimes, according to this definition, are states, the rules of the regime apply to the actions of states. However, the parties that actually engage in the activities governed by regimes are frequently private entities, such as multinational corporations, banks, fishing companies, or chemical companies. States participating in international regimes must therefore assume responsibility for ensuring that these entities comply with the norms and rules of the regime.[26]

If a convention is negotiated in anticipation of one or more later elaborating texts, it is called a **framework convention.** It is intended to establish a set of principles, norms, and goals and formal mechanisms for cooperation on the issue (including a regular conference of the parties, or

COP, to make policy and implementation decisions), rather than to impose major binding obligations on the parties. A framework convention is followed by the negotiation of one or more **protocols,** which spell out more specific obligations of the parties on the overall issue in question or on a narrower subissue. The negotiation of a framework convention and protocols may take several years, as they did in the cases of transboundary acid rain, ozone depletion, and climate change.

A nonbinding agreement could also be viewed as a regime to the extent that it establishes norms that influence state behavior. In global environmental politics, nonbinding codes of conduct and guidelines for global environmental problems such as land-based sources of marine pollution or forest management, which are referred to as **soft law,** could be considered regimes with varying degrees of effectiveness. And the Agenda 21 plan of action adopted at the 1992 Earth Summit also could be considered an "umbrella regime" for worldwide sustainable development, defining norms of behavior on a wide range of environment and development issues. Although such nonbinding agreements do influence state behavior to some extent, regimes based on legal instruments are usually far more effective. That is why some countries become dissatisfied with a given nonbinding code of conduct or other soft-law agreement and insist that it should be turned into a legally binding agreement.

An Overview of Global Environmental Regimes

Thus far, global environmental regimes have been negotiated on a wide variety of projects from whale protection to climate change to desertification. These regimes vary widely in their effectiveness, from weak to quite strong. The regime for whales grew out of the International Convention for the Regulation of Whaling (1946), which was not originally intended to be a regime for conserving whales but grew into a ban on whaling in 1985. The regime for marine oil pollution was originally the International Convention for the Prevention of Pollution of the Sea by Oil (1954), which was limited to a zone within 50 miles (80 kilometers) of the nearest coast, allowed significant deliberate oil spillage, and had no reliable system of enforcement.[27] It was so ineffective that it was replaced by the International Convention for the Prevention of Pollution from Ships (1973), also known as the MARPOL Convention, which limited oil discharges at sea, prohibited them in certain sensitive zones, and set minimum distances from land for discharge of various pollutants. It was so strongly opposed by shipping interests in crucial maritime states that it did not enter into force until a decade later.

The Convention on the Prevention of Marine Pollution by Dumping of Wastes and Other Matter, or London Convention (1972), established a regime to prohibit the dumping of some substances, including high-level radioactive wastes, and to require permits for others. It was the first marine-pollution agreement to accept the right of coastal states to enforce prohibitions against pollution. It became an important forum for negotiating further controls over ocean dumping.

Until the 1970s virtually all international treaties relating to wildlife conservation were lacking in binding legal commitments and were ineffective in protecting migratory birds and other species. The first global convention on wildlife conservation with both strong legal commitments and an enforcement mechanism was the Convention on International Trade in Endangered Species, or CITES (1973). It set up a system of trade sanctions and a worldwide reporting network to curb the traffic in endangered species, but it contained loopholes allowing states with interests in a particular species to opt out of the controls on it.

The original regime to regulate acid rain that crosses boundaries before falling was the Convention on Long-Range Transboundary Air Pollution (1979), a framework convention that did not commit the signatories to specific reductions in their emissions of the compounds. Later, however, the regime was strengthened by adding eight protocols that address long-term Financing of the Cooperative Programme for Monitoring and Evaluation of the Long-Range Transmission of Air Pollutants in Europe (1984), reduction of sulfur emissions (1985 and 1994), control of nitrogen oxides (1988), control of emissions of volatile organic compounds (1991), heavy metals (1998), persistent organic pollutants (1998), and abatement of acidification, eutrophication, and ground-level ozone (1999).

Similarly, the regime for the ozone layer was initially a framework convention, the Vienna Convention for the Protection of the Ozone Layer (1985), which did not commit the parties to reduce the consumption of ozone-depleting chemicals. The Montreal Protocol (1987) represented the first real step toward protecting the ozone layer by requiring reductions in the consumption of chlorofluorocarbons (CFCs). The regime was subsequently strengthened by a series of amendments, beginning in 1990, to include phasing out the use of CFCs and other ozone-depleting substances. The ozone-protection regime is considered the most effective of all global environmental regimes to date.

The agreement establishing a regime on transboundary shipments of hazardous wastes is the Basel Convention on the Control of Transboundary Movements of Hazardous Wastes and Their Disposal (1989), which does not prohibit the trade but establishes conditions on it. But dissatisfaction with the agreement on the part of developing countries, especially in Africa, resulted in an agreement by the parties to the Basel Convention on a complete ban on waste exports. The international regime for protection of the Antarctic environment, the Protocol on Environmental Protection to the Antarctic Treaty (1991), prohibits mining the Antarctic's mineral resources for at least 50 years.

The international regime on fisheries is composed of a number of different agreements. Key components include the 1995 United Nations Agreement for the Implementation of the Provisions of the United Nations Convention on the Law of the Sea of 10 December 1982 Relating to the Conservation and Management of Straddling Fish Stocks and Highly Migratory Fish Stocks, as well as two nonbinding agreements, the 1995 FAO Code of Conduct for Responsible Fisheries and the 1999 FAO International Plan of Action for the Management of Fishing Capacity.

A regime for biodiversity conservation was established with the signing of the Convention on Biological Diversity (1992). The biodiversity convention does not obligate signatories to any measurable conservation objectives, although it requires development of national strategies for conservation of biodiversity. The regime for climate change, the Framework Convention on Climate Change (1992), did not originally impose targets and timetables for emissions of greenhouse gases. However, with the adoption of the Kyoto Protocol (1997), parties agreed to reduce their overall emissions of six greenhouse gases by at least 5 percent below 1990 levels between 2008 and 2012. The International Convention to Combat Desertification (1994), establishing a regime for the problem of **desertification**, the destruction of formerly productive lands' biological potential, reducing them to desertlike conditions, calls for countries to draw up integrated national programs in consultation with local communities.

Theoretical Approaches to International Regimes

Several major theoretical approaches have been used to explain why international regimes come into existence and why they change.[28] These include the structural, game-theoretic, institutional bargaining, and epistemic communities approaches. Each of them may help to explain one or more international regimes, but each fails to account for all the regimes described and analyzed in this book. The structural or hegemonic power approach holds that the primary factor determining regime formation and change is the relative strength of the nation-state actors involved in a particular issue and that "stronger states in the issue system will dominate the weaker ones and determine the rules of the game."[29] This approach suggests that strong international regimes are a function of the existence of a hegemonic state that can exercise leadership over weaker states and that the absence of such a hegemonic state is likely to frustrate regime formation.

The structural approach can be viewed in two ways, one stressing coercive power, the other focusing on "public goods." In the coercive power variant, regimes are set up by hegemonic states that use their military and economic leverage over other states to bring them into regimes, as the United States did in setting up trade and monetary regimes in the period immediately after World War II.[30] The second variant views the same postwar regimes as the result of a hegemonic power adopting policies that create public goods, benefits open to all states who want to participate, such as export markets in the United States and the dollar as a stable currency for international payments.

● However useful the structural approach has been to explain the post–World War II global economic systems, it cannot explain why global environmental regimes have been negotiated. The international regimes negotiated since the 1980s, including environmental regimes, have come about despite the fact that the role of the United States, which had been the hegemon in the past, has been constrained by two factors: the rise of competing economic powers in Japan and Western Europe and, from 1981 to 1993, a U.S. ideological hostility toward international environmental regulation. The environmental regimes that have been successfully negotiated have depended on wide consensus among a number of states, not on imposition by the United States.[31]

● Another approach to regime creation is based on game theory and utilitarian models of bargaining. In game theory, bargaining situations are distinguished by the number of parties involved, the nature of the conflict (zero-sum or non-zero-sum), and an assumption that the actors are rational (they cannot pursue their own interests independently of the choices of other actors). This approach suggests that small groups of states or coalitions are more likely to be able to successfully negotiate an international regime than a large number because each player can more readily understand the bargaining strategies of other players. On the basis of this approach, Fen Osler Hampson analyzed the process of regime creation as an effort by a small coalition of states to form a regime by exercising leadership over a much larger number of national actors.[32]

Because of the importance of veto power in global environmental politics, however, relatively small groups of states are no more likely to be able to form regimes than much larger ones. If veto states are included among a small group, they will be just as prone to opposition as they would have been in a large group of states. If veto states are left outside the small group, they will still be in a position to frustrate regime formation when it is enlarged.

● A third approach, which has been called the institutional bargaining model of regime creation, hypothesizes that because states are ultimately concerned with protecting national security and maintaining economic growth, they may be incapable of adequately addressing the fundamental problems that have given rise to environmental issues. The international community's ability to preserve the quality of the planet for future generations depends on international cooperation, which, in turn, requires effective international institutions to guide international behavior. Under this approach, institutions can be defined as "persistent and connected sets of rules and practices that prescribe behavioral roles, constrain activity, and shape expectations."[33] They may take the form of bureaucratic organizations, regimes, or conventions.

The global environmental negotiations that have resulted in the formation of regimes suggest, however, that lack of clarity about the interests of the actors is seldom, if ever, the factor that makes regimes possible. As will be shown in Chapter 3, it is not imperfect information about the problems that give rise to environmental issues but other factors that have induced veto states to make concessions necessary to establish or strengthen regimes.

● The fourth approach is the epistemic communities model, which emphasizes international learning, primarily on the basis of scientific research on a given problem, as a factor influencing the evolution of regimes.[34] This approach, advanced specifically to explain both adherence to and compliance with the Mediterranean Action Plan, identifies intraelite shifts within and outside governments as the critical factor in the convergence of state policies in support of a stronger regime. The shifts empowered technical and scientific specialists allied with officials of international organizations. These elites thus formed transnational epistemic communities, that is, communities of experts sharing common values and approaches to policy problems.

The importance of scientific evidence and scientific expertise in the politics of some key global environmental issues cannot be ignored. Global warming and ozone depletion, involving threats that cannot always be detected, much less understood, without scientific research have been defined to an extent by the judgments of scientists. A significant degree of scientific consensus has sometimes been a minimum condition for serious international action on an issue. A 1985 agreement to reduce sulfur dioxide emissions by 30 percent of 1980 levels was made possible by mounting scientific evidence of the damaging effects on European forests. The impetus for an agreement to phase out CFCs in 1990 was scientific evidence that the ozone layer was much thinner than had previously been thought. The Kyoto Protocol to the Framework Convention on Climate Change was made possible, in part, by the Second Assessment Report of the Intergovernmental Panel on Climate Change (IPCC), which found that the earth's temperature had increased and that there is a "discernible human influence" on climate.

● But although scientific elites may play a supportive and enabling role in some environmental negotiations, on other issues they remain divided or even captured by particular government or private interests. And on some issues, such as the whaling ban, hazardous waste trade, the Antarctic, biodiversity loss, and ocean dumping of radioactive wastes, scientists have contributed little to regime formation and/or strengthening. In those cases, either scientific elites were not particularly influential in the policymaking process or some key actors explicitly rejected scientific findings as the basis for decision.[35]

The case studies presented in Chapter 3 suggest that theoretical approaches based solely on a **unitary actor model** (one suggesting that state actors can be treated as though they are a single entity with a single, internally consistent set of values and attitudes), ignoring the roles of domestic sociopolitical structures and processes, are likely to be poor bases for analyzing and predicting the outcomes of global environmental bargaining. Negotiating positions usually reflect domestic sociopolitical balances and may change dramatically because of a shift in those balances. Although the structure of an issue in terms of economic interests may indicate which states are most likely to join a veto coalition, it is often domestic political pressures and bargaining that tip the balance for or against regime creation or strengthening. A theoretical explanation for global environmental regime formation or change, therefore, must incorporate the variable of state actors' domestic politics.

A theoretical model of regime formation and strengthening, therefore, should link international political dynamics with domestic politics, viewing the whole as a "two-level game." While representatives of countries are maneuvering over the outcome of bargaining over regime issues, officials must also bargain with interest groups within their domestic political systems. Since the two processes often go on simultaneously, the two arenas influence each other and become part of the games going on at each level.[36]

A theoretical explanation for the formation of global environmental regimes must also leave room for the importance of the rules of the negotiating forum and the linkages between the negotiations on regimes and the wider relationships among the negotiating parties. The legal structure of the negotiating forum, the "rules of the game" regarding who may participate and how authoritative decisions are to be made, are particularly important when the negotiations take place within an already established treaty or organization. The cases of whaling and Antarctica both illustrate how these rules can be crucial determinants of the outcomes of the negotiations.

Economic and political ties among key state actors can also sway a veto state to compromise or defect. Particularly when the global environmental regime under negotiation does not involve issues that are central to the economy of the states who could block agreement, the formation or strengthening of a regime is sometimes made possible by the potential veto state's concern about how a veto would affect relations with states that are important for economic or political reasons.

Building a theoretical approach that accounts for actual historical patterns of regime formation and regime strengthening and that can predict most outcomes will require advancing a series of testable hypotheses encompassing multiple variables rather than relying on a single-variable approach. Until such explicit hypotheses are generated and tested, the study of regime formation in this book will focus primarily on identifying some common patterns through case studies, utilizing a phased process approach to the analysis of the negotiations that result in the establishment of environmental regimes.

PARADIGM SHIFT AND
ENVIRONMENTAL POLITICS

In any issue area, public policy is shaped not only by impersonal forces, such as technological innovation and economic growth, but also by people's, governments', and institutions' perception of reality. In times of relative social stability, there is a dominant social **paradigm,** a set of beliefs, ideas, and values from which public policies and whole systems of behavior flow logically. A view of the world emerges as the dominant social paradigm within a society because it has been the most useful way of thinking about and solving certain problems and is transmitted across social sectors and generations by various socialization processes. Every dominant paradigm is ultimately challenged, however, as its anomalies— the contradictions between its assumptions and observed reality—multiply and its usefulness wanes. Finally, it gives way to a new paradigm in a process called a paradigm shift.[37] The hypothesis that an alternative paradigm that is more sensitive to environmental realities may be on the rise provides a lens through which to view the issues discussed in the rest of this book.

The Dominant Social Paradigm

Because economic policy and environmental policy are so intertwined, the social paradigm that has dominated public understanding of environmental management during the period of rapid global economic growth has been essentially a system of beliefs about economics. It has been referred to as the **exclusionist paradigm** because it excludes human beings from the laws of nature. It has also been called *frontier economics*, suggesting the sense of unlimited resources that characterizes a societ open frontier.[38]

In capitalist societies this dominant social paradigm has been based primarily on the assumptions of **neoclassical economics:** first, that the free market will always maximize social welfare, and second, that there is an infinite supply not only of natural resources but also of "sinks" for disposing of the wastes from exploiting those resources—provided that the free market is operating. Humans will not deplete any resource, according to this worldview, as long as technology is given free rein and prices are allowed to fluctuate enough to stimulate the search for substitutes, so absolute scarcity can be postponed to the indefinite future.[39] Waste disposal is viewed as a problem to be cleaned up after the fact but not at the cost of interference with market decisions.[40] Because conventional economic theory is concerned only with the allocation of scarce resources, and nature is not considered a constraining factor, this paradigm considers the environment to be irrelevant to economics. (Despite a different economic and political ideology, the former Soviet Union and other communist states also shared this assumption.) The traditional legal principles of unrestricted freedom of the seas and open access to common resources such as the oceans and their living resources buttressed the exclusionist paradigm and weakened the impulse toward international cooperation for environmental protection.

Beginning in the early 1960s the dominant paradigm came under steadily mounting attack, starting in the United States, where the critique of the dominant paradigm was first articulated, and then spreading to Europe and other regions. The publication in 1962 of Rachel Carson's *Silent Spring*, which documented the dangers to human health from synthetic pesticides, was the beginning of an explosion in popular literature reflecting the new scientific knowledge about invisible threats to the environment: radiation, heavy metal toxic wastes, chlorinated hydrocarbons in the water, and others. Such research and writing helped raise awareness that public policies based on the exclusionist paradigm carry high costs to societies. The first mass movement for environmental protection, focused on domestic issues, began to develop in the United States. Parallel changes in public concern about air, soil, and water pollution also occurred in other noncommunist industrialized countries. One result of the burst of environmental activism in the United States was the passage of the National Environmental Policy Act of 1969 (NEPA), which directed federal agencies to support international cooperation in "anticipating and preventing a decline in the quality of mankind's world environment."[41]

As a result of a 1967 Swedish initiative supported by the United States, the first worldwide environmental conference in history, the

United Nations Conference on the Human Environment, was convened in Stockholm in 1972. The **Stockholm Conference,** attended by 114 states (not including the Soviet bloc states), approved a declaration containing 26 broad principles on the management of the global environment and an action plan, with 109 recommendations for international cooperation on the environment. On the recommendation of the conference, the UN General Assembly in December 1972 created the United Nations Environment Programme to provide a focal point for environmental action and coordination of environmentally related activities within the UN system.

The Rise of an Alternative Social Paradigm

The rapid rise of environmental consciousness and pressure groups in the 1960s and early 1970s was not yet accompanied by an alternative set of assumptions about both physical and social reality that could become a competing worldview. The essential assumptions of classical economics remained largely intact. Confronted with evidence that existing patterns of exploitation of resources could cause irreversible damage, proponents of classical economics continued to maintain that such exploitation was still economically rational.[42]

During the 1970s and 1980s, however, an alternative paradigm challenging the assumptions of frontier economics began to take shape. Two of the intellectual forerunners of this paradigm were the *Limits to Growth* study by the Club of Rome, published in 1972, and the *Global 2000 Report to the President* released by the U.S. Council of Environmental Quality and the Department of State in 1980.[43] Both studies applied global-systems computer modeling to the projected interactions among future trends in population, economic growth, and natural resources. They forecast the depletion of natural resources and the degradation of ecosystems. Because each of the studies suggested that economic development and population growth were on a path that would eventually strain the earth's "carrying capacity" (the total population that the earth's natural systems can support without undergoing degradation), the viewpoint underlying the studies was generally referred to as the limits-to-growth perspective.

These studies were widely criticized by defenders of the dominant paradigm, such as Herman Kahn and Julian Simon, for projecting the depletion of nonrenewable resources without taking into account technological changes and market responses. These critics argued that overpopulation would not become a problem because people are the world's "ultimate resource," and they characterized the authors of these studies that were based on global-systems models as "no-growth elitists" who would freeze the underdeveloped countries out of the benefits of economic growth.

They argued that human ingenuity would enable humanity to leap over the alleged limits to growth through new and better technologies.[44]

The development of an alternative paradigm regarding the world society and environment was set back in the United States in the early 1980s, as the Reagan administration enthusiastically embraced the exclusionist paradigm. But meanwhile, knowledge of ecological principles and their relationship to economic development issues were spreading across the globe, and the web of specialists on these linkages was thickening. A global community of practitioners and scholars was emerging, allied by the belief that economic policies based on the dominant paradigm had to be replaced by ecologically sound policies.

● By the early to mid-1980s, **sustainable development** was emerging as the catchword of an alternative paradigm. It was being heard with increasing frequency in conferences involving NGOs and government officials in the United States and abroad.[45] The publication in 1987 of *Our Common Future*, the Report of the World Commission on Environment and Development (better known as the Brundtland Report after the commission's chair, former Norwegian prime minister Gro Harlem Brundtland) popularized the term *sustainable development* and gave the new paradigm momentum in replacing the dominant paradigm.[46] Drawing on and synthesizing the views and research of hundreds of people across the globe, that report codified some of the central beliefs of the alternative paradigm.

●The Brundtland Report defined sustainable development as development that is "consistent with future as well as present needs." Its central themes criticized the dominant paradigm for failure to reconcile those needs. It asserted that the earth's natural systems have finite capabilities to support human production and consumption and that the continuation of existing economic policies risks irreversible damage to natural systems on which all life depends.

The sustainable development paradigm emphasizes the need to redefine the term *development*. It posits that economic growth cannot continue to take place at the expense of the earth's natural capital (its stock of renewable and nonrenewable resources) and vital natural support systems such as the ozone layer and climate system. Instead, the world economy must learn to live off its "interest." That means radically more efficient energy use, that is, reducing the amount of energy used per unit of gross national product and shifting from fossil fuels to greater reliance on renewable energy sources over the next several decades. It implies a rapid transition to sustainable systems of renewable natural resource management and stabilizing world population at the lowest possible level.[47] This viewpoint also suggests, although not always explicitly, the need to impose some limits on total worldwide consumption.

The sustainable development paradigm assumes the need for greater equity not only between wealthy and poor nations but also within societies and between generations (**intergenerational equity**). Highly industrialized countries such as the United States, which now use a disproportionate share of the world's environmental resources, are seen as pursuing economic growth that is inherently unsustainable, as are societies in which the distribution of land and other resources is grossly unequal. Sustainable development further holds that future generations have an equal right to use the planet's resources.[48] The paradigm recognizes that developing countries must meet the basic needs of the poor in ways that do not deplete the countries' natural resources, and it also points to a need to reexamine basic attitudes and values in industrialized countries regarding the unnecessary and wasteful aspects of their material abundance.[49]

One of the main anomalies of the classical economic paradigm is its measure of macroeconomic growth, that is, gross national product (GNP). Advocates of sustainable development have noted that GNP fails to reflect the real physical capability of an economy to provide material wealth in the future or to take into account the relative well-being of the society in general. Thus, a country could systematically deplete its natural resources, erode its soils, and pollute its waters without that loss of real wealth ever showing up in its income accounts. Because of the rise of the new paradigm, some economists began in the second half of the 1980s to study how to correct this anomaly in conventional accounting and to advocate **environmental accounting** in all governments and international organizations.[50] Critics have proposed alternatives to GNP, such as "real net national product," "sustainable social net national product," or "index of sustainable economic welfare," that include changes in environmental resources as well as other indicators that measure human welfare. Of particular importance is the United Nations Development Programme's (UNDP) annual *Human Development Report,* which uses "human indicators" to rate the quality of life in all countries by other than economic measures.[51]

The new paradigm points to the failure of markets to encourage the sustainable use of natural resources. Prices should reflect the real costs to society of producing and consuming a given resource, but conventional free-market economic policies systematically underprice or ignore natural resources.[52] Public policies that do not correct for such market failure encourage overconsumption and thus the more rapid depletion of renewable resources and the degradation of **environmental services.** (Environmental services are the conserving or restorative functions of nature, such ~rsion of carbon dioxide to oxygen by plants and the cleansing tlands.) Raising the prices of resources through taxation to make them reflect real social and environmental costs is the favored means of showing the rates of consumption of energy and tropical timber. Such **green taxes** are one tool by which the "polluter pays" principle, endorsed in the Earth Summit's Rio Declaration on Environment and Development, may be implemented. Placing an upper limit on consumption is another method.[53]

The process of paradigm shift began in the early 1990s. The sustainable development paradigm has begun to displace the exclusionist paradigm in some parts of the multilateral financial institutions, in some state bureaucracies, and in some parliamentary committees dealing with the environment and development. For instance, publications of the Asian Development Bank, the Inter-American Development Bank (IADB), and the Organization of American States (OAS) as early as 1990 impugned mistaken unsustainable development paths of the past and recommended new sustainable development strategies.[54] In the United States, in 1992 former senator and then vice president Al Gore, in his book, *Earth in the Balance*, was one of the proponents of a paradigm shift. Gore advocated a new kind of "*eco*-nomics," one that involves reorienting economic activity toward environmentally sensitive production and investment in future resources. He proposed a global Marshall Plan to stabilize population growth, develop and use "environmentally appropriate technologies," negotiate new international treaties, and increase education about global environmental issues.[55]

Nevertheless, within most of the powerful institutions in the United States and elsewhere in the industrialized world, the assumptions of the exclusionist paradigm still tend to dominate policymaking. Corporations, government ministries dealing with trade and finance, the leaders of some political parties, and some top officials of the World Bank and other multilateral institutions have been slow to change.

Governments and, more important, people, do not necessarily change their behavior even when they are aware of the seriousness of a potential threat. If there is increased public debate and education about the importance of environmentally sound development ,in conjunction with changes in economic and political power, it is possible that the paradigm shift will be accelerated. This proved to be the case during preparations for and culminating in the 1992 Earth Summit.

THE 1992 EARTH SUMMIT

The most important indication of a worldwide paradigm shift was the United Nations Conference on Environment and Development, held in Rio de Janeiro in June 1992, which was preceded by two years of discussions

UNCED, Rio, 1992. NGO representatives join hundreds of thousands who signed the Earth Pledge leading up the Earth Summit. (Photo by Charles V. Barber, World Resources Institute.)

on domestic environmental and poverty problems and global environment issues, especially questions of North-South inequities and responsibility. UNCED was a monumental effort by the international community to reach consensus on principles and a long-term work plan for global sustainable development. The conference, which came to be known as the Earth Summit, was the largest truly global summit meeting, drawing the participation of 110 heads of state, nearly 10,000 official delegates from 150 nations, and thousands of representatives of NGOs. Conceptually, its explicit focus on integrating environmental and development policies represented a major step forward from the Stockholm Conference on the Human Environment of 20 years earlier.

Stretching over two years, the negotiating process leading up to the Earth Summit included two planning meetings, four lengthy preparatory committee meetings (PrepComs), and one final negotiating session at the Rio conference itself. The major output of UNCED was a nonbinding agreement called Agenda 21 (referring to the twenty-first century), which is a global plan of action for more sustainable societies. Negotiations on Agenda 21 were the broadest and most complex international talks ever held. The 294-page comprehensive Agenda 21 encompassed every sectoral environmental issue as well as international policies affecting both environment and development, and the full range of domestic social and economic policies, all adding up to 38 chapters and 115 separate topics. The conference also produced two nonbinding sets of principles—the Rio Declaration on Environment and Development and the Statement of Forest Principles—that helped create norms and expectations. The climate and biodiversity conventions, which were negotiated independently of the UNCED process on parallel tracks, were opened for signature at the Earth Summit and are often mentioned as UNCED-related agreements.

Negotiations on Agenda 21 registered the state of international consensus on the full range of issues affecting the long-run sustainability of human society, including domestic social and economic policies, international economic relations, and cooperation on global commons issues. On domestic policies, the developing countries accepted the principles of citizen participation in sustainable development. In chapters on poverty, sustainable agriculture, desertification, and land degradation, provisions were adopted that call for decisionmaking on natural resources management to be decentralized to the community level, giving rural populations and indigenous peoples land titles or other land rights and expanding services such as credit and agricultural extension for rural communities. The chapter on major groups calls on governments to adopt national strategies for eliminating the obstacles to women's full participation in sustainable development by the year 2000.[56]

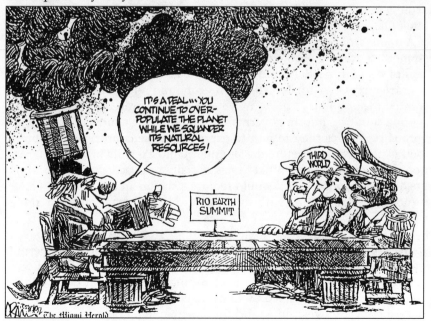

Copyright 1992 by *The Miami Herald*. Reprinted with permission.

Among the more important norms agreed to in the document, despite the reluctance of both developing countries and some industrialized countries, are provisions calling for the removal or reduction of subsidies that are inconsistent with sustainable development (such as the sale of U.S. timber from public lands at prices below the full costs of production) and the improvement of price signals through environmental charges or taxes. Implementation of those norms would be a major step toward more sustainable development worldwide.[57]

The issue of inequitable consumption patterns as a cause of global environmental degradation was elevated to a new status in international politics at the insistence of the developing countries. The issue was woven through several chapters of Agenda 21 as well as the Rio Declaration and the Statement of Forest Principles, making it a major theme of the entire conference. Industrialized countries were asked to accept responsibility to change their "unsustainable lifestyles."

Proposals by the secretariat for new initiatives on developing-country indebtedness and North-South trade were frustrated by Northern vetoes. The United States rejected a secretariat proposal for further cooperation to reduce debt owed to commercial banks by some developing countries, expansion of official bilateral debt reduction, and relief of debt owed to multilateral financial institutions.[58] Similarly, language in the negotiating text that hinted at the desirability of new commodity price arrangements was deleted at the insistence of the United States and other OECD countries.[59]

A number of proposals to create new global environmental regimes or strengthen existing ones were the subject of negotiations. On the regulation of trade in pesticides, the **Group of 77** (a coalition of developing countries pressing for North-South economic reform since the 1970s) wanted the voluntary "prior informed consent" procedure (i.e., that exporting countries inform governments of importing countries about dangerous pesticides they intend to export to those countries and obtain their explicit consent before the shipment) into a legally binding international agreement. The United States initially opposed that proposal on the dubious ground that it would require a change in U.S. laws, but after prolonged negotiations with the EPA, the U.S. delegation went along with it.[60]

The issues of depletion of the world's fish stocks and land-based sources of marine pollution were too complex and contentious to permit substantive consensus on new norms in UNCED. For example, the European states with large distant water fishing fleets were at odds with a number of coastal states, led by Canada, who argued that the Europeans and others were overfishing and this was having a negative impact on local economies. Nevertheless, delegations were able to agree to future international negotiations under UN auspices aimed at strengthening existing norms, including the possibility of legally binding rules, which have subsequently taken place (see Chapter 3).

After persistent lobbying by African delegations, UNCED agreed to the convening of an international conference on a binding desertification agreement by 1994. Most industrialized countries were very skeptical about the idea of negotiating a convention on the issue of desertification, which they believed to be an issue better addressed at the local or regional level, and the issue would not have been put on the global political agenda in the absence of the extraordinary political circumstances of the Earth Summit. The developing countries, led by the Africans, felt that desertification was an issue affecting nearly 1 billion people around the world and deserved international attention. And the small island developing states, brought together in the early 1990s by the common threat of sea-level rise from global warming, won recognition of their unique environmental and development problems. Agenda 21 called for a global conference on the sustainable development of small island developing states, which was held in 1994 and produced a detailed plan of action and commitments of financial and technical assistance from several donor countries and international organizations. While the plan of action was adopted with much fanfare, a special session of the United Nations General Assembly in 1999 determined that much more international assistance is necessary to implement the plan effectively.[61]

● The questions of financial resources, **technology transfer** (the transfer of scientific and technological knowledge, patents, or equipment, usually from the most industrialized nations to the less developed ones), education, and capacity building for implementation of Agenda 21 and global environmental agreements formed the core of the compact reached at Rio and remain a central issue today. The agreement reached in Rio was essentially that developing countries would try to put into practice more environmentally sound development policies if the industrialized countries agree to provide the necessary support, in terms of "new and additional" financial resources, technology transfer on concessional and preferential terms, and assistance with capacity building, education, and training.

UNCED as Snapshot and Dynamic Process

Did UNCED demonstrate that both North and South will block progress toward global sustainable development or that the global system is continuing to evolve toward a new social paradigm that includes norms of sustainable global human development? The answer depends on the optic used to view the outcomes.[62] The United States and other industrialized countries failed to commit significant new resources to support sustainable development and blocked secretariat proposals for change in industrialized countries' consumption patterns and in North-South economic relations. Developing countries in turn blocked the establishment of international norms for forest management and joined the United States in preventing agreement on accelerating the transition to sustainable energy systems. Furthermore, countries were not united along development lines. Developing countries themselves were split over such issues as climate change (oil producing nations vs. small island states), fisheries (distant water fishing countries vs. coastal countries), and population growth (Catholic and Muslim countries vs. more secular countries). Industrialized countries disagreed on a number of issues, including ODA levels (Nordic countries vs. the United States), fisheries (distant water fishing countries vs. coastal countries), hazardous and radioactive waste disposal, and the need to reduce excessive production and consumption patterns.

A longer-term perspective on the UNCED negotiations, however, would emphasize that they did establish new norms in a number of areas, such as popular participation in resource management as well as in international environmental negotiations, sustainable consumption patterns in industrialized countries, prices that reflect environmental costs, and reduction of subsidies for resource consumption that are inconsistent with sustainable development. Even though these norms are not legally binding and may not have been implemented in most countries in the short run, their formal adoption by consensus at a global summit meeting has made it more likely that they will be put into practice in the near future.

UNCED was also the first UN conference to truly open the doors to nongovernmental organizations (NGOs) and thus increase the transparency and democracy of the negotiations. According to Tariq Banuri of the Sustainable Development Policy Institute in Pakistan, NGOs helped create a

> civil society at the discussions, they managed to keep a check on diplomats from their own and even other countries. They were often better informed and more articulate than government representatives and better at obtaining and disseminating information than were the journalists themselves. They also engaged themselves in writing and speaking openly and forcefully on the issues involved, and ... for all these reasons, the eyes of the world became focused on the event, and therefore on the ideas behind the event.[63]

Agenda 21 also set in motion new processes both within and among nations toward progress on sustainability. It called for new international negotiations on formal regimes on desertification, overfishing, the international pesticide trade, and land-based sources of marine pollution, and on a plan of action for small island developing states. Those negotiations have either been completed or are still in process. Although Agenda 21 did not contain strong language on population, an effective women's caucus was forged in the process that became a major influence on the 1994 Cairo International Conference on Population and Development, which was widely regarded as a triumph for the population agenda.

Did UNCED help to propel an alternative social paradigm to the forefront? There is little question that the UNCED process helped advance this paradigm. In June 1992,

> virtually all of the world's heads of state met for the first time—ever—not to create or dismantle military alliances, not to discuss currency and banking reform, and not to set up rules of world trade, but to try to agree to care for the planet's biosphere. And the idea that was ratified, however little agreement was achieved on how to implement it, is this: Environment and development are inextricably linked.[64]

Likewise, Tommy Koh, the diplomat from Singapore who chaired the UNCED Preparatory Committee, argued:

> It used to be fashionable to argue in the developing countries that their priority should be economic development and that, if necessary, the environment should be sacrificed in order to achieve high economic growth. The sentiment was to get rich first and to clean up the environment later. . . . Today, developing countries understand the need to integrate environment into their development policies. At the same time developed countries have become increasingly aware of the need to cut down on their wasteful consumption patterns. . . . The new wisdom is that we want economic progress but we also want to live in harmony with nature.[65]

Yet, in spite of the recognition of the ideals behind this alternative paradigm, the Earth Summit also demonstrated that unless one deals with political reality, the most impressive statements, agendas, and manifestos would come to nothing. "Getting agreement, in principle, on protecting the environment, on saving human life, on increasing the share of global prosperity to the poorer peoples of the world is relatively simple ... The difficulty lies in achieving action. . . . The message [of Rio], despite grand speeches, appears to be 'business as usual' for many governments and businesses."[66]

The UNCED experience also marks an important new stage in the longer-term development of the national and international norms and institutions needed to meet the challenge of environmentally sustainable development. Among the results of UNCED are the creation of the United Nations Commission on Sustainable Development; new financing

● mechanisms, such as the Global Environment Facility; forums for continued interactions between diplomats, scientists, and the environmental community; and a solidified global network of environmental groups that will continue to press for change. Others, however, have presented a more skeptical view. Although numerous institutions have been created at and since UNCED, the Earth Summit failed to push the environment to the top of the international agenda in any sustained fashion.[67] Five years after Rio, the United Nations General Assembly agreed that much more needs to be done to make sustainable development a reality. It may be many more years before UNCED's true legacy is known.

CONCLUSION

Global environmental politics involve interactions among states and non-state actors transcending a single region regarding international decisions that affect the environment and natural resources. The emergence of this issue area in world politics is a reflection of the growing awareness of the cumulative stresses on the earth's resources and life-support systems from economic activities during the past century.

Much of global environmental politics focuses on efforts to negotiate multilateral agreements for cooperation to protect the environment and natural resources. These agreements constitute global environmental regimes of varying effectiveness that govern state behavior in regard to the environmental problem in question.

Divergences of environmental interests as defined by states themselves make the achievement of unanimity among the parties responsible and directly affected by an environmental problem a political and diplomatic challenge. One of the primary problems of global environmental politics is the ability of one or more states to block or weaken multilateral agreements and how to overcome such blockage. For a regime to be formed, veto states and coalitions must be persuaded to abandon their opposition to a proposed regime or at least to compromise with states supporting it.

One of the obstacles to effective international action for environmental conservation in the past has been a dominant social paradigm that justifies unlimited exploitation of nature. Despite the weakening of that paradigm and the apparent widespread recognition of an alternative sustainable development paradigm, especially in conjunction with the 1992 Earth Summit, the shift to this alternative social paradigm is far from complete. There are still some sectors of societies, particularly powerful political and economic institutions, where the traditional paradigm continues to exhibit extraordinary staying power. The subsequent chapters in this book will demonstrate the nature of the different actors involved in global environmental politics and how their interests may help to promote the alternative paradigm or retain the dominant social paradigm and just what this may entail for the future of the planet.

Theoretical approaches that have been advanced to explain the formation of international regimes generally include the structural, game-theoretic, institutional bargaining, and epistemic community models. These approaches fail to account for most global environmental regimes. To explain why environmental regimes are formed and strengthened, a theoretical approach will have to deal with the central problem of veto coalitions and why they are or are not overcome in regime negotiations. It will have to avoid relying solely on the unitary actor model and encompass domestic political forces, the structure of the negotiating forum, and the role of other international political concerns.

The subsequent chapters in this book will further explore these issues. Chapter 2 examines the actors who are responsible for the formation of global environmental policies, including the formation of environmental regimes. Although state actors are the final determinants of the outcomes of global environmental issues, since they negotiate the international legal instruments creating global environmental regimes and adopt international trade and financial policies that directly and indirectly affect the environment, nonstate actors have major roles to play as well. Nonstate actors, such as international organizations, nongovernmental organizations, and multinational corporations, help set the global environmental agenda, initiate and influence the process of regime formation, and carry out actions that directly affect the global environment.

Chapter 3 looks at the development of environmental regimes through the presentation of 10 global environmental issues on which there have been multilateral negotiations during the past 25 years. Each issue is analyzed in terms of the stages of negotiation and the role of veto coalitions in shaping the outcomes of bargaining. The cases are presented chronologically and by issue area, including atmospheric issues (transboundary air pollution, ozone depletion, and climate change), natural resources and endangered species (whaling, elephant ivory, biodiversity loss, desertification, and fisheries), pollution (toxic wastes), and the global commons (Antarctica).

The regime-building process does not end with the signing and ratification of a global environmental treaty. Therefore, Chapter 4 looks at the implementation and financing of environmental regimes, two issues that contribute to the effectiveness of an environmental regime. The first section examines the issue of compliance at the national level and examines variables that lead to a lack of compliance with an environmental agreement. The second section looks at the question of financing regimes and the various financial constraints that have contributed to an overall lack of compliance.

Chapter 5 focuses on economics and development. Environmental issues have become increasingly intertwined with the politics of international economic relations and policies in recent years as environmental issues have begun to impinge on core economic concerns of countries. As linkages with economic relations and development have multiplied, the boundaries of global environmental politics have broadened. The first part of the chapter examines North-South economic relations vis-à-vis global environmental politics. Then we analyze two political issues and processes involving the environment, economics, and development: the relationship between trade and the environment and efforts to craft a global forest regime, which demonstrate how the fears over loss of markets can block progress toward international agreement on norms for sustainable forest management. The chapter concludes with some thoughts on the future of global environmental politics.

TWO

□ □ □

Actors in the
Environmental Arena

State actors are the final determinants of the outcomes of global environmental issues. States negotiate the international legal instruments creating global environmental regimes as well as adopting international trade and financial policies that directly and indirectly affect the environment. States also decide which issues are considered by the global community both directly (by arguing for international action on an issue) and indirectly (through their membership in the governing councils of international organizations). And donor states influence environmental policies through their bilateral aid programs and donations to multilateral banks.

But nonstate actors also exert major and increasing influence on global environmental politics. International organizations help to set the global environmental agenda, initiate and mediate the process of regime formation, and cooperate with developing countries on projects and programs directly affecting the environment. Nongovernmental organizations also participate in setting the agenda, influencing negotiations on regime formation, and shaping the environmental policies of donor agencies toward developing countries. Multinational corporations both influence the bargaining over regime creation and carry out actions that directly affect the global environment.

NATION-STATE ACTORS:
ROLES AND INTERESTS

The most important actions by state actors in global environmental politics are those relating to the process of regime formation. In the negotiations on an environmental regime, a state actor may play one of four possible roles: **lead state, supporting state, swing state,** or veto or blocking state. A lead state has a strong commitment to effective international action on the issue, moves the process of negotiations forward by proposing its own negotiating formula as the basis for an agreement, and attempts to get the support of other state actors.

A supporting state speaks in favor of the proposal of a lead state in negotiations. A swing state demands a concession to its interests as the price for going along with an agreement, but not a concession that would significantly weaken the regime, such as a slower timetable for a phase-out. A veto or blocking state either opposes a proposed environmental regime outright or tries to weaken it to the point that it cannot be effective.

States may shift from what appears to be a veto role to a swing role, since threatening a veto is sometimes the best means of enhancing bargaining leverage. The Indian delegation to the London meeting of the parties to the Montreal Protocol in June 1990 at first seemed to be rejecting any agreement that would bind India to phase out CFCs in 2010 but eventually settled for a compromise that could provide financial assistance for Indian companies to purchase substitute technology.

There may be more than one lead state on a given issue. Sweden and Norway were allied from the beginning in pushing for a long-range transboundary air pollution agreement, for example. But often one state steps forward to advance a policy that puts it clearly in the lead, as did Australia on the Antarctica issue and West Germany on the climate change issue in 1990. As issues go through several stages, the role of lead state may shift from one state or combination of states to another. In the negotiation of the Vienna Convention on the Ozone Layer in 1985, Finland and Sweden took the lead by submitting their own draft convention and heavily influencing the draft put before the conference. In 1986, the United States stepped into the lead role by proposing an eventual 95 percent reduction in CFCs, and by 1989–1990 several OECD (Organization for Economic Cooperation and Development) states had become the lead states by working for a phase-out before 2000.

Lead states have a wide range of methods for influencing other state actors on a global environmental issue. A lead state may

- produce and call attention to research that defines the problem and demonstrates its urgency, as when Swedish research showed the serious damage done by acid rain;
- seek to educate public opinion in target states, as did Canada when it supplied U.S. tourists with pamphlets on acidification of its forests and waters or instructed its Washington embassy to cooperate with like-minded U.S. environmental organizations;
- take unilateral action on an issue and thus lead by example, as in the case of U.S. regulation of aerosols containing CFCs in 1979;[1]

- use its diplomatic clout to get an international organization to identify the issues as a priority, as when the United States and Canada got the OECD to take up the ozone layer and CFCs;
- rely on the worldwide network of NGOs to support its position in other countries and at international conferences, as the Alliance of Small Island States (AOSIS) did in its effort to place quantitative limits on greenhouse gas emissions beyond the year 2000 in the negotiations on the Kyoto Protocol;
- make a diplomatic demarche to a state that is threatening a veto role, as the United States did with Japan on African elephant ivory; or
- pledge to commit financial or technical resources to the problem, such as the positive incentives that developed states built into such conventions as the Montreal Protocol to ensure developing-country acceptance.

Although scientific-technological capabilities and economic power cannot ensure that a lead state will prevail on an environmental issue, they constitute valuable assets for helping to create a regime. When a big power like the United States has taken a lead role through scientific research, unilateral action, and diplomatic initiative, as it did on the issue of ozone protection in the 1970s and again in the mid-1980s, it helps to sway states that do not otherwise have clearly defined interests on the issue.

Whether a state plays a lead, supporting, swing, or veto role in regard to a particular global environmental issue depends primarily on domestic political factors and on the relative costs and benefits of the proposed regime. A third variable, which has been important in some cases, is anticipation of international political consequences, including increased prestige or damage to the country's image worldwide.

Domestic Political Factors

A state's definition of interest and choice of role on global environmental issues turn largely on domestic economic and political interests and domestic ideological currents. Whether a state actor opposes, supports, or leads on an issue depends first on the relative strength and influence of powerful economic and bureaucratic forces and of domestic environmental constituencies. Ideological factors related to broader domestic political themes also play a prominent role in the definition of interests in some cases.

Domestic economic interests are particularly prominent in promoting veto roles. When the Liberal Democratic Party dominated Japanese politics, for example, major trading companies generally received government support for their interests in whaling because of their close ties with the party.[2] Norway's fishery industry, which claims to have suffered declining fish catches because of the international protection of whales, has prevailed on the government of Norway to defend Norwegian whaling before the international community. Norway, Japan, and Greece have all tended to be swing or blocking actors on questions of marine pollution from oil tankers because of the economic importance of their shipping industries. Germany, Italy, the Netherlands, and Sweden, all of which have smaller shipping industries, were more flexible in negotiations on pollution from ships.[3]

● In some cases a state's position on a global environmental issue reflects the interests of a dominant socioeconomic elite. Indonesia, for example, has allocated control over a large proportion of its forest resources to a relatively small elite of concessionaries. In 1995, 20 Indonesian corporate conglomerates controlled more than 63 percent of the 62 million hectares of the country's timber concessions, and those businesses had close ties with the family of former president Suharto, which allowed them to ignore logging concession regulations. The Suharto regime's forest policy was dominated by a plywood exporters' cartel controlled by a timber baron crony of Suharto.[4] It is not surprising, therefore, that Indonesia opposed any proposal for new international norms on forest management in the early 1990s, or that it supported Canada's 1997 proposal for a forest convention that would allow each major timber-exporting country to create its own ecolabeling system. (See Chapter 5.)

Jeff Danziger in *The Christian Science Monitor* ©1993 TCSPS.

Government bureaucracies with institutional interests that are in direct conflict with global action on behalf of the environment are often critical factors in swing and blocking roles. During the negotiation of the Montreal Protocol in the mid-1980s, officials in the U.S. Departments of Commerce, the Interior, and Agriculture, together with the Office of Management and Budget, the Office of Science and Technology Policy, and parts of the White House staff, began in early 1987 to reopen basic questions about the scientific evidence and the possible damage to the U.S. economy from imposing additional CFC controls, but they were overruled.[5] The major obstacles to the United Kingdom's agreeing to an acid rain agreement through the mid-1980s were two public bodies, the National Coal Board and the Central Electricity Generating Board, which did everything possible to avoid having to reduce sulfur dioxide emissions.[6]

●The ability of dominant elites and bureaucratic interests to resist restrictions on their despoiling of the environment is enhanced by authoritarian political regimes that can simply suppress any opposition to their policies. The military regime that ruled Brazil from 1964 to 1985 had virtually unlimited power to determine how natural resources were exploited, permitting no opposition to its campaign to open the Amazonian rain forests to agriculture and other large-scale commercial activities. But under an elected government, with NGOs and media freer to criticize it, the government was less hostile toward international agreement to slow deforestation.

Where other motives for a lead role on a global environmental issue are present, such a role becomes far more likely if there is little or no domestic opposition to it. The United States could easily take the lead role on the issue of whaling in the 1970s and 1980s, for example, because the U.S. whaling industry had already been eliminated. Similarly, the absence of any significant bureaucratic or business interest opposing a ban on imports of African elephant ivory products made it easy for the United States to assume a lead role on that issue.

The existence of a strong environmental movement can be a decisive factor in a state's definition of its interest on an issue, especially if it is a potential swing vote in parliamentary elections. The sudden emergence of West German and French bids for leadership roles on environmental issues in 1989 reflected in large part the upsurge of public support for strong environmental protection policies in Western Europe. The West German Greens had already won 8.2 percent of the vote in the 1984 European Parliament elections, and by 1985 the Green Party, backed by popular environmental sentiment, was already a strong force in the German parliament.[7] Before the 1989 European Parliament election, polls indicated a new surge in environmentalist sentiment in West Germany and France. As a result both West Germany and France in early 1989 became part of a lead coalition of states proposing negotiations on a framework convention on climate change to stabilize carbon dioxide emissions not later than 2000, and France shifted to support of Australia's proposal for a ◀"world park" in Antarctica. Germany, the Netherlands, and Denmark have continued to be lead states on climate change, in part because they have the largest and most active environmental movements in Europe.[8] The German environmental movement's clout helped overcome the influence of the powerful German coal industry.

Australia's leadership on issues of nuclear-waste dumping in the Pacific and rejection of the Antarctic minerals treaty in favor of a comprehensive environmental protection convention for the continent was also driven in part by the rise of Australia's environmental movement as a crucial factor in Australian elections. In 1987, the Labor Party's electoral victory was attributed to a "green vote" after environmental groups called on their supporters to vote for labor candidates.[9] And the Netherlands' role as the only state within the EC to support the proposal for a global climate fund reflects a particularly strong and active environmental movement, as well as the country's political tradition of popular involvement in policy issues.

A strong environmental movement does not guarantee that the state actor will play a lead or supporting role on an issue. The U.S. environmental movement is the largest and best organized in the world, but it was unable in the late 1980s and early 1990s to sway U.S. policy in the negotiation of climate and hazardous waste trade regimes, in part because powerful interests were arrayed against it and because it was not able to influence the outcomes of congressional or presidential elections.

▪ Conversely, the absence of a strong environmental movement makes it more likely that a state will play a swing or blocking role on an international environmental issue. For example, Japanese NGOs are relatively underdeveloped in comparison with those in North America and Western Europe, and the Japanese political system makes it difficult for private interest groups without high-level political links to influence policy. So the Japanese government felt little or no domestic pressure to support regimes on African elephants, whaling, and drift-net fishing. In contrast U.S. wildlife NGOs placed a great deal of domestic pressure on the U.S. government to take a strong position on these issues.

A final domestic political factor that has occasionally shaped a country's definition of its interest in an environmental regime is the ideology or belief system of the policymaker. Despite the fact that the United States exported very little of its hazardous waste, in the UNCED negotiations the Bush administration led the veto coalition against a ban on hazardous waste exports to developing countries because of its strong hostility to the intervention of states in national and international markets.

The Bush administration also vetoed a proposal in the UNCED negotiations for targets to be set by each industrialized state for per capita energy use, regarding it as an unwarranted interference by the state in consumer preferences.[10]

Differential Costs and Benefits of Environmental Regimes

A second group of variables that shape the definition of national interest in a global environmental issue includes the degree of cost and risk that the environmental threat poses to a country as well as the costs and opportunities associated with the proposed regime.

Exceptional vulnerability to the consequences of environmental problems has driven countries to support or even take the lead on strong global action. Thirty-two small island states that are especially vulnerable to sea-level rise because of global warming formed the Alliance of Small Island States in November 1990 to lobby the climate negotiations for action to limit carbon dioxide emissions from the industrialized countries. States with densely populated coastal plains, such as Bangladesh, Egypt, and the Netherlands, are also likely to face particularly severe disruptions from storm surges, hurricanes, and typhoons due to climate change and have generally supported efforts to strengthen the UN Framework Convention on Climate Change.

Sweden and Norway, which led the fight for a Long-Range Transboundary Air Pollution Convention in the 1970s, have been the major recipients of sulfur dioxide from other European countries and also have acid-sensitive soils and lakes. The damage from acid rain therefore appeared earlier and was more serious in those Nordic countries than in the United Kingdom or West Germany. Similarly, Canada has a higher proportion of soil that is vulnerable to acid deposition than does the United States and receives far more sulfur dioxide from U.S. factories than it sends across the border, so it has pushed the United States for stronger action on the issue.

The costs of compliance with a given global environmental regime may differ dramatically from one country to another, and such differences have sometimes shaped the roles played by states in regime negotiations. The negotiation of the Montreal Protocol provides several examples of states whose roles were linked with economic interests. UNEP executive director Mostafa Tolba is reported to have observed, "The difficulties in negotiating the Montreal Protocol had nothing to do with whether the environment was damaged or not. . . . It was all who was going to get the edge over whom."[11] Because of an earlier unilateral ban on aerosols using ozone-depleting chemicals, the United States was ahead of members of the European Community and Japan in finding substitutes for CFCs in aerosol cans. So it joined Canada and the Nordic states in supporting such a ban. Western Europe and Japan rejected a ban on aerosols in the early 1980s because they did not yet have technological alternatives. The Soviet Union initially resisted the idea of a CFC phase-out in 1986–1987, fearing it would be unable to develop new technologies to replace CFCs. China and India, who were minor producers at the time but were already gearing up for major production increases, also feared that the transition to ozone-safe chemicals would be too costly without noncommercial access to alternative technologies. Moreover, India's chemical industry planned to export half its projected CFC production to the Middle East and Asia.

The anticipated economic costs of compliance were the underlying issue during the negotiations that resulted in the Kyoto Protocol to the UN Framework Convention on Climate Change. Achieving reductions in greenhouse gas (GHG) emissions is easier and/or cheaper for some countries to implement than others. For example, the European Union states are generally net importers of fossil fuels and have learned how to reduce energy use without compromising economic growth. Since the EU states saw that their cost of compliance would be relatively low, they were able to play a lead role in the negotiation of the protocol. In March 1997, the EU called for a 15 percent reduction of emissions across the EU by 2010, taking into consideration internal burden sharing. This burden sharing would entail that those countries able to reduce their GHG emissions at the lowest cost would carry the burden for those countries where reductions would have a greater economic burden.

International Political-Diplomatic Considerations

A state's definition of its interest is sometimes influenced by anticipated benefits or costs of lead or veto roles to the state's international relations. A state may hope to gain international prestige by assuming a lead role. Or it may decide against a veto role in order to avoid international opprobrium or damage to its relations with other countries for whom the issue is of significantly greater concern.

Concern for national prestige—a state's reputation or status in the international community—was once confined to the issue area of international security. But in the early 1990s a few states had begun to regard leadership on the global environment as a means of enhancing their international status. Both the United States and Germany made bids for leadership on a possible world forest convention in 1990–1991, in large part because both anticipated that such leadership would enhance their environmental image around the world. The European Union had aspirations for a lead role on climate change and in the Rio conference in order to signify its emergence as a global power. In 1994, EU environment commissioner Yannis Paleokrassas hailed the prospect of a regionwide carbon tax, which would give the EU a lead role on climate change and lead to "the resumption of world environmental and fiscal leadership by the European Union," thus suggesting that it would gain a new kind of international prestige.[12]

●At the 1992 Earth Summit in Rio, the image of the United States was seriously tarnished because it stood alone in rejecting the Convention on Biological Diversity. Germany and Japan, among other countries, shared the unhappiness of the United States with some provisions of the Biodiversity Convention but shunned a veto role, fearing damage to their prestige. In a telling display of anger, a Bush administration official charged that Germany and Japan had departed from the U.S. position on the convention in part to demonstrate their new status as emerging world powers.[13]

A state's concern about how a veto role might affect its image is sometimes focused on a particular country or group of countries. In the case of the international trade in hazardous wastes, France and the United Kingdom were swayed by the desire to maintain close ties with former colonies to modify their veto of a hazardous waste trade ban in 1989. And Japan avoided a veto role on banning African elephant ivory in 1989 largely because it feared damage to its relations with its most important trading partners, the United States and Europe.

Subnational Actors

National governments, despite their assertion of exclusive rights to act in international relations, are no longer the only governmental actors in global environmental politics. In recent years cities, states, and provinces have shown increased interest in adopting their own environmental and energy policies that could have a major impact on global environmental problems, especially global warming.

● Large cities are major producers of greenhouse gases because of their heavy concentrations of transportation, which is the single biggest source of carbon dioxide emissions. So urban policies, if effective, could substantially reduce greenhouse gas emissions. The governments of 14 major cities in North America, Europe, and the Middle East joined in the Urban CO_2 Reduction Project in 1990 in order to develop strategies for reducing greenhouse gas emissions at the local level. In November 1993, Portland, Oregon, became the first U.S. city to formally adopt a comprehensive global warming strategy. It declared a goal of reducing its carbon dioxide emissions 20 percent below 1988 levels by the year 2010, primarily by reducing automobile travel and encouraging less polluting transport.[14] In the Netherlands, 54 municipalities formed a Climate Alliance aimed at developing their own local greenhouse policies.[15] In preparation for UNCED, mayors from around the world organized forums to prepare proposals for Agenda 21, including recommendations on transportation. Since Rio they have continued to promote their own projects for sustainable development.[16]

Federal states could have even greater impact on global warming by adopting similar plans. Californians claim their state is the seventh largest economy in the world. If California were to decide on an ambitious strategy for reducing greenhouse gases, it would be as important as most members of the **Group of Eight** industrialized nations (the United States, Canada, the United Kingdom, Japan, Germany, France, Italy, and Russia) in influencing the success of a global regime for global warming. In fact, such a plan was proposed as part of the Proposition 128 environmental initiative that was on the ballot in California in 1990. The initiative, which would have approved a plan to reduce the state's emissions of carbon dioxide by 20 percent by the year 2000 and 40 percent by 2010, was defeated but got a respectable 37 percent of the vote.[17]

Municipal and state governments are not likely to usurp national government functions in regime strengthening. But they may reinforce and supplement the decisions of national governments on the regime on climate change, especially as the world becomes increasingly urbanized.

INTERNATIONAL
ORGANIZATIONS AS ACTORS

The influence of international organizations (IOs) on global environmental politics has greatly increased since 1972. Also referred to as intergovernmental organizations (IGOs), IOs are formed by member states either for multiple purposes, as in the case of the United Nations, or various regional associations, such as the Organization of American States, or for more specific purposes, as in the case of the specialized agencies of the United Nations, such as the Food and Agriculture Organization (FAO) and the World Health Organization (WHO). IOs range in size and resources from the World Bank, which has a staff of over 6,000 and lends billions of dollars annually, to UNEP, with its annual budget for the biennium 2000–2001 of only $120 million and a professional staff of 275. These organizations are staffed by officials from many nations, who tend to share common approaches to functional problems. Although they are ultimately accountable to governing bodies made up of the representatives of their member states, staff can take initiatives and influence the outcomes of global issues. The professional skills of these bureaucrats can be an important factor in environmental negotiations, as was obvious in the resourcefulness of the UNCED secretariat. IO bureaucracies have widely varying degrees of independence. Those at UNEP and the FAO must take their cues from their governing councils on setting agendas, sponsoring negotiations, and implementing development and environment programs; at the World Bank, which is dependent on major donor countries for its funds, the staff nevertheless has wide discretion in planning and executing projects.

An IO may influence the outcomes of global environmental issues in the following four ways:

- It may set the agenda for global action, determining which issues the international community will deal with.
- I may convene and influence negotiations on global environmental regimes.
- It may develop normative codes of conduct (soft law) on various environmental issues.
- It may influence state policies on issues that are not under international negotiation.

No IO influences global environmental politics by performing all of these functions; IOs tend to specialize in one or more political functions, although one may indirectly influence another.

Setting Agendas and Influencing Regime Formation

In the past, the agenda-setting function of global environmental politics was dominated by UNEP because of its unique mandate, growing out of the 1972 Stockholm Conference, to be a catalyst and coordinator of environmental activities and focal point for such activities within the UN system. Through the decisions of its Governing Council, composed of 58 UN member governments elected by the General Assembly, UNEP regularly identified the critical global environmental threats requiring international cooperation in the 1970s and 1980s. In 1976, for example, UNEP's Governing Council chose ozone depletion as one of five priority problems, and consequently UNEP convened a meeting of experts in Washington, D.C., that adopted the World Plan of Action on the Ozone Layer in 1977—five years before negotiations on a global agreement began.

◆UNEP played a similar role in initiating negotiations on climate change. It cosponsored with the Rockefeller Brothers Fund the Villach and Bellagio workshops that helped create scientific consensus and raised worldwide consciousness about the threat of global warming. Along with the World Meteorological Organization (WMO), it sponsored the Intergovernmental Panel on Climate Change to study scientific and policy issues in preparation for negotiations on a global convention on climate change. UNEP convened international negotiations on many of the major environmental conventions of the past two decades: the Vienna Convention for the Protection of the Ozone Layer (1985), the Montreal Protocol on Substances that Deplete the Ozone Layer (1987), the Basel Convention on the Control of Transboundary Movements of Hazardous Wastes and Their Disposal (1989), and the Convention on Biological Diversity (1992). In 1995 the UNEP Governing Council decided that UNEP would convene together with FAO an intergovernmental negotiating committee with a mandate to prepare an international legally binding instrument for the application of the Prior Informed Consent (PIC) procedure for certain hazardous chemicals in international trade. The PIC Convention was adopted in Rotterdam in September 1998. UNEP is also sponsoring negotiations on a legally binding instrument to control persistent organic pollutants, which is expected to be adopted in May 2001.

UNEP also has sought to shape the global environmental agenda by monitoring and assessing the state of the environment and disseminating the information to governments and nongovernmental organizations. UNEP's Earthwatch program includes a series of systems directly under UNEP's control as well as a loose network of UN agencies that also carry out global environmental monitoring. But although monitoring and assessment are essential to stimulating international cooperation on environmental threats, donor countries have not supported those activities adequately. As a result, serious gaps remain in the data, such as the lack of accurate remote sensing images of Indonesia's tropical forests.[18] And many developing countries have regarded this program as a way for industrialized countries to "spy" on them—especially in regard to deforestation—and have reduced funding for it in the UNEP Governing Council since 1993.[19]

Former UNEP executive director Mostafa Tolba influenced environmental diplomacy through direct participation in the negotiations. During the negotiations on the Montreal Protocol he lobbied hard for a complete phase-out of CFCs in informal talks with the chiefs of EC delegations.[20] At the London conference of the parties in 1990, he convened informal meetings with 25 environmental ministers to work out a compromise on the contentious issue of linking protocol obligations with technology transfer. He also urged a compromise to bridge the gap between U.S. and Western European timetables for a CFC phase-out. During the negotiations on the Convention on Biological Diversity, Tolba took over the negotiations at the final session, when there appeared to be gridlock on key issues regarding the financing mechanism, and he virtually forced the acceptance of a compromise text. (See Chapter 3.)

Tolba sometimes openly championed the developing countries against the highly industrialized countries. At Basel in 1989, for instance, he fought for a ban on shipping hazardous wastes to or from noncontracting parties and for a requirement that exporters check disposal sites at their own expense. Opposed by the waste-exporting states, Tolba and the developing countries lost on both issues.[21]

In the 1990s UNEP's role in agenda setting and convening regime negotiations was sharply reduced by several factors. Despite his siding with them on the emotional waste trade issue, the developing countries began to lose confidence in Tolba and UNEP by 1990. They felt he was not sufficiently committed to their agenda and put too much emphasis on climate change, ozone depletion, and loss of biodiversity, which they considered "Northern" issues. When UNCED was being organized in the United Nations General Assembly (UNGA), the Group of 77 sought emphasis on environmental problems of primary concern to developing nations: drinking water and sanitation, urban pollution, desertification, and so on. It succeeded in naming the twentieth anniversary of the Stockholm environmental conference the 1992 UN Conference on Environment *and Development* and assigned organizing responsibility to the UN secretariat rather than to UNEP. At the same time, the UNGA took the climate negotiations out of the hands of UNEP and WMO and gave them to an ad hoc UN body, the Intergovernmental Negotiating Committee (INC), which reported directly to the General Assembly.

And after the Earth Summit conference in 1992, the UNGA established the United Nations Commission on Sustainable Development (CSD) to monitor and coordinate implementation of Agenda 21. The creation of the CSD and the replacement of Tolba with a new executive director, Elizabeth Dowdeswell, further reduced UNEP's role in agenda setting for global environmental politics. Among other things, Dowdeswell alienated key donor countries by failing to consult them adequately. There is no doubt that UNEP has had its share of successes; however, there have been dramatic changes in international environmental policymaking in recent years and UNEP has not demonstrated the ability to keep pace. Chronic financial problems, the absence of a clear focus and mission for the institution, problems of location (Nairobi, Kenya), and management difficulties have all contributed to the erosion of UNEP's participation in the international environmental policymaking process.[22]

In February 1998, Dr. Klaus Töpfer was appointed as UNEP's new executive director. By the 1999 meeting of the UNEP Governing Council, UNEP had begun to demonstrate that it was trying to adapt itself to new challenges and the full and complex agenda of global environmental concerns. As a result, donor pledges to UNEP's Environment Fund have increased, demonstrating renewed faith in the organization, its leadership, and its work program. UNEP, however, has lost its lead position in agenda setting and initiating negotiations to various other institutions within the UN system.

Given its position as a highly visible and well-attended UN commission, the 53-member CSD has an opportunity to play a pivotal role in agenda setting. The Commission has been successful in generating greater concern for some issues on the international sustainable development agenda. By creating the Intergovernmental Panel on Forests and, subsequently, the Intergovernmental Forum on Forests, the CSD was able to focus the forest issue and create more understanding that forests are owned by someone and give livelihood to many people. Freshwater resources and energy are two issues that did not receive much attention in Rio and are now at the top of the international agenda (at least the CSD's agenda for the period 1998–2001), largely due to the work of the commission. Similarly, the CSD's discussions on sustainable production and consumption patterns and the need for technology transfer, education, and capacity building in developing countries have raised the profiles of these issues.

However, when it comes to putting new issues on the international agenda, the CSD has not been as successful. To its credit, the CSD has put the issues of transport and tourism on the agenda and has advanced the discussions on finance so that new issues such as private direct investment, airline fuel taxes, and a tax on foreign financial transactions have also been added to the international sustainable development agenda. Given the wide range of sustainable-development-related issues that could be placed on the agenda, these issues are only the tip of the iceberg.[23]

Developing Nonbinding Norms

Another way that international organizations influence global environmental politics is to facilitate the negotiation of common norms or rules of conduct that do not have binding legal effect on the participating states. A variety of creative nontreaty measures, often called soft law, have been developed to influence state behavior on environmental issues, including codes of conduct, declarations of principle, global action plans, and other international agreements that create new norms and expectations without the binding status of treaties.[24]

These nonbinding agreements are negotiated by groups of experts representing their governments convened by one of the IOs. Most UN agencies have contributed to this process, but UNEP has done the most to promote it. In the case of UNEP's guidelines for the management of haz-ardous waste, for instance, an ad hoc working group of experts helped draft guidelines in 1984. In 1987, the same process produced a set of guidelines and principles aimed at making the worldwide pesticide trade more responsive regarding threats to environmental health. Other exam-ples include the 1980 International Program on Chemical Safety and the 1985 Action Plan for Biosphere Reserves, each of which has become the recognized standard in the field.

•The FAO has drafted guidelines on the environmental criteria for the registration of pesticides (1985) and the International Code of Conduct on the Distribution and Use of Pesticides (1986). A set of criteria for food reg-ulations, the Codex Alimentarius, also developed under the FAO's aegis, could be used in a trade dispute to have a national environmental health standard declared an illegitimate barrier to trade. The FAO Code of Con-duct for Responsible Fisheries, which was adopted in 1995, sets out prin-ciples and international standards of behavior for responsible practices with a view to ensuring the effective conservation, management, and de-velopment of living aquatic resources.

Soft-law agreements are often a good way to avoid the lengthy process of negotiating binding agreements. They do not require enforcement mechanisms and can sometimes depend on the adherence of networks of bureaucrats who share similar views of the problem. But in cases where soft-law regimes are adopted only because key parties are unwilling to go beyond nonbinding guidelines, the norms agreed on may be less strin-gent and the compliance may be haphazard at best. The FAO Code of Conduct on pesticide trade, negotiated from 1982 to 1985, and the 1985 Cairo guidelines on international hazardous waste trade are examples of this pattern.

•Soft law may be turned into binding international law in two ways: Principles included in a soft-law agreement may become so widely re-garded as the appropriate norms for a problem that they are ultimately absorbed into treaty law; or political pressures may arise from those dis-satisfied with spotty adherence to soft-law norms to turn a nonbinding agreement into a binding one.

Influencing National Development Policies

A fourth way that IOs affect global environmental politics is to influence the environmental and development policies of individual states outside the context of regime negotiations. National policy decisions on such is-sues as what goals should be set for population growth rates, how much of the government budget should be allocated to human resource devel-opment, how to manage forests, how to generate and use energy supplies, and how to increase agricultural production determine how sustainable the national economies and societies will be. IOs influence such policies, and thus the sustainability of societies, in several ways:

- They provide financing for development projects, as well as advice and technical assistance that help shape the country's development strategy.
- They undertake research aimed at persuading state officials to adopt certain policies.
- They focus normative pressure on states regarding sustainable development policy issues.

The FAO, for example, has had a major impact on the policies of the developing world—much of which critics charge has been negative—through its promotion of commercial exploitation of forests and export crops, large-scale irrigation projects, and heavy use of chemical inputs.[25] As the lead agency in the Tropical Forest Action Plan (TFAP), which was supposed to help reduce the rate of tropical deforestation through increased investments in forests, the FAO steered most of the new investments into commercial development of tropical timber rather than toward conservation or sustainable use. Its main constituency in regard to forest issues was the government forestry departments, whose interests were to promote vigorously the sale of timber resources.[26] NGOs monitoring the TFAP wanted a new structure that would take the program out of the FAO's Forestry Department, but the FAO Director-General resisted the suggestion.[27]

On a much smaller scale, FAO has also used research to promote sustainable alternatives to the conventional agricultural development model. FAO's program on integrated pest control in South and Southeast Asia, launched in the early 1980s, helped spread integrated pest management (IPM) techniques to farmers in several Asian countries. The research done by the FAO showing the superiority of natural pest control strategies over reliance on chemical pesticides helped convince key Indonesian government officials in 1986 to adopt IPM as an alternative to heavy reliance on pesticides and to train Indonesian farmers to make their own informed decisions about pest management.[28]

In the early 1990s, the organization was restructured for the first time for the purpose of integrating sustainability into its programs and activities.[29] And in 1993, the FAO received a new mandate from its governing body to focus more on the consequences of the earth's shrinking natural resource base, sustainable agricultural and rural development, and food security through protection of plant, animal, and marine resources. Since 1993 the FAO has focused extensively on implementation of sustainable agriculture, supported the work of the Commission on Sustainable Development's Intergovernmental Panel on Forests (and its successor the Intergovernmental Forum on Forests), and cosponsored with UNEP the negotiation of the Rotterdam Treaty for the application of the Prior Informed Consent (PIC) procedure for certain hazardous chemicals in international trade, among other things. The FAO also embarked upon the revision of the 1983 International Undertaking on Plant Genetic Resources. The International Undertaking addresses the conservation, exploration, collection, documentation, and sustainable use of plant resources for food and agriculture. It is being updated to harmonize with the goals of the Convention on Biological Diversity and, once revised, may be adopted as a protocol to the treaty.[30]

● The FAO Committee on Fisheries (COFI), consisting of FAO member states, was established in 1965 as a subsidiary body of the FAO Council and has remained the only global forum for consideration of major issues related to fisheries and aquaculture policy. Until the late 1980s, COFI focused on problems of developing coastal states in the development of their fisheries, especially after they acquired 200-mile coastal fishing zones in the 1970s. But when the pressures of overfishing on global fish stocks became increasingly difficult to ignore, COFI and the FAO Secretariat became more aggressive in pushing for new international norms for sustainable fisheries.

The FAO Secretariat has helped mobilize international support for more sustainable fisheries management by collecting and analyzing data on global fish catch, issuing annual reviews on the state of the world's fisheries, and organizing technical workshops. These efforts have focused government and NGO attention on such issues as excess fishing capacity and fisheries subsidies.

In 1991 COFI recommended that the FAO should develop the concept of responsible fisheries in the form of a code of conduct, and the FAO Secretariat convened negotiations on the Code of Conduct for Responsible Fisheries in 1994 and 1995. The Code of Conduct is the most comprehensive set of international norms for sustainable fisheries management that currently exists and, despite its not being legally binding, has great potential to influence state and producer practices. The main constraint on the code is the absence of an effective system for monitoring and reporting on compliance. The FAO Secretariat, which has the responsibility for monitoring and reporting on compliance, has chosen to make only the most general report on the code's implementation. The secretariat's ability to play that role is constrained, in turn, by its dependence on key fishing states for its budget.

● UNDP, with a budget of over $2 billion annually, a staff of 5,300 worldwide, and liaison offices in 132 countries, is the largest single source of multilateral grant development assistance. Moreover, it has projects in every developing country, allocating its funds for five-year periods according to a formula based primarily on population and per capita GNP, and is the only UN agency with resident representatives in each member country. Prior to the preparations for UNCED, however, UNDP gave little attention to the environment or sustainable development as a mission and lacked the expertise to provide environmentally sound technical advice to developing countries.

In 1994, in direct response to UNCED, UNDP administrator Gus Speth, a well-known environmentalist, made a strategic decision to strengthen UNDP's environment and sustainable development capacity by establishing the Sustainable Energy and Environment Division (SEED). Since its origin, SEED has worked to support UNDP's overall efforts to help countries successfully design and carry out programs that support the implementation of Agenda 21 and the Rio Conventions. One of SEED's primary objectives is to bridge the perceived "gap" between environmental programs and development programs to ensure that the needs of humans are met while protecting the planet's natural resources and ecosystems.[31] UNDP is also one of the three implementing agencies of the Global Environment Facility and is the lead UN agency in building the capacity of developing-country governments for sustainable development under its Capacity 21 program. UNDP also assists in building capacity for good governance, popular participation, private and public sector development and growth with equity, all of which are necessary to promote sustainable human development.

In spite of UNDP's intentions, a recent study[32] examined UNDP's regular portfolio of projects and determined that UNDP had not been as "proenvironment" as it seemed. For example, UNDP reduced the number of projects and total funding for new and renewable energy from 22 projects for a total of $22.6 million in 1993, to only 11 projects for a total of $5.1 million in 1996.[33] Furthermore, in fiscal 1997, UNDP continued to provide four times more grant funding for conventional sources of energy (petroleum, coal and gas) than it did for "new and renewable sources of energy."[34] To its credit, UNDP has taken some key steps toward greater emphasis on new and renewable energy, including its Initiative for Sustainable Energy, a policy document that serves as the basis for national and regional training events for UNDP and government staff, and a change in the project approval and implementation process.[35] Speth stepped down as UNDP administrator in June 1999, and many are curious as to whether or not environment will remain a strong focus under Speth's successor, Mark Malloch Brown, formerly the World Bank's Vice President for External Affairs and United Nations Affairs.

IOs may influence state policy by focusing normative pressures on states regarding the environment and sustainable development even when no formal international agreement exists on the norm.[36] UNDP has gone the farthest of any UN agency in this regard, asserting the allocation of a minimum level of resources for human resource development (health, population, and education) by both donor countries and developing-country governments as a norm in the context of what it calls "sustainable human development." Through its annual *Human Development Report*, which ranks nations on the basis of their provision of these social services, UNDP pressures developing countries to devote more of their budgets to these social sectors. UNDP has also begun to inject norms into UN-related international forums, including the World Summit for Social Development. UNDP's normative advocacy has made some developing countries uncomfortable.[37]

**Multilateral Financial
Institutions as Actors**

In terms of direct impact on the development and environmental policies of developing states, the most powerful IOs are the multilateral financial institutions, including the World Bank, the International Monetary Fund, and the regional banks, because of the amount of financial resources that they transfer to developing countries each year in support of particular development strategies and economic policies. Within these IOs, in which voting is weighted according to the size of a country's contributions, the donor countries are the dominant players. The United States has the most power in the World Bank and the Inter-American Development Bank (IADB), as does Japan in the Asian Development Bank.

•The World Bank's influence on the policies of its borrowers has been viewed by environmental activists as contributing to unsustainable development. The Bank has been driven by the need to lend large amounts of money each year; by a bias toward large-scale, capital-intensive, and centralized projects; and by its practice of assessing projects on the basis of a quantifiable rate of return while discounting longer-term, unquantifiable social and environmental costs. In the 1970s and 1980s, the Bank supported rain forest colonization schemes in Brazil and Indonesia, cattle-ranching projects in Central and South America, and tobacco projects in Africa that contributed to accelerated deforestation and a cattle development project in Botswana that contributed to desertification.[38]

In response to persistent, well-orchestrated pressure from NGOs and U.S. Congress criticism of such egregious loans, the World Bank began a process of evolution in the mid-1980s toward greater sensitivity to the environmental implications of its lending. It refused to provide new support for some of the worst projects in Brazil and Indonesia, created an Environment Department, began to build an environmental staff, and financed more explicitly environmental programs.

Under pressure to become part of the solution to global environmental problems rather than a contributor to the problem, the Bank has taken a number of steps directly related to these issues since 1990. In 1990–1991, it became an implementing agency of the nascent Global Environment Facility (GEF), the multilateral fund to finance the additional costs to countries of projects that have global environmental benefits, as well as of the Multilateral Fund of the Montreal Protocol. It thus had the largest portfolio of global environmental projects of any multilateral institution, albeit funded by other donors.

With regard to forests the Bank has combined investments in conservation and capacity building in selected tropical forest countries with policy dialogues aimed at eliminating the worst distortions in the sector. It also adopted a new forest policy in 1991 that precluded support for commercial logging in primary tropical forests. The biggest obstacle to success in the Bank's approach was lack of political will on the part of governments of states with intensive exploitation of forests.

In Indonesia, the Bank implemented two loans in the late 1980s and early 1990s for development of a forest database and institution building, but a later project with ambitious policy and institutional reform goals had to be abandoned during preparation because the Suharto government resisted key policy reforms.[39] In 1998, the Bank negotiated a major structural adjustment loan with Indonesia as part of the economic rescue package, which included pledges to carry out some far-reaching reforms in the logging-concession system. But when Indonesia failed to deliver on its pledges, the Bank was unwilling to suspend payments because its interests in reviving the economy trumped environmental concerns. (See the discussion of adjustment lending below.)

Perhaps reflecting an implicit recognition of the past failure of the Bank to leverage changes in the forest management policies of clients, in 1998 it tried a different strategy on forests: it launched the World Bank–World Wide Fund for Nature Forest Alliance. The Forest Alliance represents a sharp shift in the Bank's approach to an open acknowledgment of the critical problems of commercial logging, the illegal practices in the forest sector, and the frequently corrupt nexus between officials and economic elites and to the use of a combination of resources, technical assistance, and public pressures on government. It is also distinct in the identification of measures and ambitious global forest policy goals: 50 million hectares of new forest protected areas, 50 million hectares of threatened forests put under sustainable management, and 100 million hectares each of the world's tropical and boreal/temperate forests under independently certified sustainable management by 2005.

On biodiversity, the Bank adopted a new policy of not supporting any projects that would result in significant conversion or degradation of habitats that are officially designated as critical—a limitation that severely limits its application. In 1996, the Bank presented its first "biodiversity assistance strategy" to the second meeting of the Conference of the Parties to the Convention on Biological Diversity, emphasizing the importance of integrating biodiversity concerns into country assistance strategies.

As an implementing agency of the GEF and in implementing its "biodiversity assistance strategy," the Bank had pledged publicly to integrate global environmental concerns into its lending portfolio. And in 1996 it established a program to identify opportunities for promoting both development objectives and global environmental benefits in loan projects in the process of preparing country lending strategies for each client government. But the Bank devoted too few budgetary resources and too little staffing to the program, and as a result its Country Assistance Strategies, written in 1996 and 1997, seldom made the linkages between renewable resource problems and biodiversity loss.[40] As a result, lending for biodiversity in the Bank's regular loan portfolio did not increase from 1994 through 1997, compared with the six-year period prior to 1994.[41] However, during the same period, the Bank did invest an additional $73.2 million of its own funds in eight biodiversity loans that were made more attractive to borrowers by linking them with GEF grants.[42]

With regard to climate change, the Bank's longtime role as financier of large conventional fossil fuel power loans has been in sharp conflict with the UN Framework Convention on Climate Change's objective of greenhouse gas emissions reductions. From 1990 through 1997, the Bank approved 170 loans in the electric power sector totaling more than $24 billion, mostly for governments that have no obligations to reduce their greenhouse gas emissions, resulting in an additional 10 billion tons of carbon over the lifetime of the projects.[43] So it was impossible for the Bank to claim that it was supporting the treaty's aim of reducing greenhouse gases.

The Bank has defended its lending for fossil fuel power plants by arguing that the climate change convention does not require non-Annex I (developing) countries to reduce their emissions and, therefore, does not permit the World Bank to "force" a country to accept a higher-cost energy alternative.[44] But the Bank has established environmental conditions on lending in the energy sector (including a ban on nuclear power projects) in the absence of international agreements requiring any such restrictions and against the wishes of its clients.[45]

The World Bank Group's energy strategy, adopted in 1998, called for lending only to the countries committed to energy efficiency through policy reform, but the Bank did little to encourage states to undertake a major shift to renewable energy development. World Bank lending for end-use energy efficiency was much greater in the post-GEF period, but lending for renewable energy (other than geothermal) in the GEF period was actually less than in the pre-GEF period. Country Assistance Strategies that included large power sector loans conveniently ignored their global environmental implications.[46] The Bank itself conceded that lending for energy efficiency and renewables was still "modest," largely because "environmentally friendly energy projects are more labor-intensive, borrower commitment to fundamental reform is often weak and energy efficiency and renewable energy are relatively new business products for which skills and experience are scarce."[47]

Structural adjustment, usually involving coordinated lending by the World Bank and the International Monetary Fund (IMF), can strongly influence the policies of heavily indebted developing countries on key issues of sustainability. Structural adjustment programs require the borrowing country to reduce domestic demand through removing subsidies and cutting government budgets, devaluating currencies, and tightening credit while increasing exports in order to achieve a positive trade balance and pay off debts. IMF and World Bank officials have argued that economic distortions such as overvalued exchange rates, artificially low agricultural prices, and subsidies actually hurt the poorest segments of society and create perverse incentives for activities that degrade the environment.[48] Some analysts have argued that the consequences of these programs (greater industrial unemployment and fewer primary health care services) have worsened the plight of the poor, caused increased population migration onto marginal lands, and created pressure for more rapid logging of forests and more intensive cultivation, whereas others have found no clear pattern of adverse environmental impacts of adjustment lending.[49]

In theory, structural adjustment lending can be either bad or good for the environment, depending on the environmental and socioeconomic situation and the conditions for policy reform that are required. If policy reforms are needed to eliminate distortions that result in mining of natural resources, their inclusion in a structural adjustment loan agreement could help overcome major political resistance to reform. But as the Indonesian case study below shows, structural obstacles in the nature of the World Bank and the IMF may constrain the use of structural adjustment lending to achieve major policy reforms that are not directly related to short-term resumption of economic growth and positive trade balances.

The IMF has been far slower than the World Bank and regional banks to acknowledge the need to take environmental considerations explicitly into account in its lending operations, defining its role as limited to helping countries achieve balance of payments and pay off their international debts. Only in 1991 did the IMF executive board consider for the first time the extent to which the IMF should "address environmental issues." It decided that the IMF should avoid policies that might harm the environment but that it should not do any research or build up its own expertise on possible environmental consequences of its policies.[50] In May 1993, an IMF official, meeting for the first time with NGOs, suggested that the IMF must pursue its macroeconomic objectives "separate" from issues of sustainable development.[51] More recently, the IMF and the World Bank have put in place a joint initiative for Heavily Indebted Poor Countries (HIPC Initiative). The Initiative is aimed at reducing the debt-service burden of eligible countries to sustainable levels and helping them exit from the debt-rescheduling process, provided they adopt and pursue strong and sustained programs of adjustment and reform. Implementation of this Initiative should help eliminate external debt as an impediment to achieving sustainable development.[52]

The IMF claims that its mandate and the expertise of its staff limit its ability to address environmental issues. Since the World Bank addresses environmental issues and supports an extensive work program on environmental and other sectoral issues, the Executive Board of the IMF decided early that the IMF should not duplicate the work of the Bank in this area. The IMF's involvement is thus limited to only those areas that have a serious and perceptible impact on the macroeconomic outlook of a country or on the effectiveness of macroeconomic policy instruments in achieving domestic and external stability.

Even in these respects, the IMF sometimes runs into obstacles. At times, a member country does not have a National Environmental Action Plan or a stated national strategy to protect the environment. In some cases, even where such plans or strategies do exist, they are not specific enough to allow the IMF staff to consider their macroeconomic implications. Sometimes, the authorities themselves are not fully committed to environmental objectives because of pressure from one or more interest groups or because these objectives conflict with short-run economic growth or with some other objective of the country's policymakers. Thus, the IMF argues, it can only integrate environment into its policy dialogue to the extent that member countries allow it to do so.[53]

When Indonesia's economy collapsed in 1997–1998 and had to be rescued by major loans from the IMF and the World Bank, it presented a unique opportunity to hold the government of Indonesia accountable for eliminating the most distorted and corrupt features of its forest exploitation system. The policy reforms negotiated by the IMF with the Suharto regime in early 1998 included pledges to reform the logging concession system and to "reduce land conversion targets to environmentally sustainable levels." The latter pledge referred to the clear-cutting of forests that had already been logged over but were still productive to plant oil palm or timber plantations, which was rapidly becoming as important a source of logs as commercial logging concessions. Conversion of forests to oil palm plantations was usually accomplished by burning logging refuse after clear-cutting the forests, and was the single largest cause of the catastrophic forest fires that raged in Indonesia in 1997–1998.[54]

In July 1998, the World Bank followed the IMF agreement with its own $1-billion structural adjustment loan to post-Suharto Indonesia, which went further on forest policy reform: It required that the Indonesian government prepare an accurate map of the forest areas of key provinces based on recent satellite imagery and identify priority conservation areas. Pending completion of the mapping exercise, the government was required by the loan agreement to "implement and maintain a moratorium on conversion of state forest areas." Any future conversion or change in forest land use status was to be reviewed through a transparent and consultative process involving both nongovernment stakeholders and interdepartmental dialogue within the government. Finally the agreement required the government to publish a list of all applications already received prior to the date of the agreement and to "subject them to public review prior to final approval."[55]

But the government failed to make good on its pledges. The Forestry Ministry argued that it could not turn down applications from companies that had already made some investment in the conversion process. Some applications were still being approved, despite the pledged moratorium. Moreover, no list of applications was ever published, nor any public review carried out. The World Bank's Jakarta office was unable to obtain any information on approvals or rejections during the first six months of 1999.

Nevertheless, despite this clear failure to comply with the terms of a critical forest policy reform requirement, the World Bank went ahead with disbursement of the second tranche of $400 million in February 1999. Then it signed a second adjustment loan in May 1999, which was disbursed immediately upon signing. World Bank staff said privately that the Bank could only pick a few policy conditionalities as the basis for deciding whether to go ahead with disbursement and with a new loan.

The World Bank thus let the biggest opportunity it is likely to have to leverage policy reform in the Indonesian forest sector go by without decisive action. The failure to hold Indonesia accountable for the most elementary forest policy reforms cannot be explained in terms of the Bank staff involved but clearly reflected the political preferences of the finance ministries of the major funders of the World Bank and the IMF, starting with the United States, Germany, Japan, and the United Kingdom.

Regional and Other Multistate Organizations as Actors

In recent years, regional groupings of states have played an increasing role in environmental politics. Some, such as the regional fishing organizations, are specific functional groups that have taken on environmental responsibilities out of necessity. Others have a broad political or economic agenda but have taken on significant environmental functions. The European Union is the most advanced of the latter group in that it is the only such regional organization whose decisions obligate its members. It is often represented by its own delegation in negotiations and is more often than not a party in its own right to various international environmental conventions, as are its member states.

The Organization for Economic Cooperation and Development (OECD) is also a player on the international environmental stage. The OECD has played a major role in promoting sustainable consumption and production within its member states and has provided a great deal of background information and support to its members on such issues as climate change mitigation, trade- and environment-related issues, and transport and the environment.

The Organization of African Unity (OAU) has also undertaken several regional environmental initiatives. It is trying to demonstrate regionally appropriate sustainable development strategies, and it organized strong opposition to importation of all hazardous wastes into its region. It hosted the negotiations of the Bamako Convention on trade in hazardous wastes and argued consistently for a worldwide ban on trade in hazardous wastes under the Basel Convention. The OAU also submitted a number of proposals that were incorporated into the 1994 Convention to Combat Desertification.

The Organization of American States (OAS) was the first regional organization to hold a presidential summit on the environment when it convened the Summit of the Americas on Sustainable Development in Bolivia in December 1996. The Unit for Sustainable Development and Environment (USDE) is the principal technical arm of the OAS General Secretariat for responding to the needs of member states on issues relating to sustainable development within an economic development context. With the objective of establishing concrete means to strengthen sustainable development, at the Bolivia Summit the heads of state and government conferred responsibility to the OAS for formulating a strategy for the promotion of public participation in decisionmaking for sustainable development. The USDE coordinated the formulation of the Inter-American Strategy for Public Participation in Environment and Sustainable Development Decision-Making in the Americas, which was adopted in December 1999. This project focuses on the exchange of experiences and information between government and civil society; legal and institutional mechanisms facilitating civil-society participation; capacity building; and national- and regional-level consultation processes.

• Asia-Pacific Economic Cooperation (APEC), which was formed in 1989 in response to the growing interdependence among Asia-Pacific economies, also deals with three categories of environmental issues, including air, atmospheric and water pollution, especially those related to energy production and use, resource degradation, and demographic shifts, including rural out-migration, food security, and urbanization. APEC had a major setback in 1998 as a result of the spread of the Asian financial crisis. However, at their November 1998 meeting in Kuala Lumpur, Malaysia, the APEC Economic Leaders reiterated their "commitment to advance sustainable development across the entire spectrum of our workplan including cleaner production, protection of the marine environment and sustainable cities."[56] However, what concrete actions APEC or its member countries are willing or able to implement remains to be seen.

There are also regional organizations created for explicit environmental purposes. One such organization is the South Pacific Regional Environment Programme (SPREP), which was created in 1982. SPREP has created a framework for environmentally sound planning and management that is suited to the South Pacific region. SPREP's action program aims to build national capacity in environmental and resource management to improve and protect the environment. SPREP has also provided capacity building, training, and support for its member states to improve their ability to represent their interests in international negotiations on such issues as climate change, as well as in United Nations global conferences.[57]

The Central American Commission on Environment and Development (CCAD) was organized for regional cooperation on development. It developed a Central American agenda in preparation for UNCED, a common position on hazardous waste, and an Alliance for Sustainable Development to coordinate policy.[58] In response to the disasters caused by Hurricane Mitch in 1998, CCAD and the Secretariat of the System for the Central American Integration (SICA) are preparing an Action Plan for the Integrated Management of Water Resources in the Central American Isthmus. The CCAD has also negotiated a regional forestry treaty and is building regional environmental institutions.[59]

NONGOVERNMENTAL
ORGANIZATIONS AS ACTORS

The emergence of the global environment as a major issue in world politics has coincided with the rise of NGOs as a major force in the politics of the environment.[60] Although business organizations are included in the United Nations definition of an NGO,[61] the term is used here to mean a private, nonprofit organization that is not beholden either to government or to a profit-making organization.

NGO influence on global environmental politics has been based on one or more of three factors: first, NGOs' expert knowledge and innovative thinking about global environmental issues, acquired from specializing in issues under negotiation; second, their dedication to goals that transcend narrow national or sectoral interests; and third, their representation of substantial constituencies within their own countries that command attention and that sometimes influence policies and even tight electoral contests.

In the industrialized countries, most NGOs that are active in global environmental politics fall into one of three categories: organizations that are affiliated with international NGOs (INGOs), which are NGOs with branches in a number of countries; large national organizations focused primarily on domestic environmental issues; and think tanks, or research institutes, whose influence comes primarily from publishing studies and issuing proposals for action.

INGOs may be a loose federation of national affiliates or have a more centralized structure. Friends of the Earth International (FOEI), based in Amsterdam, is a confederation of 60 national, independent affiliates, half of which are in developing countries. At an annual meeting, delegates democratically set priorities and select five or more campaigns on which they cooperate each year. Greenpeace is one of the largest INGOs, with more than 2.4 million financial supporters/members and offices in 40 countries.[62] Its international activities are tightly organized from a well-staffed headquarters (also in Amsterdam) and guided by issues and strategies determined at an annual meeting.

The Switzerland-based World Wildlife Fund (WWF)—also known in Europe as the Worldwide Fund for Nature—is the world's largest and one of the most experienced independent conservation organizations, with around 5 million supporters and a global network of 27 national organizations, 5 associates, and 21 program offices. Its focus traditionally has been the protection of wildlife, but recently it has also been involved in policy issues such as trade and structural adjustment. In recent years, the U.S. affiliate has established extensive development and conservation projects in Latin America and Asia, which give the organization international credibility and valuable links with local groups around the world. The European Environmental Bureau (EEB), organized in 1974, is now a confederation of 130 national-level environmental organizations in 24 countries. The EEB works on issues within the EU as well as on EU policies toward global environmental issues and has direct access to the European Commission, which also contributes financially to its work. It includes the full range of European NGOs, and its style of operation is moderate rather than confrontational. Affiliates of all the INGOs make extensive use of fax, e-mail, and the Internet, greatly improving their ability to act expeditiously in concert on key issues.

More recently, in May 1999, a group of more than 60 representatives of NGOs from Europe and the United States agreed to establish the Transatlantic Environment Dialogue (TAED) to bring together environmental citizens' organizations and other NGOs to influence policies at the national and global levels. The TAED plans to work on climate change, biodiversity conservation, trade and environment, agriculture and environment, and industry and environment.[63]

In the second category of NGOs are the big U.S. environmental organizations, all of which have international programs. Some, such as the Sierra Club, the National Audubon Society, and the National Wildlife Federation (NWF), were formed in the late nineteenth and early twentieth centuries around conservation issues. Other organizations with a broad national agenda, including Environmental Defense (formerly the Environmental Defense Fund, or EDF) and the Natural Resources Defense Council (NRDC), which have used legal, economic, and regulatory processes to affect national policy and have become very important actors on international atmospheric and climate issues, arose in the early 1970s. Along with FOE/USA, they have played effective roles in the negotiations on climate and ozone and have also helped reshape the policies of the multilateral development banks. Still other organizations with more specific agendas have become internationally active on their issues, including Defenders of Wildlife and the Humane Society on marine-mammal issues. Total membership in these national environmental organizations increased in the 1980s to an estimated 13 million and leveled off in the 1990s.

Environmental think tanks, normally funded by private donations or contracts, rely primarily on their technical expertise and research programs to influence global environmental policy. Examples are the Worldwatch Institute, whose publications have often identified new problems and suggested alternative approaches to international issues, and the World Resources Institute (WRI), which publishes reports on the global environment and policy studies on specific issues. The International Institute for Environment and Development (IIED) in London drew early attention to the environment/poverty connection in developing countries. In a few countries, government-funded but nevertheless independent institutes seek to directly influence the policies of their own governments and of international negotiations. The International Institute for Sustainable Development (IISD) of Canada and the Stockholm Environment Institute of Sweden have played such roles. All of these organizations collaborate with colleagues in other countries.

Environmental NGOs in developing countries tend to be as much concerned with poverty and other development issues as with strictly environmental issues. They tend to stress issues such as land use, forest management and fishing rights, and redistribution of power over natural resources, rather than ozone depletion and global warming.[64] But there are many exceptions, such as the Chilean and Argentinean NGOs' interest in the ozone layer and the NGOs in low-lying coastal areas or small islands who are concerned about climate change. Developing-country NGOs often have become involved in international policy issues through opposition to multilateral-bank projects and government policies that displace villages or threaten rain forests, and they tend to regard transnational corporations as enemies of the environment. Inherently critical of their governments on most domestic policies, NGO members who are committed to environmental protection often have been harassed, subjected to political repression, and jailed. In some countries, however, they have acquired political legitimacy and even a measure of influence on national environmental policy issues. In many countries, the widespread, effective, visible participation of NGOs in the UNCED process added to their stature at home.

Developing-country NGOs often form national-level coalitions, such as the Brazilian NGO Forum, which had over 1,000 organizations affiliated with it at the time of UNCED; the Indonesian Environmental Forum (WALHI), which unites hundreds of environmental organizations countrywide; and the Kenya Environmental Non-Governmental Organization (KENGO), founded in 1982, which now includes 68 environmental groups and has ties with groups in 22 other African countries. Indigenous minorities in the five Amazon Basin countries have organized their own national-level coalitions, which in turn have formed a coordinating body (called COICA, for its Spanish name) to lobby for a voice in all Amazon development projects affecting them. Indeed, UNCED recognition of indigenous groups in Chapter 26 of Agenda 21 and their highly visible participation at the Rio conference have given a boost to the rights of indigenous peoples and given them a modest influence on international environmental negotiations.

Broad international coalitions of NGOs working on a specific environmental issue have also become a means of increasing NGO influence. The

Antarctic and Southern Oceans Coalition (ASOC) is a consortium of 200 environmental organizations in 33 countries that lobbied against the Antarctic minerals treaty and for an Antarctic environmental protocol. The Climate Action Network, formed in November 1989, has over 250 member organizations from around the world that share a common concern for the greenhouse effect and wish to cooperate in the development and implementation of short- and long-term strategies.

North-South NGO alliances have sometimes been very effective in influencing international events. An alliance between U.S. NGOs and indigenous opponents of rain forest destruction brought worldwide attention to Brazilian policy in 1986. Together they helped stop the World Bank's Polonoreste project, an Amazonian road-building and colonization scheme, persuaded President José Sarney to halt the tax incentives for agriculture and ranching that had stimulated the Amazon land boom, and persuaded members of the U.S. Congress and officials of the Inter-American Development Bank to support extractive reserves.[65]

The Internet has facilitated North-South NGO cooperation on a number of issues. For example, in 1997 a coalition of Northern and Southern NGOs, ranging from the Third World Network in Malaysia to the Council of Canadians used the World Wide Web, electronic mail, and electronic conferencing to quickly organize opposition to the Multilateral Agreement on Investment (MAI). The prospective treaty to liberalize international investment rules was being negotiated behind the closed doors of the OECD.[66] In December 1998, the OECD canceled negotiations, acknowledging that the NGOs had aroused enough opposition in many countries to derail the process.

But relations between Northern and Southern NGOs are not always smooth. At climate change negotiations in February 1991, developing-country NGOs charged that they had not been consulted by Northern NGOs advocating steeper curtailment of CO_2 emissions, the burden of which they thought would fall on developing countries. There was a similar division in the pre-UNCED discussions of a forest treaty. In this matter, also, the Southern NGOs' position tended to parallel their governments'. There is sometimes a Southern resentment of Northern NGOs, especially at the big international conferences such as UNCED, where the better-prepared, better-financed U.S. and European NGOs are heavily represented. Despite these tensions, however, there were many instances of close North-South cooperation in lobbying during UNCED, as well as jointly issued statements on key issues. For example, the Brazilian NGO Forum and CAPE '92, a coalition of six leading U.S. environmental organizations, issued a joint paper on financial resources and mechanisms with specific proposals on sources of funding and environmental commodity agreements.

One organization through which NGOs influence environmental politics is the International Union for the Conservation of Nature (IUCN). It has 895 member groups, including individual government agencies and NGOs, and it can draw on the work of six international commissions composed of 8,000 volunteer scientists and other professionals. Governed by a General Assembly of delegates from its member organizations that meets every three years, the IUCN has had a major influence on global agreements on wildlife conservation. While IUCN actions tend to be limited by state member agencies and often embrace only broad consensus positions, IUCN has been successful in drafting environmental treaties and assisting in monitoring their implementation.

**Influencing Environmental
Regime Formation**

NGOs influence international regimes in five ways. They may

- influence the global environmental agenda by defining a new issue or redefining an old one;
- lobby or pressure their own or other governments to accept a more advanced position toward an issue, by advancing new proposals, by carrying out consumer boycotts and educational campaigns, or by bringing lawsuits;
- propose entire draft texts of conventions in advance of conferences;
- lobby and participate in international negotiations; or
- monitor the implementation of conventions and report to the secretariat and/or the parties.

An example of influencing the global environmental agenda is the role that WWF and Conservation International (CI) played in 1988–1989 in creating a new issue of banning commerce in African elephant ivory by publishing a report on the problem and circulating it to parties of the Convention on the International Trade in Endangered Species (CITES). In 1987, despite momentum toward an Antarctic minerals convention, the Antarctic and Southern Oceans Coalition, in which Greenpeace, Friends of the Earth, and WWF were the biggest and most active organizations, put forward a detailed proposal for an Antarctic World Park that would exclude mineral exploration. Two years later, the World Park proposal was the basis for a new policy rejecting a treaty to govern future minerals exploitation in Antarctica.

Pressing for changes in the policy of a major actor is sometimes the best means for NGOs to influence an international regime. In the case of protecting the ozone layer, the U.S. Clean Air Coalition, a group of national environmental organizations, successfully lobbied for a ban on aerosols and regulation of CFCs. They lobbied for a total phase-out of CFCs before negotiations on the Montreal Protocol began, contributing to U.S. international leadership on this issue. Similarly, three U.S. NGOs working with protreaty biotechnology firms were a major influence on the Clinton administration's decision to reverse the Bush administration's position and sign the biodiversity convention in 1993.[67] Although effective consumer boycotts are rare, an NGO-organized boycott affected the whaling issue in 1988 when 100 school districts and several fast-food and supermarket chains boycotted Icelandic fish because of Iceland's prowhaling stand and brought a temporary halt to that country's whaling.[68]

In the negotiations on Antarctic minerals, a coalition of 20 Australian NGOs were instrumental in converting Australian prime minister Bob Hawke in 1989 to reject the Antarctic minerals treaty that his negotiators had just helped negotiate and adopt the Antarctic World Park in its place. And when Italy, Belgium, and other countries supported the Australian position, it was in large part due to effective lobbying by NGOs affiliated with the ASOC.[69] Greenpeace's monitoring and reporting on the toxic waste trade was a key factor in encouraging a coalition of countries to push for a complete ban on North-South waste trade under the Basel Convention.

A more specialized way for NGOs to influence international regimes is to write a draft convention well in advance of the negotiations. Few NGOs have the staff resources to devote to such a task, and only IUCN has succeeded in getting draft conventions to be used as the basis for negotiations. The Convention Concerning the Protection of the World Cultural and Natural Heritage, signed in 1972 in Paris, was based on a draft produced by IUCN. CITES, signed in 1973, was the result of an IUCN initiative that went through three drafts over nearly a decade.[70]

NGOs have become especially active and well organized in lobbying at international negotiating conferences. The conferences of the parties to most environmental conventions permit NGO observers, enabling NGOs to be actively involved in the proceedings. Certain NGOs specialize in the meetings of particular conventions and have acquired over the years a high level of technical and legal expertise. The Humane Society of the United States has been lobbying at meetings of the International Whaling Commission (IWC) since 1973, and Greenpeace has been active in the conference of the parties to the London Convention since the early 1980s. The Antarctic and Southern Oceans Coalition began attending meetings of the Antarctic Treaty Consultative Parties to lobby on Antarctic environmental issues in 1987, when those meetings were first opened up to NGO observers.

The Climate Action Network was extremely active in the negotiation of the Framework Convention on Climate Change and the Kyoto Protocol and continues to participate in the meetings of the conference of the parties to the convention. The Climate Action Network lobbied extensively for greater commitments toward the reduction of greenhouse gas emissions beyond the year 2000 during the Kyoto Protocol negotiations.

NGOs also influence international conferences primarily by providing scientific and technical information or new arguments to delegations that are already sympathetic to their objectives. In the process leading up to the whaling moratorium, NGOs supplied factual information on violations of the whaling convention as well as scientific information not otherwise available to the delegations.[71] In some circumstances, however, NGOs may have particularly strong influence on a key delegation's positions, as happened with the biodiversity negotiations in 1991–1992, when WWF/Australia and other NGOs represented on the Australian delegation were consulted on all major issues in the convention before the delegation adopted positions.[72] The Foundation for International Environmental Law and Development (FIELD) has assisted the Alliance of Small Island States within the context of the climate change negotiations. FIELD has been instrumental in providing AOSIS with advice and legal expertise, which has enabled the Alliance to wield unexpected influence in the climate negotiations.[73] Greenpeace provided a great deal of technical support to African and other developing countries, which were supporting a ban on the dumping of hazardous wastes in developing countries during the negotiation of the Basel Convention.

NGOs can also provide useful reporting services during these conferences. *ECO* has been published by NGOs at numerous UN-sponsored environmental conferences since 1972 and provides a combination of news stories and commentary. The *Earth Negotiations Bulletin*, published by IISD, has provided objective reports of United Nations environment and development negotiations since 1992.[74] The reporting of ongoing negotiations is something countries cannot do easily or effectively on their own. If any one government were to attempt to provide such reporting, the reports would be derided as biased. If the UN or a formal secretariat published daily reports, they would have the status of official documents, and member governments would have difficulty agreeing on content, style, tone, and so forth. However, since the NGO community is already providing the information, in a fair manner and free of charge, there is little incentive for governments to step in.[75]

NGOs can also influence regime formation by monitoring compliance with an agreement once it goes into effect. Investigation and reporting by NGOs can bring pressure on parties that are violating provisions of an agreement. They can demonstrate the need for a more effective enforcement mechanism (or for creation of a mechanism where none exists) or help build support for the further elaboration or strengthening of the existing regime rules.

This NGO function has been especially important with regard to CITES and whaling regimes. The international Trade Records Analysis of Flora and Fauna in Commerce (TRAFFIC), a joint wildlife trade monitoring program of WWF and IUCN, has played a vital role in supplementing the CITES secretariat in monitoring the compliance of various countries with CITES bans on trade in endangered species.[76] Climate networks in the United States and the EU produced specific critical reviews of countries' national climate action plans even before the climate treaty came into effect. Greenpeace's aggressive reporting of hazardous wastes dumped in violation of the Basel and Bamako agreements helped create a climate in which a full ban on international shipping of such wastes to non-OECD countries was accomplished in 1994.

NGOs and International Institutions

Influencing the structure and policies of major international institutions active in global environmental politics poses a different set of challenges to NGOs. The international NGO community has taken on a wide range of global institutions, from the World Bank and the GEF to the International Tropical Timber Organization (ITTO) and the World Trade Organization (WTO). These institutions have different characteristics that help to explain the degree of success of NGO efforts to influence the policies and structures of each.

The most successful such NGO effort was influencing the restructuring of the Global Environment Facility, on which both Southern and Northern NGOs were in full agreement. The NGOs were highly critical of the GEF as administered by the World Bank during its 1991–1993 pilot phase. They supported the developing-country position for a secretariat independent of the World Bank and for project approval by a council of all treaty parties.[77]

Primarily because of the importance of the U.S. Congress in approving funding for the multilateral development banks, U.S. NGOs have been effective in forcing some changes in the lending of multilateral development banks (MDBs).[78] Between 1983 and 1987, U.S. environmental NGOs in alliance with congressional fiscal conservatives persuaded congressional appropriations subcommittees to sponsor legislation directing the U.S. executive directors of the MDBs to press for environmental reforms. As a result, by 1986, the United States began voting against particularly egregious World Bank loans, prompting former World Bank president Barber Conable's 1987 commitment to greater attention to the environment.

In the late 1980s, NGO campaigning for bank reform began to focus on issues of public participation and accountability. About 150 NGOs worldwide participated in some fashion in a campaign to spur greater openness and accountability and to encourage debt reduction and development strategies that were more equitable and less destructive to the environment. Today, partly as a result of this high-profile pressure, about half of the Bank's lending projects have provisions for NGO involvement, up from an average of only 6 percent between 1973 and 1988. The Bank has even included NGOs such as Oxfam International in multilateral debt relief discussions. Even the IMF is recognizing the role of NGOs. In June 1998, the IMF Board of Directors met with several NGO leaders to discuss their proposals to increase the fund's transparency.[79]

Much more difficult still for NGOs is the trade and environmental issue, to which they turned their attention only in 1990. The General Agreement on Tariffs and Trade (GATT) has one single-minded goal, determined half a century ago, to reduce tariffs and other trade barriers. The GATT has never had provisions for NGO observers. Environmental activists have been campaigning for increased transparency, participation, and accountability in the WTO, portraying it as a secretive organization lacking in accountability. They argue that NGOs have a crucial role to play in making the world trading system more transparent and accountable.[80] Prior to the third WTO ministerial talks in Seattle in December 1999, it was believed that although NGO demands for participation are unlikely to be met in the near future, it was apparent that governments were attempting to engage in a more open manner with development and environmental organizations.[81] However, in the aftermath of the Seattle meeting and the massive protests both inside and outside the negotiations, it is not clear just what role NGOs will play and how much influence they will have in the future. (See Chapter 5.)

NGOs in UNCED and the Post-UNCED Process

UNCED represented a new level of NGO participation in global environmental politics. In fact, NGOs' unusual degree of access to meetings and delegations, especially at the Preparatory Committee meetings, has become the standard by which subsequent UN conferences are judged. NGO success at Rio helped open up subsequent UN conferences on human rights, population, social development, women, and human settlements to greater NGO participation. A record number of NGOs participated in the UNCED process: About 200 NGOs were accredited to the second PrepCom for UNCED in Geneva in March 1991, and nearly 500 NGOs brought some 1,200 people to the final PrepCom for UNCED in New York in March 1992. About one-third of them were from developing countries, as nearly 100 developing-country NGOs were helped in financing the trip to New York by a fund established by the UNCED secretariat (which recognized the NGOs as potential allies) and supported by some governments and private foundations.[82]

The UNCED preparatory process enhanced NGO influence in other ways: NGOs in industrialized countries were encouraged to form new cross-sectoral coalitions that integrated environment and development issues. Two coalitions that have been particularly effective in the post-UNCED era have been the Women's Caucus and the CSD NGO Steering Committee. The Women's Caucus was created in 1991 by the Women's Environment and Development Organization (WEDO) as a means of bringing activists together. The Women's Caucus has played a pivotal role in UN conferences, including the Earth Summit, the 1994 International Conference on Population and Development and the 1995 Fourth World Conference on Women, as well as meetings of other United Nations bodies, such as the CSD. Every morning during negotiating sessions, and at the actual conferences or meetings, hundreds, sometimes thousands, of representatives of NGOs have met to develop strategies for common-ground advocacy and coordination, based on line-by-line analyses of official documents by WEDO's international working group which, after consultation, suggests policy improvements in language. The aim of WEDO's linkage strategy is to prevent collective amnesia by governments and to make steady progress in formulating and implementing improved public policies not only for women but also for all people.[83] Many credit the Women's Caucus for effectively lobbying for most of the language on the role of women in Agenda 21, as well as language on the empowerment of women and sustainable development in the Programme of Action adopted at the International Conference on Population and Development.

The CSD NGO Steering Committee was formed in 1994 by representatives of NGOs and other "major groups" present at annual sessions of the CSD. Members of the committee are elected by region, issue, and major group. The system of regional representation has helped to ensure that there are more Southern than Northern NGO representatives on the committee. Two cochairs, one from the North and one from the South, are chosen by all NGOs who participate. The Steering Committee's key roles include sharing information with organizations around the world and making necessary arrangements to strengthen NGO input into official UN processes. The committee has also overseen the work of caucuses meeting to focus on specific issues. This has allowed for selection of NGO spokespeople in key areas, which has in turn enhanced input into the intergovernmental process. Because the Steering Committee's goal is not to formulate policy but to coordinate development of common NGO positions, it has gained the support of a wide range of organizations, who appreciate that greater dialogue and cooperation is in the interest of all NGO participants in the work of the CSD.[84] These developments have represented a maturing process since 1992, when differing objectives and philosophies often prevented NGOs from working together effectively.

The NGO Steering Committee has also worked with the CSD Secretariat in organizing dialogue sessions between representatives of governments and major groups on the issues being discussed during the Commission's substantive session each year. The outcomes of these dialogue sessions have then been incorporated into the decisions and recommendations that have then been adopted by the commission. This represents much more than government acceptance of NGOs' observing the negotiations. Within the CSD, NGO input is now being institutionalized and incorporated into the intergovernmental decisionmaking process.

CORPORATIONS AS ACTORS

Private business firms, especially multinational corporations, are important actors in global environmental politics because their interests are so directly affected by environmental regulation. Often they oppose national and international policies that they believe would impose significant new costs on them or otherwise reduce expected profits. Corporations have worked to weaken several global environmental regimes, including ozone protection, climate change, whaling, the international toxic waste trade, and fisheries. Sometimes they may prefer an international agreement if it has weaker regulations on their activities than those that they would expect to be imposed domestically.

When they face strong domestic regulations on an activity with a global environmental dimension, however, corporations are likely to support international agreements that would impose similar standards on competitors abroad. For example, on fisheries management issues, U.S. and Japanese fishing industries are more strictly regulated on various issues of high seas fishing, particularly quotas on bluefin tuna and other highly migratory species, than those of other Asian fishing states (Republic of Korea, China, Taiwan, and Indonesia). So their respective fishing industries pushed the United States and Japan to take strong positions on regulation of high seas fishing capacity in FAO negotiations in 1998.

The interests of a particular industry in regard to a proposed global environmental regime are often far from monolithic. On ozone, climate change, biodiversity, and fisheries, industries have been divided either along national lines or between different sectors or subsectors of industry. On climate, European-based energy firms have been more willing to see such an agreement as a business opportunity, because they have had experience in using greater energy efficiency to become more profitable, whereas U.S.-based firms, who have little or no such experience, have been much more resistant to such plans.

But even the U.S.-based energy industry is not united on the climate change issue. Three major energy companies (Shell, Sunoco, and BP Amoco) have decided to seek a seat at the table rather than remain in opposition to the Kyoto Protocol, joining the Pew Center on Global Climate Change to discuss ways to make the market-based mechanisms in the protocol work better.[85] And U.S. automobile manufacturers, who were once central players in the antiprotocol Global Climate Coalition, have distanced themselves from U.S. oil and coal industries because they have begun to see opportunities for future markets under the Kyoto Protocol.

When some companies see a positive stake in a global environmental agreement, however, they can dilute the influence of those determined to weaken it. In the case of the biodiversity convention, the Industrial Biotechnology Association (IBA) opposed the convention in 1992, fearing that the provisions on intellectual property rights would legally condone existing violations of those rights.[86] But the issue was not a high priority for most of the industry, and two of its leading member corporations, Merck and Genentech, believed the convention would benefit them by encouraging developing countries to negotiate agreements with companies for access to genetic resources. After those companies joined environmentalists in calling for the United States to sign the convention in 1993, the IBA came out in favor of signing it.[87]

Similarly, U.S. industries interested in promoting alternatives to fossil fuels began lobbying at meetings of the Intergovernmental Negotiating Committee for the climate convention in August 1994 and sharply reduced the influence of pro–fossil-fuel industries, which had previously monopolized industry views on the issue. Similarly, insurance agencies have been more and more concerned about increased hurricane and storm damage that may be caused by global warming. As a result, they have become proactive in supporting targets and timetables for greenhouse gas emissions reductions. The insurance industry has focused on raising awareness on the issue of climate change and its implications, including through applied research projects looking into the impacts of windstorms and floods. The Insurance Industry Initiative, which was set up by UNEP in 1996, is increasing its political efforts to create a wider and more responsive lobby group with which it can steer the debate within the UN Framework Convention on Climate Change.[88]

Corporations have significant assets for influencing global environmental politics. They have good access to decisionmakers in most governments and international organizations and can deploy impressive technical expertise on the issues in which they are interested. They have national and international industrial associations that represent their interests in policy issues. In some circumstances, however, their influence is reduced by the perception that they represent narrow self-interest rather than global human interests.

Corporate Influence on Regime Formation

Corporations may influence global environmental regimes either indirectly by influencing regime formation or directly by undertaking business activities that weaken a regime or contribute to its effectiveness. To influence the formation of regimes, they may

- shape the definition of the issue under negotiation in a way that is favorable to their interests;
- persuade an individual government to adopt a particular position on a regime being negotiated by lobbying it in its capital; or
- lobby delegations to the negotiating conference on the regime.

The greatest success of corporations in defining an issue so as to shape the process of regime formation in their favor was the International Convention for the Prevention of Pollution of the Sea by Oil (1954). The seven major oil companies and global shipping interests (most of which were owned directly or indirectly by the oil companies) were the only actors with the technical expertise to make detailed proposals on the issue of maritime oil pollution. The technical papers submitted by the International Chamber of Shipping (ICS), composed of 30 national associations of shipowners, and the International Marine Forum, representing the interests of major oil companies, defined the terms of the discussion of the convention.[89] That ensured that the convention would be compatible with oil and shipping interests—and quite ineffective in preventing oil pollution of the oceans. That degree of success in defining an issue is unlikely to recur in the future because both governments and NGOs now have more expertise on issues being negotiated and NGOs are better organized and more aggressive.

In most global environmental issues, corporations have relied on their domestic political clout to ensure that governments do not adopt strong policies adversely affecting their interests. The domestic U.S. industry most strongly opposed to a ban on hazardous waste trade, the secondary-metals industry, helped persuade U.S. officials to block such a ban in the negotiation of the Basel Convention. And on ozone depletion, Japan agreed to a phase-out of ozone-depleting chemicals only after some of its largest electronic firms said they would phase out their use by 2000.

In the case of the climate change regime, industry lobbying in the United States succeeded in reducing the flexibility of the executive branch in the negotiations. Some of the most powerful trade associations launched the Global Climate Information Project (GCIP) in 1997. Through a multi-million-dollar print and television advertising campaign, the GCIP cast doubt upon the desirability of emissions controls in the Kyoto Protocol, which was entering the final stages of negotiation, arguing that it would raise taxes on gasoline, heating oil, and consumer goods and reduce the competitiveness of American businesses. An alliance of business and labor succeeded in getting the U.S. Senate to vote 95–0 for a resolution stating that the president should not sign any protocol that requires greenhouse gas reductions without commitments from developing countries, or that would result in serious harm to the economy of the United States.[90]

Industry associations have been actively involved in influencing the conferences negotiating on several global environmental regimes. In certain cases where the industry had particular technical expertise or relatively unchallenged influence over the issue, it was represented on one or more key countries' delegations. In the negotiations on Antarctic minerals in the mid-1980s, the American Petroleum Institute, the main umbrella organization for the U.S. oil industry, was represented on the U.S. delegation.[91] And the Japanese commissioner to the International Whaling Commission has generally been the president of the Japanese Whaling Association.[92]

In conclusion, Mr President, we at Exxon feel that human survival may simply not be economic.

Copyright Richard D. Willson. Reprinted with permission.

Like NGOs, representatives of corporate interests lobby negotiations on environmental regimes primarily by providing information and analysis to the delegations that are most sympathetic to their cause. In the case of the climate change negotiations, for example, coal interests were very active in advising the U.S., Russian, and Saudi delegations on how to weaken the regime.[93] And oil industry representatives were successful in lobbying for weak environmental controls in the Antarctic minerals regime being negotiated in the 1980s.

Corporations also may facilitate or delay, strengthen or weaken, global environmental regimes by direct actions that have an impact on the environment. These actions may be taken unilaterally or may be the result of agreements reached with their respective governments. Such actions may be crucial to the ability of a government to undertake a commitment to a regime-strengthening policy. The climate-change and ozone-protection regimes are particularly sensitive to the willingness of corporations in key countries to take actions that would allow the international community to go beyond the existing agreement.

In the ozone-protection issue, the U.S. chemical industry delayed movement toward any regime for regulating ozone-depleting CFCs in the early 1980s, in part by simply reducing their own research efforts on CFC substitutes.[94] Subsequently, CFC producers gave impetus to an accelerated timetable for CFC phase-out by unilaterally pledging to phase out their own uses of CFCs ahead of the schedule already agreed to by the Montreal Protocol parties. In 1989, Nissan and Toyota pledged to eliminate CFCs from their cars and manufacturing processes as early as the mid-1990s. In 1992, Ford Motor Company pledged to eliminate 90 percent of CFC use from its manufacturing processes worldwide by the end of that year and to eliminate all CFCs from its air conditioners and manufacturing by the end of 1994.

In the case of climate change, the Japanese auto industry, which accounts for 20 percent of Japan's overall carbon emissions, adopted a goal of improving fuel efficiency by 8.5 percent above its 1990 level by 2000, thus encouraging a Japanese government commitment to the national goal of stabilization of carbon emissions at 1990 levels by 2000.[95] In the Netherlands a number of industrial sectors, including iron and steel, glass, cement, and textiles, signed long-term agreements with the Dutch government in 1992 to improve their energy efficiency by 20 percent from the 1989 level by the year 2000.[96] BP Amoco is arguably the most forward-thinking large energy company in the world with respect to climate change policy. BP Amoco recognized that the outcomes of intergovernmental negotiations would increasingly constrain fossil fuel energy choices and that the company would be better positioned if it took early action and involvement in the issue. In fact, one of BP Amoco's corporate goals is to reduce greenhouse gas emissions by 10 percent from a 1990 baseline over the period to 2010.[97]

Industry and Nonregime Issues

Corporations have their greatest political influence on a global environmental issue when there are no negotiations on a formal, binding international regime governing the issue. Under those circumstances, they are able to use their economic and political clout with individual governments and international organizations to protect their freedom to carry out economic activities that may be damaging to the environment.

For example, in the past the agrochemical industry enjoyed strong influence on the FAO's Plant Protection Service, which is responsible for the organization's pesticide activities. The industry's international trade association even had a joint program with the FAO to promote pesticide use worldwide until the 1970s.[98] This influence was instrumental in carrying out the industry's main strategy for avoiding binding international restrictions on its sales of pesticides in developing countries: a voluntary "code of conduct" on pesticide distribution and use, which was drafted by FAO between 1982 and 1985 in close consultation with the industry. More recently, however, the UNEP Governing Council at its 19th session in 1997, established an intergovernmental negotiating committee for an "International Legally Binding Instrument for Implementing International Action on Certain Persistent Organic Pollutants," including pesticides.[99]

The logging of tropical rain forests for timber exports is another example of a global environmental issue on which multinational corporations have had a major influence. Major Japanese trading companies, such as Mitsubishi Corporation, have been heavily involved in logging operations in the Philippines, Indonesia, Malaysia, Papua New Guinea, Brazil, and Siberia. U.S. companies have also been involved in Southeast Asia. These companies have provided much of the financing for logging in those countries and then imported the raw logs—sometimes illegally harvested—or wood chips to Japan. They have also purchased timber from Myanmar, Thailand, Vietnam, Cambodia, and Laos. And they have had the cooperation of the Japanese government, which subsidized the construction of roads to be used by the Japanese-financed logging in Malaysia and Papua New Guinea.[100] Close ties between state leaders—such as former President Suharto of Indonesia and Chief Minister Taib Mahmud of Sarawak, Malaysia—and corporate executives have shielded destructive loggers throughout the Asia-Pacific. These ties have distorted state policies, including reforestation and conservation guidelines, sustainable management plans, tax and royalty rates, processing incentives, and foreign investment regulations. In this context, state implementers, in exchange for gifts, money, and security, often ignore or assist illegal loggers, smugglers, and tax evaders.[101] The governments of some of the tropical forest countries were the main actors in fending off any move to establish an international regime for managing tropical forests, but multinational corporations played a critical role in establishing and maintaining the international system of exploitation of those forests.

Although corporations have resisted strong international environmental agreements when they were not in their interest, in recent years a number of corporations have been positioning themselves as advocates of global sustainable development, including DuPont, BP Amoco, and Royal Dutch Shell. Under greater public scrutiny of their environmental behavior and pressure from consumers for environmentally friendly products, these corporations have discovered that pollution prevention is good for profitability. The result is the emergence of a group of corporate leaders who support some of the main aspects of the new paradigm of sustainable development and support the development of certain environmental regimes.

In the 1980s, a number of European and U.S. corporations participated in two world industrial conferences on environmental management, a joint endeavor of UNEP, the International Chamber of Commerce, and the U.S. Business Roundtable, intended to improve corporate environmental practices through voluntary initiatives. In 1991, at the request of UNCED Secretary-General Maurice Strong, Swiss industrialist Stephan Schmidheiny enlisted a group of 48 chief executive officers of corporations from all over the world to set up the Business Council on Sustainable Development (BCSD) to support the objectives of the Earth Summit. The BCSD issued a declaration calling for the prices of goods to reflect environmental costs of production, use, recycling, and disposal and for changes in consumption patterns.[102]

In January 1995, the BCSD and the World Industry Council for the Environment (WICE), an initiative of the International Chamber of Commerce (ICC), merged into a coalition of 125 international companies united by a shared commitment to the environment and to the principles of economic growth and sustainable development. Its members are drawn from 30 countries and more than 20 major industrial sectors. The resulting World Business Council on Sustainable Development (WBCSD) has since been working to develop public-private partnerships in support of the Kyoto Protocol. It has also published a trade and environment report that looks at the merits of voluntary as opposed to regulatory measures and states the case for the establishment of a bridging mechanism to harmonize international trade law with multilateral environmental agreements. Other programs address corporate social responsibility, eco-efficiency, and technology and innovation.[103]

CONCLUSION

From the promotion of ideas that lead to the shift to an alternative social paradigm, to the establishment of global environmental regimes, state and nonstate actors play key roles in the formation of environmental policies, at both the national and the international levels. State actors have the primary roles in determining the outcomes of issues at stake in global environmental politics, but nonstate actors—IOs, NGOs, and corporations—influence the policies of individual state actors toward global environmental issues as well as the international negotiation process itself. Whether a state adopts the role of lead state, supporting state, swing state, or veto state on a particular issue depends primarily on domestic political factors and on the relative costs and benefits of the proposed regime. But international political-diplomatic consequences can also affect the choice of role.

International organizations, especially UNEP, WMO, and FAO, have played important roles in regime formation by setting the international agenda and by sponsoring and shaping negotiations on global environmental regimes and soft-law norms. The CSD has called attention to issues that should be on the international agenda as well as areas where there has been a failure to implement recommendations contained in Agenda 21. The Bretton Woods institutions and certain UN agencies, particularly UNDP and FAO, influence state development strategies through financing and technical assistance. IOs also seek to exert influence on state policy through research and advocacy of specific norms at the global level.

NGOs influence the environmental regimes by defining issues, swaying the policy of a key government, lobbying negotiating conferences, providing information and reporting services, drafting entire convention texts, and monitoring the implementation of agreements. They have also sought to change the policies and structure of major international institutions, such as the World Bank and the GATT, with varying degrees of success. They have been more successful when the institution in question is dependent on a key state for funding and less successful when the institution is not so dependent or has no tradition of permitting NGO participation in its processes.

Corporations have been active in international relations longer than NGOs and have influenced regime creation. They can sometimes employ special political assets, including particular technical expertise, privileged access to certain government ministries, and political clout with legislative bodies, to veto or weaken a regime. They can also directly affect the ability of the international community to meet regime goals by their own actions. They are able to maximize their political effectiveness in shaping the outcome of a global environmental issue when they can avert negotiations on a binding regime altogether.

THREE

□   □   □

The Development of
Environmental Regimes:
Ten Case Studies

The development of global environmental regimes may involve four processes or stages: issue definition, fact-finding, bargaining on regime creation, and regime strengthening. Within each environmental issue the sequencing of these stages and the length of time that each takes vary greatly. The stages are not always distinct; the definition stage may overlap the fact-finding stage, which may, in turn, overlap the bargaining stage. Nevertheless, examining negotiations through the use of stages or phases can provide a framework that reduces some of the complexities of multilateral negotiation to a more manageable level for understanding and analysis. It essentially divides the negotiation process into a number of successive, often overlapping, phases, in each of which there is a particular focus of attention and concern by the negotiators.

Issue definition involves bringing the issue to the attention of the international community and identifying the scope and magnitude of the environmental threat, its primary causes, and the type of international action required to address the issue. An issue may be placed on the global environmental agenda by one or more state actors, by an international organization (usually at the suggestion of one or more members), or by a nongovernmental organization. The actors who introduce and define the issue often publicize new scientific evidence or theories, as they did in the case of ozone depletion, acid rain, and climate change. But issue definition may also involve identifying a radically different approach to international action on a problem, as it did in the cases of whaling, hazardous waste trade, African elephants, and Antarctic minerals.

Fact-finding involves efforts to build consensus on the nature of the problem and the most appropriate international actions to address it

79

through an international process of studying the science, ecology, and economics surrounding the issue. In practice, the fact-finding process may vary from well developed to nonexistent. In the most successful cases, a mediating international organization has brought key policymakers together in an attempt to establish a baseline of facts on which they can agree. In cases where there is no such mediated process of fact-finding and consensus building, the facts may be openly challenged by states that are opposed to international action. The fact-finding stage often shades into the bargaining stage. Meetings ostensibly devoted to establishing the scope and seriousness of the problem may also try to spell out policy options. During this stage, a lead state may begin to advance a proposal for international action and try to build a consensus behind it. International cleavages and coalitions begin to form.

The nature of global environmental politics raises fundamental questions concerning the bargaining process. To be truly effective, a regime to mitigate a global danger such as ozone depletion or climate change must have the participation of virtually all the states contributing to the problem. However, at some point negotiators must determine whether to go ahead with a less than optimal number of signatories or to accommodate veto state demands. Can a regime successfully address the problem without the participation of key nations? On the other hand, can an agreement be considered a success if it has universal support but has been weakened by compromises with veto states?[1] The outcome of the bargaining process depends in part on the bargaining leverage and cohesion of the veto coalition. The veto states can prevent the creation of a strong international regime by refusing to participate in it or weaken it by insisting on a regime that has no teeth. However, one or more key members of the veto coalition usually make major concessions to make regime creation or regime strengthening possible. In certain cases, a regime may actually be created without the consent of key members of the veto coalition and thus remain a relatively ineffective regime, as in the case of acid rain.

The regime-building process does not end with the signing and ratification of a global environmental convention. Once established, a regime can be strengthened, its central provisions made clearer or more stringent through further bargaining. The strengthening of a regime may occur either because new scientific evidence becomes available on the problem, because there are political shifts in one or more major states, or because the existing regime is shown to be ineffective in bringing about meaningful actions to reduce the threat.

The process of regime strengthening is encouraged by the review process that takes place at the periodic meetings of the Conference of the

Parties mandated by most global environmental conventions. Regime strengthening may take one of three possible forms:

- The Conference of the Parties can formally amend the treaty, as has been done in the case of uplisting the African elephant in CITES and the moratorium on commercial whaling adopted by the International Whaling Commission.
- The Conference of the Parties can adopt a protocol that establishes concrete commitments or targets, as in the cases of the Parties to the Vienna Convention negotiating the Montreal Protocol, the Parties to the UN Framework Convention on Climate Change negotiating the Kyoto Protocol, and the Parties to the Convention on Long Range Transboundary Air Pollution negotiating protocols on sulfur dioxide, nitrogen oxide, and volatile organic compounds.
- In some treaties the Conference of the Parties can make decisions requiring important new actions by the Parties without either amending the convention or creating a new protocol, as in the cases of the tightening of phase-out schedules in the Montreal Protocol, the ban on hazardous waste exports to developing countries in the Basel Convention, and the adoption of conservation measures by regional fisheries commissions.

The adoption of protocols has been used successfully to strengthen regimes that began as a framework convention. A framework convention does not establish any detailed, binding commitments, such as targets or timetables for national actions, usually because the negotiators have not been able to reach agreement on such measures. Rather the framework convention requires sharing of information, study of the problem, and perhaps national plans or strategies aimed at reducing the threat. The creation of a conference of the parties allows further negotiations on more concrete, binding actions on the issue, taking the form of one or more protocols.

This two-stage approach has allowed the international community to establish the institutional and legal framework for regime strengthening even when there was no agreement on the specific actions to be taken. However, the framework convention-protocol approach has been criticized for taking too much time. For example, it took over six years to negotiate the Climate Change Convention and the Kyoto Protocol, and it is still uncertain how long it will take the Protocol to enter into force. But it would not have been possible to reach agreement on targets and timetables any earlier. It is domestic political forces in veto states that dictate the pace of progress toward stronger regimes, not the choice of approach.

Regime strengthening by formal amendment normally requires either consensus of the Parties or, if that is not possible, a "supermajority" (either two-thirds or three-fourths of those present and voting).[2] But most treaties also allow parties to opt out of the amendment if they do not support it. CITES and the International Whaling Commission allow amendment by two-thirds and three-fourths majorities, respectively, but both have opt-out provisions for amendments. These opt-out provisions applied to the decisions on uplisting of African elephants and the moratorium on commercial whaling, respectively. The Basel Convention requires specific steps to "opt in" by all parties willing to be bound by the amendment. These arrangements allow changes to take effect without long ratification delays but also risk effective action being blocked by key states that do not support it. Protocols to a framework convention are treated as an entirely new agreement and must be ratified by a certain number of signatories, as specified in the protocol itself, thus requiring that each party "opt in."

Some environmental regimes allow new or stronger actions to be mandated without a formal amendment or protocol procedure. The Montreal Protocol allows a supermajority to "adjust" technical appendices or annexes that are binding on all the Parties. Thus the Conference of the Parties can amend the technical annexes by a supermajority without either "opt-out" or "opt-in" requirements. The London, Copenhagen, and Montreal Amendments, which changed the chemicals covered by the Protocol as well as the targets and timetables for their phase-out, applied to all Parties, regardless of whether or not they supported them. The Basel Convention allows "substantive decisions" to be made by a two-thirds majority of those present and voting, without any opt-out provision for those who oppose it, which is how the ban on the trade in hazardous wastes was adopted.

In this chapter, we analyze 10 global environmental issues on which there have been multilateral negotiations during the past 25 years. Each issue is analyzed in terms of the stages of negotiation and the role of veto coalitions in shaping the outcomes of bargaining. This sample of issues represents a wide range of environmental and political circumstances. It shows the similarities and differences in the political processes and provides a basis for addressing the question of why states agree to cooperate on global environmental issues despite divergent interests. The cases are presented chronologically and by issue area. The first six regimes were negotiated prior to UNCED and address atmospheric issues (transboundary air pollution and ozone depletion), endangered species (whaling and elephant ivory), pollution (toxic waste trade), and the global commons (Antarctica). The four post-Rio regimes address climate change, biodiversity loss, combating desertification, and sustaining global fisheries.

TRANSBOUNDARY AIR POLLUTION
(ACID RAIN)

Transboundary air pollution, or acid rain, is an issue on which a veto coalition has been divided and weakened over time by defections, permitting a strengthening of a regime that was initially extraordinarily ineffective. New scientific evidence was a major force for change in the position of key states, who switched from being part of the veto coalition to advocating a strong international regime for the reduction of acid rain. But the evidence has made no impact on the policies of the states remaining in the veto coalition.

Emissions of sulfur dioxide and nitrogen oxide became an international problem after developed countries raised the heights of their industrial chimneys by as much as six times in the 1960s in order to disperse pollutants into the atmosphere. Previously industries had polluted only the area immediately surrounding them, but now they exported their acid rain to other countries downwind of the sites.

The definition of transboundary air pollution as an issue in global environmental politics began in the late 1960s with Sweden as the lead actor. The first Swedish move was to introduce new scientific evidence that the acidification of Swedish lakes was related to sulfur dioxide emissions from outside Sweden. Sweden's efforts to put the issue of long-range transboundary air pollution on the international agenda were advanced by Sweden's offer to host the first UN environmental conference in 1972 in Stockholm.

There was still relatively little or no interest on the part of other European states. But Sweden and other Nordic states succeeded in getting the Organization for Economic Cooperation and Development (OECD) to agree to monitor transboundary air pollution in Europe in 1972, thus successfully completing the definition process. The OECD monitoring program from 1972 to 1977 was an international fact-finding program that established that pollution was being exported across boundaries and that the problem required international cooperation. In 1977, these monitoring programs were unified under a program sponsored by the UN Economic Commission for Europe (ECE) and thus included the communist states of Eastern Europe.

Within the ECE those states that had been the victims of this export of acid rain—notably Sweden, Finland, and Norway—took the initiative to negotiate for stringent and binding regulations on emissions of sulfur dioxide and nitrogen oxide.[3] But the industrialized states that were net exporters of acid rain formed a veto coalition, in large part because of their reliance on coal-fired power stations, which accounted for two-thirds of all sulfur dioxide emissions. Its members were the United States, the United

Kingdom, the Federal Republic of Germany, Belgium, and Denmark, with the United Kingdom and the FRG in the lead role. The veto coalition rejected any agreement that included specific commitments to reduce emissions. Only after pressures from France, Norway, and Sweden did the FRG and UK accept vague obligations to endeavor "as far as possible" to reduce transboundary air pollution. The Convention on Long-Range Transboundary Air Pollution, concluded in Geneva in 1979 with 35 signatories, was a toothless agreement that failed to effectively regulate emissions or transboundary fluxes of acid rain.[4] It did, however, set up an assembly of signatory parties to meet annually to review the implementation of the agreement, thus providing the institutional basis for a process of regime strengthening.

That process was impelled by new and more convincing scientific evidence of damage to European forests and historic buildings from acid rain. Some major exporters of acid rain—especially the FRG—began to change their stance in the early 1980s. At the first meeting of the assembly of signatory parties in 1983, Norway and Sweden proposed a program to reduce emissions of sulfur dioxide by 30 percent of 1980 levels by 1993 and were supported by three defectors from the veto coalition: the FRG, which had begun to experience forest damage, and France and Italy, which had less reason to hold out because they relied heavily on nuclear and hydroelectric power.[5] However, the United States and the United Kingdom continued to oppose formal pledges of emissions reductions.

In an unusual departure from diplomatic tradition, some states committed themselves formally to larger unilateral reductions, thus setting the standard by which other states would be judged. At a conference in Ottawa in March 1984, 10 states pledged to reduce sulfur dioxide emissions by 30 percent and to substantially reduce other pollutants, especially nitrous oxide, thus forming the "Thirty-Percent Club." The club propelled agreement on the Protocol on the Reduction of Sulfur Emissions or Their Transboundary Fluxes by at Least 30 Percent (also known as the Helsinki Protocol), signed by 21 states in 1985. The protocol came into force in September 1987, but it lacked the adherence of three major exporters of acid rain: the United States, the United Kingdom, and Poland, which together represented more than 30 percent of total world emissions of sulfur dioxide.[6]

The second sulfur protocol was signed in Oslo, in June 1994, by 28 parties to the Convention, and sets different requirements for each country, the aim being to attain the greatest possible effect for the environment at the least overall cost. It also contains some specific requirements, not very rigorous, for large combustion plants. The text for basic obligations says that parties shall control and reduce their sulfur emissions in order to protect human health and the environment from adverse effects, and that they shall ensure that sulfur depositions do not, in the long term, exceed critical loads. The scientific analysis underpinning the protocol showed that if the long-term goal is to be attained, sulfur emissions would have to be reduced by at least 90 percent. If all the signatories stick to their undertakings, the total European emissions of sulfur can be expected to fall by 50 percent by 2000, and by 58 percent by 2010, as from 1980. This protocol came into force in August 1998.[7]

In negotiations on reducing nitrogen oxide emissions, three dramatically different positions were advanced by states and NGOs. Austria, the Netherlands, Sweden, Switzerland, and West Germany advocated a 30 percent reduction in emissions by 1994, but the United States demurred, arguing that it should be credited with previous abatement measures. (Environmental organizations, on the other hand, called for a 75 percent reduction over 10 years.[8]) The Protocol Concerning the Control of Emissions of Nitrogen Oxides or Their Transboundary Fluxes (better known as the Sofia Protocol), signed by 23 European countries, the United States, and Canada in 1988, also reflected compromise between the lead states and the veto coalition. It required only a freeze of nitrogen oxide emissions or transboundary flows at 1987 levels while allowing most countries to postpone compliance until 1994 by providing credits for reductions in previous years—a concession to U.S. demands.

Four additional protocols have since been adopted by the parties, contributing significantly to the strengthening of the regime. In November 1991, the parties adopted a protocol on volatile organic compounds (VOCs, i.e., hydrocarbons), which is the second major air pollutant responsible for the formation of ground-level ozone. The VOC negotiations elicited three broad sets of national positions. The majority of countries were willing to sign an across-the-board 30 percent reduction protocol. Countries with low ozone problems due to meteorological and geographical conditions, including the USSR, Norway, and Canada, however, wanted to commit only to reducing VOCs in regions responsible for transborder fluxes. Most Eastern European countries wanted to commit only to a freeze. In the end 21 parties signed a protocol that merely listed three different forms of regulation (based on the three sets of national positions).[9] Most of the signatories committed themselves to reducing their emissions by at least 30 percent by 1999, with five different base years between 1984 and 1990, since countries were permitted to select their own base year. Because ratification was long and drawn out, the protocol did not enter into force until September 1997. Nevertheless, between 1988 and 1995 the European emissions of VOCs had fallen by about 15 percent.

The Protocol on Heavy Metals was adopted in June 1998 in Aarhus, Denmark. It targets three particularly harmful metals: cadmium, lead, and mercury. The Protocol aims to cut emissions from industrial sources, combustion processes, and waste incineration. The Protocol also requires Parties to phase out leaded gasoline. It also introduces measures to lower heavy-metal emissions from other products, such as mercury in batteries, and proposes the introduction of management measures for other mercury-containing products, such as thermometers, fluorescent lamps, dental amalgam, pesticides, and paint.

The Protocol on Persistent Organic Pollutants (POPs) was also adopted in June 1998. Canada and Sweden were the lead states on POPs, because POPs tend to bioaccumulate in the Arctic and have had an impact on Arctic populations in both countries. The fact-finding process took place in a special task force established to investigate POPs, which met from 1991 to 1994. Formal negotiations began in 1997. A major part of negotiating the protocol was deciding which substances the protocol would cover. Most of the European countries, led by Sweden, advocated a large list of POPs, whereas the United States, as a veto state, favored a more limited list. Negotiators resolved most of the disputes over the POPs to be included by setting up a set of criteria and then screening the POPs and ranking them based on their toxicity and bioaccumulation potential and then assessing long-range transport risk. The United States did succeed in blocking inclusion of pentachlorophenol under the protocol. The United States argued that this wood preservative, which is widely regulated in Europe, should not be considered a POP and threatened not to sign the protocol if pentachlorophenol was included. The United States was successful in its efforts, primarily because Sweden and other countries felt that it was crucial that the United States be a party to the protocol and were willing to leave off pentachlorophenol at this stage, since there are provisions for placing additional POPs under the protocol.[10] The protocol focuses on 11 pesticides, 2 industrial chemicals, and 3 byproducts/contaminants. The ultimate objective is to eliminate any discharges, emissions, and losses of POPs. The protocol bans the production and use of some products outright and schedules others for elimination at a later stage. The protocol includes provisions for dealing with the wastes of products that will be banned.[11]

The Protocol to Abate Acidification, Eutrophication and Ground-Level Ozone was adopted in Gothenberg, Sweden, in December 1999. The Protocol aims to cut emissions of sulfur, nitrogen oxides, volatile organic compounds, and ammonia from energy generation, industrial sources, motor vehicles, agriculture, and products. The Protocol sets reduction targets for all four pollutants. By 2010, Europe's sulfur emissions should be cut by 63 percent, its NOx emissions by 41 percent, its VOC emissions by

40 percent, and its ammonia emissions by 17 percent compared to their 1990 levels. Each country's individual ceilings depend on the impact that its emissions have on public health and on the vulnerability of the environment that they pollute. Countries whose emissions have the most severe health or environmental impact and whose emissions are the cheapest to reduce will have to make the biggest cuts.

In summary, a small group of blocking states, usually led by the United Kingdom and/or the United States, has either refused to join acid rain agreements or demanded that they be watered down. Like other regimes negotiated in the 1970s and 1980s, the international regime for acid rain has lent itself to strengthening through a mechanism for regular review and action and the negotiation of protocols, although the protocol negotiations themselves involved some of the same challenges by the same blocking states as the original treaty.

OZONE DEPLETION

International negotiations to reverse the depletion of the ozone layer illustrate both the role of a veto coalition in weakening a global regime and the dissolution of that coalition because of a combination of scientific evidence and domestic political pressures in key states. The agreement ultimately produced by the bargaining process and continually strengthened since now stands as perhaps the strongest and most effective international environmental regime.

Ozone is an unstable molecule composed of three atoms of oxygen that has the property of being able to absorb certain wavelengths of ultraviolet radiation in the upper part of the earth's atmosphere, approximately 6–30 miles above the earth's surface. If these ultraviolet rays were to reach the earth's surface in excessive quantities, they could damage and cause mutations in human, animal, and plant cells. In the 1970s scientists discovered that depletion of the ozone layer was being caused by human-made chemicals called chlorofluorocarbons (CFCs). Subsequently, scientists have determined that ozone-depleting compounds contain various combinations of the chemical elements chlorine, fluorine, bromine, carbon, and hydrogen and are often described by the general term *halocarbons*. The compounds that contain only carbon, chlorine, and fluorine are CFCs. CFCs, carbon tetrachloride, and methyl chloroform are important human-made ozone-depleting gases that have been used in many applications including refrigeration, air conditioning, foam blowing, and the cleaning of electronics components and as solvents. Another important group of human-made halocarbons is the halons, which contain carbon, bromine, fluorine, and (in some cases) chlorine and have been mainly used as fire extinguishers.

The political definition of the ozone depletion issue began in 1977 when the United States, Canada, Finland, Norway, and Sweden urged UNEP to consider the international regulation of ozone. A UNEP experts' conference in 1977 adopted the World Plan of Action on the Ozone Layer. The definition that emerged, however, was based on scientific uncertainty about the causes and seriousness of the problem. Although international action to regulate CFC use was suggested as a policy option, even the most enthusiastic proponents did not see it as an urgent problem.

Issue definition continued as the Coordinating Committee on the Ozone Layer, consisting of representatives of governmental agencies and NGOs, was established by UNEP to determine the extent of the problem. The fact-finding process was protracted because scientific estimates of the likely depletion fluctuated widely during the late 1970s and early 1980s. The methods of estimating future depletion of the ozone were still being refined, in fact, when UNEP moved to the stage of multilateral negotiation on a framework convention for protection of the ozone layer in 1981.[12] The Ad Hoc Working Group of Legal and Technical Experts for the Elaboration of a Global Framework Convention for the Protection of the Ozone Layer, which included representatives from 24 nations, began meeting in January 1982.

The bargaining process actually began, therefore, before there was a clear definition of the issue by proponents of international action. The United States, which alone accounted for 30 percent of worldwide production, was prepared to be the lead state in part because it had already been forced by domestic pressures to regulate CFCs, at least in aerosol cans, and wanted other states to follow suit. But it was essential to any ozone-protection regime that the other CFC-producing states be part of the agreement. The European Community, with four major producing states (the UK, France, Germany, and Italy) accounting for 45 percent of world CFC output and exporting a third of their production to developing countries by the mid-1980s, constituted a potential veto coalition. Germany was willing to support controls on CFCs, but the EC position was controlled by the other three producing countries, which wanted to preserve their industries' overseas markets and avoid the costs of adopting substitutes for CFCs.[13] Japan, which was a major user of CFCs, also became part of the coalition.[14]

The large developing countries—India, China, Indonesia, Brazil, and Mexico—also had some potential as a veto coalition. Their bargaining leverage depended on their potential capacity to produce CFCs and thus remain independent of industrialized-country exports. Although they produced less than 5 percent of the world's CFCs, their production was rising at 7 to 10 percent annually and, if not curtailed, could have reduced the impact of an ozone agreement by as much as 50 percent.[15] No developing country played an active role in the early negotiations, and India remained outside the negotiations altogether until after the Montreal Protocol was signed in 1987. However, these states did take advantage of their potential veto power to hold out for a fund for developing countries to switch to substitutes for CFCs as the price for signing the Montreal Protocol and did not sign it until after the Montreal Protocol Fund was created in 1990.

The first proposal by the lead states (the United States, Canada, and the Nordic states) was for the simultaneous negotiation of a framework convention and associated protocols, with binding obligations to reduce CFC use. The veto coalition steadfastly rejected any negotiation of regulatory protocols, arguing that the state of scientific knowledge was not sufficient to support such a protocol. The United States began in 1985 to define the issue as one of heightened urgency because of new evidence of the possibility of a collapse of the ozone layer at a critical point.[16] But the veto coalition held firm. The only agreement that could be forged, therefore, was a framework convention. The 1985 Vienna Convention for the Protection of the Ozone Layer was essentially an agreement to cooperate on monitoring, research, and data exchanges. It imposed no specific obligations on the signatories to reduce production of ozone-depleting compounds. Indeed, it did not even specify which compounds were the cause of ozone depletion. But because of a last-minute U.S. initiative, there was agreement to resume negotiations on a binding protocol on ozone protection.

Negotiations on such a protocol began in December 1986, with the lead states advocating a freeze followed by a gradual 95 percent reduction in production of CFCs and other ozone-depleting substances over 10–14 years. The industrialized-country veto coalition, supported now by the Soviet Union, continued to advocate a production cap (meaning further growth) on the grounds that the evidence of danger from the ozone hole was not clear. The Toronto Group (including Canada, Finland, Norway, Sweden, Switzerland, and the United States) offered a 50 percent cut as a compromise, but as late as April 1987 the EC position was that it would not agree to more than a 20 percent reduction. Only at the Montreal conference in September 1987 did the EC Commission's representative agree to the 50 percent reduction. The evolution of the EC position from a production cap may have reflected several factors: disunity within the EC (with West Germany, Denmark, Belgium, and the Netherlands all urging strong regulation), the personal role played by UNEP Executive Director Tolba, relentless diplomatic pressures by the United States, and reluctance to be blamed for the failure of the conference.

The Montreal Protocol on Substances That Deplete the Ozone Layer was a compromise under which industrialized countries pledged to reduce CFC production by 50 percent of 1986 levels by 1999. Developing countries were permitted to increase their use of CFCs substantially for the first decade up to 0.66 pounds (0.3 kilograms) per capita annually.

The estimated net reduction in CFC use to be brought about by the agreement was less than half of the 85 percent generally regarded as necessary even to stabilize the level of ozone depletion. The protocol also permitted the continued production of some ozone-depleting chemicals and neglected to specify that alternatives to CFCs and halons must not be damaging to the ozone layer. It failed to include provisions for international monitoring of production and consumption of ozone-destroying chemicals and contained no real penalties for noncompliance.[17] Nor did it include a fund to defray the costs of substitutes for CFCs in the developing countries, a requirement urgently sought by the developing countries but successfully opposed by a veto coalition of the United States, Japan, and the EC. For this reason, three of the most important members of the potential developing-country veto coalition (China, India, and Brazil) refused to sign the Montreal Protocol. But Mexico and Indonesia chose to sign the agreement, a move perhaps reflecting their greater vulnerability to trade sanctions against nonparticipants.

Within months of the Montreal accord, however, new scientific evidence gave the process of regime strengthening a strong impetus. British scientists discovered an "ozone hole," that is, springtime decreases of 40 percent of the ozone layer over Antarctica between 1977 and 1984. Then a 1988 report by 100 leading atmospheric scientists concluded that the Northern Hemisphere ozone layer had also been reduced up to 3 percent between 1969 and 1986. As a result, the EC decided in March 1989 to phase out all CFC production by the year 2000. At the first meeting of the parties in Helsinki in May 1989, the veto coalition began to shift its position dramatically: The EC members were among 80 nations—not including Japan or the Soviet Union—voting for a complete CFC phase-out by the year 2000 in a nonbinding declaration. In London in June 1990 at the second meeting of the parties, a new coalition of 13 industrialized states pushed for a 1997 deadline for final elimination of CFCs. The four leading CFC-producing states (the United States, Britain, France, and Italy), joined by the Soviet Union, favored a phase-out by 2000, thus constituting a new veto coalition against the proposed faster deadline.

The final London amendment on timetables for phasing out ozone-depleting chemicals not controlled under the original protocol may be viewed as a considerable victory for the lead states: Carbon tetrachloride was to be phased out by 2000, and methyl chloroform was to be eliminated five years later. Hydrochlorofluorocarbons (HCFCs), which were many times less damaging to the ozone layer than CFCs but were expected to increase rapidly in the future, remained uncontrolled.[18]

The 1990 London meeting of the parties also created the Multilateral Fund for the Implementation of the Montreal Protocol, the first such fund established under an environmental agreement. The Fund meets the incremental costs to developing countries of implementing the control measures of the protocol and finances all clearinghouse functions, that is, country studies, technical assistance, information, training, and costs of the Fund secretariat. The fund is administered by an executive committee made up of seven donor and seven recipient countries, carefully balanced geographically. The Fund has been replenished three times: U.S. $240 million (1991–1993), U.S. $455 million (1994–1996), and U.S. $466 million (1997–1999). As of March 31, 2000, the contributions made to the Multilateral Fund by some 32 industrialized countries amounted to U.S. $1.01 billion.[19]

After more evidence of the seriousness of ozone-layer depletion in the winter of 1991–1992, the 90 parties agreed to further strengthen the regime at the meeting of the parties in Copenhagen in 1992. They accelerated the ban on all CFCs by four years and shortened timetables on other ozone-depleting chemicals. They also added HCFCs to the chemicals to be phased out: From a cap (3.1 percent of 1989 consumption of both CFCs and HCFCs weighted by ozone-depleting potential), HCFCs are to be reduced gradually by 35 percent in 2004 to a complete ban by 2030, with all but 0.5 percent of HCFC use to be phased out by 2020.[20]

The European Commission proposed in 1993 that HCFC use be phased out by 2015, but the United States opposed this proposal, arguing that it would reduce total damage to the ozone layer by less than 0.5 percent and that a significant proportion of the substitutes for HCFCs would be hydrofluorocarbons (HFCs), which are also potent greenhouse gases. In 1995 Sweden and other states proposed to phase out HCFCs by 2010 and to cut in half the cap from which the phase-out would be implemented. That would have reduced damage to the ozone layer much more than the earlier EC proposal, but the United States opposed the proposal, largely because it wanted to allow U.S. firms that had invested heavily in HCFC technologies as substitutes for CFCs to recoup their investments over 30 years or longer. The United States also pointed out that a rapid phase-out of methyl bromide (a fumigant used in agriculture) would have a much greater impact on the ozone layer than speeding up the HCFC phase-out.

Even before the 1992 Montreal Protocol meeting, U.S. NGOs demanded a five-year phase-out of methyl bromide (the second most widely used insecticide in the world by volume) because it is a threat to human health and the ozone layer. Most of the production and use of methyl bromide is in the industrialized countries, but use is also growing in the developing world.[21] The 1993 Bangkok meeting of the parties agreed on the need to strengthen the treaty by phasing out methyl bromide.[22] The United States had already unilaterally frozen its production until 2001, when it will cease abruptly. Germany, Switzerland, and the Netherlands, which had virtually eliminated agricultural uses because of water contamination, and Italy and Denmark will phase out by 2001.[23] And in December 1993, the EU environmental ministers agreed to a 25 percent reduction by 1998.

The tenth anniversary of the Montreal Protocol was marked in Montreal at the ninth meeting of the parties in September 1997. The parties agreed to move up the phase-out of methyl bromide to 2005 from 2010. Developing countries, previously committed only to a freeze by 2002, agreed to a 20 percent reduction by 2005 and a phase-out by 2015. In addition to the $10 million agreed on in 1996 for funding demonstration projects testing the feasibility of methyl bromide alternatives, the Multilateral Fund agreed to make $25 million per year available in both 1998 and 1999 for activities to phase out methyl bromide in developing countries.

Another issue addressed by the 1997 meeting was the illegal trade in CFCs that emerged in the 1994–1995 period as the United States and Europe approached their respective cutoff dates for CFC manufacture, thus creating a new market for the less expensive CFCs that were being banned. In response, the parties agreed to a new system of licensing for all imports and exports of CFCs and on regular exchanges of information between parties on illegal trade in CFCs.[24] The new system became effective at the start of 2000. This was the first time that any concrete action was taken to address this growing problem of illegal trade in controlled substances. Nevertheless, proposals by the European Community and Switzerland to accelerate the phase-out of the consumption of HCFCs and to introduce production control were not accepted.[25]

The Protocol was most recently strengthened at the eleventh meeting of the Parties in Beijing in December 1999. The Beijing amendment bans trade in HCFCs with countries that have not yet ratified the Protocol's 1992 Copenhagen amendment, which introduced the HCFC phase-out. It also requires developed countries to freeze the production of HCFCs in 2004 at 1989 levels and developing countries to do so in 2016 with a similar baseline of 2015. Production of 15 percent above baseline will be permitted to meet the "basic domestic needs" of developing countries. In addition, the production of bromochloromethane (a recently developed ozone-depleting chemical) is to be completely phased out in all countries by 2002.

The ozone protection regime continues to face implementation challenges, especially as the cutoff dates for the manufacture of numerous ozone-depleting substances approaches, including the phase-out of CFC production in developing countries. However, the Protocol has been successful. In 1986 the total consumption of CFCs worldwide was about 1.1

FIGURE 3.1   CFC Production (As Reported to the Ozone Secretariat, UNEP)

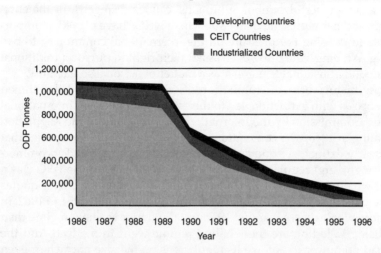

SOURCE: Ozone Secretariat, UNEP, Nairobi, Kenya.

million tons; by 1996 this had come down to about 160,000 tons. It has been calculated that without the Montreal Protocol, global consumption would have reached about 3 million tons in the year 2010 and 8 million tons in 2060, resulting in a 50 percent depletion of the ozone layer by 2035.[26] (See Figure 3.1.) The Montreal Protocol is the best example so far of a regime that has been continually strengthened in response to new scientific evidence and technological innovations.

WHALING

The fight to ban whaling worldwide illustrates the transformation of an international regime from one that permitted virtually unregulated exploitation of an endangered species into a global conservation regime, despite the continued resistance of a veto coalition led by a powerful blocking state: Japan. The process of decisionmaking on all commercial whaling, which took place entirely within the International Whaling Commission (IWC) on the basis of a majority vote, favored the forces supporting a ban. Even so, the power of the veto coalition, based on the ability to bolt the agreement at any time, has not yet been broken.[27]

Whaling is not an enterprise of significant economic dimensions worldwide. Nevertheless, it has generated great emotion, and opposing parties have often taken positions with little reference to science. For many environmental NGOs in the United States and Western Europe, whaling is a powerful symbol of humans' callous disregard for the environment and has represented an issue where NGOs have played an important role in keeping the pressure on the international community to ban whaling. Whaling states, however, assert their right to pursue a traditional livelihood in a sustainable manner as a matter of national sovereignty.

A long history of overexploitation of whales, which had threatened many species with extinction, led to the establishment of the International Whaling Commission by the International Convention for the Regulation of Whaling in 1946. The convention prohibited killing certain species that were nearly extinct, set quotas and minimum sizes for whales commercially caught, and regulated the seasons for whaling. But the IWC was a club of whaling nations. It met in secret each year to haggle over quotas that were set so high that the kill more than doubled from 1951 to 1962. In fact, more whales were being killed annually under the new regime than were being killed before the whaling regime went into effect. And the IWC had no power to enforce its regulations on the size of catch or even its bans on the killing of endangered species. Although the major whaling nations that were responsible for most of the catch were members of the IWC, many developing countries, including China, South Korea, Brazil, Chile, Ecuador, and Peru, refused to join or to abide by its restrictions. They allowed "pirate" whalers, often financed by and selling to the Japanese, to operate freely.

The process of fact-finding and consensus building played virtually no role in relations among the members of the IWC. There was no international organization to facilitate consensus building on the scientific facts on whaling. For many years scientific evidence was subordinated to the political and economic interests of the whaling nations; IWC's scientific committee routinely produced data and analysis supporting continued commercial exploitation. By the 1960s, the survival of the largest species, the blue whale, was in doubt, the finback stock was dwindling, and younger and smaller whales were being taken.

The plight of the whales seized the imagination of Americans who were beginning to learn more about the intelligence of whales and dolphins and led to popular demand in the United States for meaningful international protection. The United States, impelled by the Endangered Species Act (1969), declared eight whale species endangered in 1970 and then took the lead in defining the whaling issue internationally.[28] The United States led a regime transformation not by a process of fact-finding and consensus building within the IWC but by creating a three-fourths majority needed under the treaty for a whaling ban.

At the 1972 Stockholm Conference, the United States proposed an immediate moratorium on commercial whaling, which was adopted unanimously by 52 nations. But a whaling moratorium had to be passed by the

IWC to have the force of law, and a similar proposal in the IWC was defeated 6 to 4, with 4 abstentions. The whaling states (Norway, Japan, the Soviet Union, Iceland, Chile, and Peru) constituted a veto coalition that was also a majority in the IWC.

The charter of the IWC, which did not limit membership to whaling states, provided a way to overcome the veto coalition by recruiting non-whaling states to the Whaling Commission. That is exactly what the United States, Sweden, and some other conservationist states did between 1979 and 1982. They recruited first the Seychelles and then seven other developing states, most of which viewed the whaling issue from their perspective that the oceans and their natural resources are the "common inheritance of mankind."[29]

The United States, as the lead state, also sought to weaken the veto coalition through the threat of economic sanctions. It used domestic legislation to ban imports of fish products and denial of fishing permits within the U.S. 200-mile zone to any country violating international whale-conservation programs. This put pressure on Chile and Peru, both heavily dependent on U.S. fishing permits and markets, to go along with a whaling moratorium.

In order to be adopted by the IWC, a moratorium required a three-fourths majority of the membership. By 1982, enough developing-country nonwhaling nations had entered the IWC to tilt the balance decisively. A five-year moratorium on all commercial whaling, to take effect in 1985, was passed 25 to 7, with 5 abstentions. The veto coalition, consisting of four states (Japan, Norway, Peru, and the USSR) that accounted for 75 percent of the kill and almost all the consumption of whale meat and other whale products, filed formal reservations to the moratorium but chose not to openly defy it when it went into effect.

Instead, Japan, Norway, and the Soviet Union all formally ended commercial whaling activity by the 1987–1988 whaling season. Then Japan, Iceland, and Norway unilaterally began carrying out what they called "scientific" whaling, which is permitted by the whaling convention. Most IWC members found no scientific merit in this whaling, conducted by commercial ships, which killed hundreds of minke whales annually. But the United States failed to ban imports of $1 billion in Japanese seafood annually because of the likelihood of Japanese retaliation on U.S. fish exports, choosing only the lesser sanction of denying the Japanese permission to fish in U.S. waters. And the United States, fearful of being denied use of its Air Force base in Reykjavik, reached two successive bilateral agreements with Iceland condoning its "scientific" whaling in 1987 and 1988. Only a boycott of Icelandic fish products by conservationists persuaded Iceland to pledge a halt in whaling, at least until 1991.[30] The Soviet Union, meanwhile, just continued whaling, bringing in the second largest catch in the world in the 1980s.[31] False reporting of the Soviet catch during those years may very well have skewed the decade's estimates of surviving stocks.

The "scientific" whaling policy was only a temporary stratagem pending a renewed effort to roll back the moratorium, as shown by the whaling states' request for a change in the status of the Northeast Atlantic minke whales from "protection stock" to "sustainable stock," thus opening the way for resumption of harvesting. At the 1990 IWC meeting, however, with the five-year moratorium ending, the United States led a majority of IWC members in blocking a proposal allowing limited commercial whaling in the Atlantic and extending the moratorium for another year instead. At the meeting, Iceland, Japan, and Norway resorted to the ultimate weapon of threatening to quit the IWC if the moratorium was not overturned at the following year's meeting.

Prior to the 1993 Kyoto IWC meeting, both Japan and Norway again prepared for another effort to end the whaling ban. Norway announced its intention to resume modest commercial whaling (160 minkes from the North Atlantic) in the 1993 season, reportedly because Prime Minister Gro Harlem Brundtland needed the Arctic whaling communities' votes in a tight upcoming election. Japan planned to request a resumption of commercial whaling of a limited number of Antarctic minkes and of 50 more by village fishermen off the Japanese coast. Meanwhile both governments spent large sums on public relations in nonwhaling countries in support of their arguments that minke whales were no longer endangered and that whaling villages, severely impoverished by the moratorium, were being denied the right to pursue a cultural tradition.[32] And Japan induced six Caribbean IWC members to support its position by providing funds for new fishing vessels and by paying their annual IWC membership fees.[33]

But the Kyoto meeting again extended the whaling moratorium for another year, rejecting Japan's requests. Norway resumed limited whaling in 1993 and came under increased pressure when the Clinton administration certified that Norway was eligible for U.S. trade sanctions and the U.S. House of Representatives called unanimously for the application of such sanctions. President Clinton delayed the application of sanctions, pending efforts to convince Norway to end its defiance of the moratorium.

More important, the whale protection regime was further strengthened at the IWC meeting in Mexico in 1994 by the adoption of a long-term ban on all whaling below 40 degrees south latitude, creating a whale sanctuary that could protect up to 90 percent of the estimated 3.5 million great whales remaining. The big loser in the vote was Japan, which was taking 300 minkes from the Antarctic annually, ostensibly for "scientific" purposes.

Meanwhile, both Japan and Norway continued to be determined to defy the whaling ban. In 1997, Norway hunted five times as many whales as it did in 1992, and Japan continued to hunt whales in an international whale sanctuary established in the Antarctic in 1994.[34] Japanese officials claim that the Antarctic whale hunt is for scientific research, but every year the whale meat is sold on the open market for tens of millions of dollars. The 1,700 tons of whale meat from the 1997 "research" hunt sold in Japanese fish markets for an estimated $50 million.[35]

At the 1997 IWC meeting in Monaco, Ireland's commissioner, Michael Canny, tabled a proposal to end the ban on commercial whaling and bring commercial whaling back under the control of the commission. Central to the Irish proposal was that the commission should formally adopt the Revised Management Procedure (RMP), which is a new means of calculating commercial catch limits for whales. The RMP had been under discussion by the IWC since the early 1990s and would permit a carefully limited catch of a whale species whose populations can be scientifically demonstrated to be large enough. Far more conservative than previous management procedures, the RMP would allow catch limits only up to 1 percent of the estimated population. The greater the uncertainty in population estimates, the lower the catch limit. In addition, catches decrease in inverse relation to the size of previous hunting, thus ensuring protection for depleted populations.

To further strengthen the safeguards, and strictly limit the possibility of commercial whaling spreading beyond Japan and Norway, Canny also proposed that any future commercial whaling be restricted to the coastal waters of those countries already killing whales and be limited to minke whales only, and that all meat be used solely for local consumption. At the same time, scientific whaling would be phased out—and, in the interim, any catches for such "research whaling" purposes would be counted against any quotas devised under the RMP.

Many NGOs have expressed concern that adoption of the Irish plan would open the door to resumed commercial whaling worldwide. The ideal scenario, for many NGOs, would be a complete end to commercial whaling, although there is currently no credible strategy for achieving it. The premise behind the Irish initiative is that commercial whaling is under way and now the IWC needs to cap the burgeoning commercial whaling industry before it grows totally out of control and to bring commercial whaling back under the aegis of the commission.[36] Meanwhile, more than 120 NGOs signed a statement calling on the Irish government to withdraw the proposal, urging the IWC to carry out a fully comprehensive assessment of environmental threats to whales, and calling on the IWC to retain and enforce the moratorium for at least 50 years while this program of work is undertaken.[37]

At its fifty-first meeting in May 1999 in Grenada, the IWC again considered an Irish proposal to lift the 13-year-old ban with the above conditions. After two days of acrimonious debate, it was voted to defer the vote until 2000, despite the fact that a majority of the 34 governments present appeared to support the proposal.[38] Many of the nations who have spoken most loudly in support of whale protection did not openly support the Irish proposal. Nervous about being criticized by some environmental and animal welfare organizations, they were reluctant to endorse any plan that would officially allow commercial whaling, even though the present strategy of a simple ban on whaling is allowing more and more whales to be killed each year.[39]

The IWC did take action on a proposal to lift a ban on trade in certain populations of minke whales. Legalized trade would create new financial incentives for whalers to go after ever higher catches once again. By a vote of 21–10, the IWC asked the Convention on Trade in Endangered Species (CITES) "not to change the status of any whales until the commission gives permission." Nevertheless, Japan and Norway, who received considerable support for lifting trade restrictions on minke whales at the 1997 CITES conference, tried again in April 2000 but were defeated.[40]

The bitter stalemate over the moratorium on commercial whaling has raised concern about the IWC's role in the future. Norway has for years ignored the IWC moratorium on commercial whaling because the commission has been so highly polarized. Some NGOs, including WWF, fear more countries will follow Norway's lead.

In the IWC differences persist between governments as well as among NGOs on the best way to manage a species, in this case, whales. The argument centers around what constitutes sustainability and what strategies are best to achieve and sustain it. As whale counting has greatly improved over the years and scientists are better able to determine the health and number of different whale populations, some scientists, NGOs (such as WWF), and states argue that a complete moratorium on whaling is not the answer to effective whale management, nor is it possible, given Japan and Norway's (the veto states) refusal to uphold the moratorium.

There continues to be a broad global consensus against hunting any whale species that could be endangered and on the need to take the precautionary approach in making such determinations. Even the whaling states do not disagree with that norm, and it will have to be the basis for any detailed set of rules for managing whale stocks that is adopted by the IWC in the future.

THE TRADE IN IVORY
FROM AFRICAN ELEPHANTS

The issue of saving the African elephant by preventing illegal trade in ivory from its tusks illustrates how the transformation of a veto state into a supporter of the regime can be brought about through diplomatic pressures. This case, like those of whaling and Antarctica, illustrates the importance of bans or prohibitions as an effective mechanism for regulating activities that threaten the environment, natural resources or wildlife. The context of that transformation suggests that such pressures, taking advantage of the potential embarrassment that could be created by a veto of the regime, were successful in part because the issue did not touch on interests considered to be crucial by the veto state.

The umbrella regime for dealing with illegal traffic in wildlife products is the Convention on International Trade in Endangered Species, commonly known as CITES, which was adopted in 1973. CITES combats commercial overexploitation of wild animals and plants by imposing trade sanctions against violators. It set up a secretariat, provided by UNEP, and a conference of the parties, which meets every two years to decide how to regulate trade in species in different degrees of danger. The treaty created three categories of species according to the threat to their existence, with various levels of controls over each: Those in Appendix I are threatened with extinction and are not to be traded except for scientific or cultural endeavors. Those listed in Appendix II are not yet endangered but are believed to merit monitoring and thus require export permits from the country of origin; those in Appendix III require export permits only if the country of origin has listed them in this appendix.

Nations that are the sources of wildlife trade generally support CITES because it helps them protect their valuable wildlife resources from poachers and illegal traders; importing countries often support it because it protects the interests of their legitimate dealers. In the negotiations on CITES the threat of a veto coalition forced the convention's strongest proponents to allow a party to the agreement to enter a reservation to the listing of a species as controlled or banned if the party claims an overriding economic interest in exploiting the species. Such a reservation makes that party in effect a nonparty with regard to that particular species.

The international trade in exotic wildlife is an enormous and lucrative business, worth billions of dollars and involving hundreds of millions of plants and animals and their parts and derivatives annually, of which a significant amount is illegal.[41] The worldwide market for live animals as well as for their parts and derivatives is an important cause of species loss, representing a systematic overexploitation of natural resources.[42]

The ivory ban negotiations were triggered by the dramatic crash in African elephant populations in the 1980s—from 1.3 million in 1979 to 625,000 in 1989—which was due partly to loss of habitat but mostly to killing for commercial sale of the ivory tusks.[43] In 1989, the market was worth an estimated $50–60 million annually. Tusks removed from dead elephants, usually killed by poachers, were shipped from African countries to be processed in the United Arab Emirates, Hong Kong, Macao, or

China. Most of the worked-ivory products were sold in highly industrialized countries. Although the United States and Western Europe have significant markets for ivory products, Japan dominates the world market, importing more than 80 percent of all African ivory products, making it the potential leader of a veto coalition.[44]

As the largest consumer of illegal wildlife in the world, Japan was the leading blocking or veto state on many wild species. Japan made nine reservations to CITES when it ratified the convention and by 1985 added five more, and it refused to ban the import of a number of endangered species. Confronted with international criticism of its policies, however, Japan withdrew eight of its reservations between 1987 and 1994 and in 1987 passed a tough new law punishing traders in protected species.

The African elephant was listed under Appendix II of CITES beginning in 1977, and in 1985 a system of ivory export quotas in the countries with elephant herds was established by CITES to control the international traffic. But in 1988 the World Wildlife Fund and Conservation International (CI) redefined the issue, calling for a worldwide ban on trade in African elephant ivory. They sponsored a study of the African elephant by a group of elephant scientists, trade specialists, and economists in 1989 that made the case for placing the African elephant in Appendix I of CITES. The report concluded that the sustainable level of ivory production was 50 metric tons annually, whereas the world had been consuming 770 metric tons per year for a decade.[45]

The NGO report on the African elephant also represented the beginning of a relatively brief process of fact-finding. But that process failed to achieve a consensus on the facts. There were countercharges by some other elephant conservation specialists that the NGO report was based on inaccurate trade figures and had deliberately exaggerated the reduction in the elephant population.[46] Countries accepted or rejected the report depending on what policy they wished to support for other reasons.

The bargaining stage began when an odd international coalition including Kenya, Tanzania, Austria, the Gambia, Somalia, Hungary, and the United States initiated an effort to list the African elephant in Appendix I and ban trade in ivory products entirely. These efforts took place at the Seventh CITES Conference of the Parties in October 1989. Another unlikely coalition, uniting foes in southern Africa's struggle over apartheid (Botswana, Malawi, Mozambique, Zambia, South Africa, and Zimbabwe), opposed the listing. Underlying their resistance to the ban was the fact that although Africa's elephant population had declined by roughly one-half over the previous decade because of poaching and ivory trade, Botswana, South Africa, and Zimbabwe had succeeded in increasing their elephant herds by providing economic incentives to localities for conservation by allowing limited hunting for elephants and commercial trade in elephant parts.

After the conference defeated a compromise proposed by the CITES Secretariat that would have distinguished between herds that needed the protection of an ivory trade ban and those that did not, a two-thirds majority put all African elephant herds in Appendix I but also created a special review process to consider the possible transfer of some of the sustainably managed herds before the next CITES meeting.[47] The southern African states lodged reservations against the ban and announced plans to sell their ivory through a cartel, with the proceeds to be used to finance conservation.[48]

It was Japan, however, not the African states, that determined the viability of the regime. A major consumer nation that had much to lose, Japan was expected to veto the ban. Nevertheless it decided not to enter a reservation. Under heavy pressure from NGOs, the United States, and the EC—and hoping to host the 1992 Conference of the Parties—Japan changed its policy and agreement was possible. Once the ban was in place, world prices for raw ivory plunged by 90 percent, radically reducing incentives for poaching and smuggling.[49]

Three southern African countries (Zimbabwe, Namibia, and Botswana) continued to call for an end to the ivory trade ban by proposing that the African elephant be "downlisted" from CITES Appendix I to Appendix II. Proposals to that effect were made at CITES meetings in 1992 and 1994 by the three countries but were withdrawn in the face of opposition from most African states, including three range states (Kenya, Tanzania, and Angola), as well as from the United States, Australia, and France and other EU member states. In an attempt to find some common ground on the issue, elephant range countries met in Senegal in November 1996 to try to develop a more constructive regionwide dialogue. Although no agreement was reached on the future of the CITES ivory ban, the discussions represented the first successful fact-finding process since the beginning of the negotiations on the ivory ban.[50]

At the tenth Conference of the Parties in June 1997 in Harare, Zimbabwe, the debate over the proposal by the three southern African range states and Japan for a "split" downlisting of the elephant populations in their countries was long and acrimonious. The three range states argued that their herds had grown to a combined total of about 150,000, and that continued inability to exploit their herds commercially was costing them revenues that could be used to increase their conservation budgets. The Zimbabwean tourism minister charged that some opponents of the ivory trade were opposing it on racial grounds. But the United States and other opponents of downlisting expressed fears that this partial easing of the trade ban would result in a new flood of illegal trade in ivory, citing deficiencies in enforcement and control measures in the three African countries and Japan that had been identified by the CITES panel of experts. They pointed out that, without adequate controls in place, it would be extremely difficult to track where elephant tusks originated.

In the end, a committee of 19 CITES members worked out a deal under which each of the three states could get permission to sell a strictly limited "experimental quota" of ivory under a stringent set of conditions. The decision was made by a majority vote of 76 countries, with 21 voting against and another 20 abstaining in a secret ballot. The United States and Australia opposed the compromise, but the EU member states had failed to reach a consensus and had abstained.[51]

The limited trade was to take place only 18 months after the downlisting took effect, and only after the CITES Standing Committee had ensured that the deficiencies found by its expert panel had been remedied, and that an adequate system of international reporting and monitoring to track illegal hunting of elephants and trade in elephant products had been set up.[52]

The first legal sale of ivory in a decade took place on April 9, 1999, when 14 metric tons of stockpiled elephant tusks were auctioned to Japanese buyers in Windhoek, Namibia. Sales in Zimbabwe and Botswana also took place in April 1999. On July 17, 1999, all the ivory from the experimental sales was imported into Japan. The CITES Secretariat worked to ensure that all ivory tusks and derived products were duly registered in Japan and that all the funds obtained by the three countries were invested in elephant conservation, as required by the decision.[53]

At the eleventh Conference of the Parties in April 2000 in Nairobi, Kenya, delegates voted to continue the ban on elephant ivory sales. The elephant populations of Botswana, Namibia, South Africa, and Zimbabwe will remain on CITES Appendix II, but there will be a zero quota for ivory sales, which means that no ivory sales can take place before the next CITES meeting in 2002, when the ivory ban will be revisited. Africa's other elephant populations remain on Appendix I. The African elephant range states will continue to seek a continentwide consensus on a long-term conservation strategy for the elephant. In addition, efforts will be made to improve data on elephant populations and poaching incidents.

The split downlisting of African elephants in the three range states has not ended the controversy over African elephant ivory. Conservation groups continue to be sharply divided, with those in the three range states that stand to gain new income from the sale generally supporting the decision and most others opposing it. It is too soon to say whether it represents, on balance, a strengthening of the regime by establishing stronger national and international controls over illegal hunting and trade in elephant ivory, or a weakening of the regime by compromising the global trade ban.

Although the elephant ivory case shows the political difficulty of achieving political consensus on a complete ban, it also underlines the value of such a ban as a mechanism for discouraging activities that threaten the environment—in this case rampant elephant poaching in the range states. In a situation marked by weak domestic regulatory systems, as in the case of the hazardous waste trade case, the strategy for saving African elephants had to shift from government to market and from range state to importing states.[54]

During the negotiations that resulted in the ivory ban, the southern African states were not a true veto coalition, however, because their position reflected an alternative wildlife management scheme that had worked in southern African countries to accomplish the same objective: saving the African elephant. As in the whaling case, this raises the question of how best to save an endangered species. Do we need to have a ban on trade in African ivory or will an alternative elephant management scheme work? However, in the negotiations, the real issue was how Japan would deal with the issue in CITES. By demanding a reservation on African ivory, Japan would have frustrated international efforts to ban the trade. Now that limited trade in ivory has resumed, with the full support of the African countries, new coalitions could develop at future CITES meetings as the consequences of the Harare and Nairobi decisions are determined.

INTERNATIONAL TOXIC WASTE TRADE

The United Nations Environment Programme estimates that between 300 and 500 million tons of hazardous waste are generated each year.[55] Industrialized market economies generate more than 90 percent of the world's hazardous wastes, and as laws regulating hazardous waste disposal grow in those countries, individual firms have sought cheaper sites for their disposal. It is generally accepted that about 10 percent of generated hazardous wastes are shipped across international boundaries. The OECD estimates that about 80 percent of the legal trade occurs between OECD countries, with 10 to 15 percent going to Eastern Europe and the remainder to developing countries.[56]

North-South hazardous waste shipments increased through the 1970s and 1980s, and unsafe and illegal waste dumps were discovered in several developing countries. It was found that an estimated $3 billion worth of hazardous wastes, representing one-fifth to one-tenth of the total annual global trade in such wastes, was exported from industrialized countries to developing countries, most of which lack the technology or

Copyright the Los Angeles Times News Syndicate. Reprinted with
permission.

administrative capacity to dispose of them safely. These states, particularly the poorer states in Africa, Central America, and the Caribbean,
have been tempted by offers of substantial revenues for accepting the
wastes. In many cases the trade was illegal, the result of bribery of officials to allow the wastes to enter the country covertly.

The main exporters of hazardous wastes in 1993 were Canada, Germany, the Netherlands, Switzerland, and the United States, countries
that all have stringent environmental regulations. The United States exported only 1 percent of its hazardous wastes, mostly to Canada and
Mexico. Nevertheless, it was the United States that led the veto coalition
in the 1980s, because of an ideological rejection of any limitation on its
right to export.

The issue definition stage on the international trade in hazardous
wastes began in 1984–1985, when a UNEP working group of legal and
technical experts elaborated a set of guidelines (the Cairo Guidelines) on
the management and disposal of hazardous wastes. The Guidelines specified prior notification of the receiving state of any export, consent by the
receiving state prior to export, and verification by the exporting state that
the receiving state has requirements for disposal at least as stringent as
those of the exporting state.

But this process did not satisfy key actors, notably the African states who were among the major recipients of illegal hazardous waste exports. The issue of banning international hazardous waste trade, as opposed to regulating it, was defined primarily by African states, who characterized the trade as a form of exploitation of poor and weak states by advanced countries and businesses. This definition of the problem drew support from some officials in the industrialized states. The Dutch minister of environment, for example, called it "waste colonialism."[57] In 1988, parliamentarians from the European Community joined with representatives from 68 developing states from Africa, the Caribbean, and the Pacific (ACP) in demanding arrangements banning international trade in wastes. The Nonaligned Movement also called for industrialized countries to prohibit waste exports to developing countries.

The bargaining stage began in 1987 when UNEP organized a working group to negotiate a global convention to control international trade in hazardous wastes. During the next year and a half major differences emerged between African and industrialized countries. The African states wanted a total ban on such waste exports, as well as export-state liability in the event of illegal traffic in wastes, because the developing countries had neither the administrative, technical, nor financial ability to enforce a ban on their own. The waste-exporting states wanted a convention that would permit the trade, providing importing countries were notified and agreed to accept it—what was called an informed-consent regime.

The final bargaining stage took place in Basel, Switzerland, in March 1989, where the veto coalition, led by the United States, took advantage of the fact that the waste-exporting states could have continued to find poor countries willing to accept wastes. The veto coalition gave the waste-importing states a choice: Accept an informed-consent regime or get none at all. The Organization of African Unity (OAU) proposed amendments to prevent the export of wastes to countries that lack the same level of facilities and technology as the exporting nations and to require inspection of disposal sites by UN inspectors, but the industrialized countries rejected the amendments.[58]

The Basel Convention on Control of Transboundary Movements of Hazardous Wastes and Their Disposal allowed hazardous wastes to be exported to countries whose facilities for storage are less advanced than those of the exporting country as long as the importing state had detailed information on the waste shipment and gave prior written consent. Agreements between signatory states and nonsignatory states were permitted by the convention, although they were supposed to conform to the terms of the convention. Critics charged that the convention did not go any further than existing regulations in industrialized countries, which had failed to curb legal or illegal waste traffic. Moreover, the convention's enforcement provisions were weakened by lack of precision on key definitions, such as "environmentally sound" and "hazardous wastes," and by lack of liability provisions.[59]

As in other global environmental issues, the signing of the Basel Convention began a new phase of maneuvering and bargaining for a stronger regime, but it did not take place in the Basel Convention Conference of the Parties alone. Within months the veto coalition was splitting under pressure from developing countries. In April 1989, 30 states (not including the United States) and the EC pledged publicly to dispose of wastes at home and to ban the export of hazardous wastes to countries that lack the legal and technological capacity to handle them.[60] Later in 1989, after extended negotiations, the EC also reached agreement with the 68 former European colonial ACP states to ban waste shipments to all 68 members, after ACP negotiators rejected a proposed EC exception for countries with "adequate technical capacity."[61] This concession by the EC appears to have reflected particular conditions affecting member states: a French decision to give priority to cultural and economic ties with France's former colonies, heavy pressure on the United Kingdom from its former colonies, and a weak commitment by West Germany to the veto coalition because of its lack of interest in exporting to developing countries.

In January 1991, 12 African states, under the auspices of the OAU, signed the Bamako Convention, banning the import into their countries of hazardous wastes from any country. This underlined the African determination to end the international hazardous waste trade. These multilateral and unilateral bans on hazardous waste trade created, in effect, a stronger waste trade regime outside the Basel Convention, although it excluded Latin American and Asian states.

The Basel Convention came into effect in May 1992 without ratification by any of the major exporting states that had been the victorious veto coalition in the negotiations. None of them was ready to push for the convention's implementation, and it remained a very weak regime.[62]

But in less than two years, the rapidly growing demand for a complete ban on hazardous waste trade would transform the Basel Convention from a weak regime into a strong one. By early 1994 over 100 countries had banned the import of hazardous wastes, although not all of them had the administrative capacity to do so unilaterally.[63] Some of the credit must go to Greenpeace, which published an exposé volume of 1,000 cases of illegal toxic waste exports.[64] The Clinton administration decided in 1994 to reverse U.S. policy toward hazardous waste trade. In preparation for the March 1994 Geneva meeting of the Basel Convention parties, which the United States would attend only as an observer (since it had not ratified the Convention), the administration announced its intention to call for a ban on all hazardous waste exports to developing countries, and a ban on such exports to any country within five years—exempting only scrap metal, glass, textiles, and paper, which are widely traded for recycling.[65]

But at the Geneva meeting, a broader coalition of states pressed for a complete ban on hazardous waste exports from OECD countries to non-OECD countries, including those exported for recycling.[66] It was argued that shipments of recyclables were often not recycled but just dumped in a developing country and that the OECD countries would never be forced to reduce their own excessive waste as long as they could ship it out. The G-77 was the lead state coalition calling for such a complete ban to go into effect immediately. Denmark was only a step behind, calling for such a ban to begin in 1995. The United Kingdom, Australia, Germany, the Netherlands, Japan, Canada, and the United States wanted to exempt recyclables. China and the former socialist states of Central and Eastern Europe came out in favor of the G-77 proposal.

It was here in a new issue definition phase that Greenpeace, who had been a major player in the issue definition phase in the 1980s, stepped in again as a key player by pointing to the widespread dumping of hazardous wastes that were being labeled recyclables. Greenpeace reported that from 1980 to 1988, only 36 percent of the schemes where the destination was reported claimed a further-use or "recycling" destination.[67] By 1989 this had risen to 76 percent. In 1990 it was 83 percent, in 1991 it was 87 percent, in 1992 it was 88 percent, and in 1993 it had risen to 89 percent.[68] Greenpeace, which in the course of seven years closely examined over 50 recycling operations in non-OECD countries, also brought the not so pretty pictures and chemical analyses to the conference halls in Geneva to demonstrate to delegates that often shipments labeled "recyclables" were not recycled but just dumped in a developing country.[69]

Despite intensive lobbying by exporting countries, particularly for allowing bilateral agreements on hazardous waste exports for recycling, the G-77 would negotiate only on the timetable for its implementation. Confronted with non-OECD unity, the veto coalition began to divide, as the Netherlands shifted to the G-77 position. Italy offered a new proposal for a total ban that was ultimately endorsed unanimously by the Secretariat of the European Council of Ministers.

The remaining veto states could get no more than a delay in the implementation of a total export ban. The 64 nations that were party to the convention adopted by consensus a total immediate ban on hazardous waste exports from OECD countries for final disposal to non-OECD countries and an end to *all* hazardous waste exports, including recyclables.[70] The United States, Germany, and the European Commission did not accept the verdict of the COP as final, arguing that the ban did not constitute an amendment of the Convention and was not binding international law.

The most controversial aspect of the ban amendment (also known as Decision III/1) is the ban on exports of wastes intended for recovery and recycling, such as scrap metal. Because of the economic interests of the veto coalition, and, increasingly, some developing countries as well, in the maintenance of a lucrative trade in wastes for recycling, the ban may or may not be endorsed. The amendment has still not been ratified by two-thirds of the parties who were present at COP-3 in 1995 in order to enter into force. The debate had centered on the question of which wastes were defined as "hazardous" for the purposes of recycling and recovery. To help remedy this situation, a Technical Working Group was assigned the task of drawing up a list of banned (and exempt) wastes and to report to the fourth Conference of the Parties, which was held in February 1998. At COP-4, parties accepted the lists that the Technical Working Group had created: List A (wastes characterized as hazardous and subject to the ban), List B (wastes exempt from the ban), and List C (wastes not yet assigned to Lists A or B). The Technical Working Group is now working on categorizing the List C wastes, which include polyvinyl chloride (PVC), among other wastes.[71] Agreement on these lists added clarity with respect to which wastes are covered within the scope of the convention and defused the most vociferous industry argument that nobody knew what the ban was banning. It was hoped that these definitions would help speed up the ratification and implementation of the ban amendment.[72]

The strong regime on international hazardous waste trade that emerged from the 1994 COP represented a complete reversal of the original Basel Convention regime. In an astonishingly short time, an international environmental issue that had deeply divided North and South moved decisively to conclusion. The Convention has been central to the elimination of some of the worst forms of toxic waste dumping by industrialized countries on developing countries. The evolution of the Basel Convention shows how veto power can dissipate under pressure from a strong coalition, including all of the developing countries with the added support of a number of key OECD countries. The pressure and publicity generated by the activities of several key NGOs, especially Greenpeace, also had an impact on overriding the veto coalition. Once the hazardous waste trade issue became a matter of political symbolism uniting developing countries behind the demand for a complete ban, it eliminated the leverage of waste export states that had weakened the waste trade regime in 1989.

THE ANTARCTIC ENVIRONMENT

The regime for Antarctica was fundamentally redefined when what started as negotiations to regulate mineral exploitation concluded in a regime to protect the environment. The usual roles of state actors are reversed in this case: The veto coalition was composed of states who wished to ban economic activities that could imperil the environment. Antarctica also illustrates how important the "rules of the game" are for global environmental politics: The Antarctic Treaty system requires an unusually high degree of consensus to make binding decisions. The difficulties of creating a new regime within that framework were ultimately advantageous to those campaigning for environmental protection in the region.

Antarctica, which constitutes about 10 percent of the earth's land and water areas, is the only continent that has not been exploited for economic purposes. But it is believed to contain considerable mineral wealth, including reserves of uranium, gold, silver, and other precious metals under the Antarctic Peninsula and oil and natural gas offshore.[73] Given the extreme conditions in Antarctica, which increase the likelihood of accidents and decrease the ecosystem's ability to recover from disruption, ecologists fear that mineral exploitation would pose serious threats to the environment.

Antarctica is governed by the Antarctic Treaty of 1959, which bans military activities and radioactive wastes in the continent and sets it aside as a research preserve. The original 12 signatories to the Antarctic Treaty (Argentina, Australia, Belgium, Chile, France, Japan, New Zealand, Norway, South Africa, the United Kingdom, the United States, and the Soviet Union) include 7 that have made territorial claims in Antarctica and 5 others that insist on viewing the continent as the common property of humankind.

Antarctica is under the collective management of 38 states, called the Antarctic Treaty Consultative Parties (ATCPs), including the 12 original signatories and 26 other states who have since signed the treaty and have been accepted by the original signatories as having done substantial scientific research activity in Antarctica. Other states, even if signatories to the Antarctic Treaty, may attend the meetings of the ATCPs only as observers. Thus the ATCPs are a relatively exclusive club, consisting of countries with the resources for scientific research.[74]

The Antarctic Treaty was supplemented by three agreements to protect the environment: Agreed Measures on the Conservation of Antarctic Fauna and Flora in 1964, the Convention for the Conservation of Antarctic Seals in 1972, and the Convention on the Conservation of Antarctic Marine Living Resources (CCAMLR) in 1980. But compliance with all these agreements is voluntary; the treaties failed to establish an environmental review body or regulatory authority, thus leaving individual member states to interpret agreements and resolutions on environmental protection. The CCAMLR requires a consensus of parties on conservation measures and therefore limits environmental protection to what is acceptable to the most shortsighted party.

Protesters at the McMurdo U.S. base point up the danger of exploiting
Antarctic mineral deposits. (Photo by Midgley.)

In 1972 the Second World Conference on National Parks, cosponsored
by the IUCN, noted the "great scientific and aesthetic value of the unal-
tered natural ecosystems of the Antarctic" and called for the negotiation
of a "world park" regime that would ban all mineral exploration in the
continent. The proposal was formally supported by New Zealand in 1975
but never raised in meetings of the ATCPs.

Meanwhile most of the ATCPs, driven by sudden price increases in the
international oil market, agreed that an international regime was needed
to govern eventual exploration for Antarctic oil and gas resources. The
United States, in particular, believed that Antarctica might become a vital
source of supply in the future and was one of the few ATCPs to oppose a
moratorium on exploration until a minerals regime was negotiated. No
issue definition process was carried out by the ATCPs before the bargaining process began. By 1977, the ATCPs were already discussing the principles of such a regime.[75]

Negotiations began in 1981 and continued in secret for the next seven
years.[76] A division developed between the most enthusiastic pro-mining
states (the United States, West Germany, Japan, Britain, and France) and
states geographically closer to Antarctica (Australia, Argentina, and
Chile), which wanted stronger conservation provisions.[77] The latter coali-

tion won some concessions from the most pro-mining states, but it agreed to a regime that could have permitted minerals exploitation in Antarctica.

The Convention on the Regulation of Antarctic Mineral Resources Activities (CRAMRA, 1988) would have blocked any exploration for minerals in the absence of a consensus of all members that the activity would not violate specific environmental standards, thus reversing the rule in the CCAMLR that economic activities can proceed unless there is a consensus on measures to restrict them.[78] Nevertheless, environmentalists doubted that the ATCP states could be counted on to put environmental protection ahead of economic development once the race for mineral wealth began and feared that the regulatory committees provided for in the treaty would be subject to political horse-trading at the expense of the environment.[79]

Before the new convention could go into effect, the political process took a sudden dramatic turn, as a veto coalition quickly took shape behind Australia. In May 1989 Australia, influenced by the environmentalist vote in the previous election, announced that it would not sign the convention but would work for a comprehensive environmental protection convention, including a provision for an Antarctic World Park, first proposed by IUCN. To take effect, the minerals treaty required the ratification of 16 of the 20 ATCPs who were signatories as well as all 7 of those with territorial claims. That meant that Australia could single-handedly veto the minerals regime.

Australia's pronouncement simultaneously redefined the issue and began a new phase of bargaining. In August, France—another claimant state—jointly proposed with Australia that Antarctica be designated as a nature preserve, asserting that mining was not compatible with environmental protection there. Belgium, Italy, Austria, Greece, India, and the European Parliament then joined the call for making Antarctica a permanent wilderness preserve. Finally, New Zealand, formerly a strong supporter of the minerals regime process but under strong pressure from environmentalists, abandoned the minerals treaty in early 1990 and indicated that it would work with France and Australia to protect Antarctica from mining. With the tide now running against the minerals regime, the UN General Assembly voted overwhelmingly in 1989 in favor of an Antarctic World Park.

The United States at first strongly resisted Australia's initiative, but it was soon subject to its own domestic pressures. After the U.S. Congress passed two pieces of legislation prohibiting mining activities in Antarctica indefinitely and backing the world park proposal, the United States countered with a proposal for a legally binding moratorium, though still not a permanent ban, on minerals exploration in Antarctica. At the 1990 ATCP meeting the parties agreed to pursue the negotiation of a new "comprehensive legal instrument" on the environmental protection of Antarctica, which would prohibit any exploration for mineral resources in the region.

At a special meeting of the treaty parties in December 1990, the concept of a long-term legal moratorium was discussed, but there was no agreement on how long it should last or what would follow its termination. The United States, the United Kingdom, and Japan led a new veto coalition that resisted an indefinite ban. But at the second session of the meeting in April 1991, Japan broke ranks and joined the advocates of such a ban. A compromise proposal was tabled for a 50-year ban on mineral-related activity in Antarctica that could be lifted only with the support of all 26 of the present ATCPs, thus continuing to give each of them a veto.

At another meeting in Madrid two months later, the proposal was supported by every ATCP except the United States. After two weeks of intensive lobbying by other states, the United States agreed to a new compromise that would permit a repeal of the mineral ban by three-fourths of the 26 ATCPs,[80] and the Environmental Protocol to the Antarctic Treaty was signed. The protocol entered into effect on January 14, 1998.

The agreement on a 50-year mining ban represented another stunning reversal of a regime negotiated earlier. The collapse of the proposed minerals regime was in large part due to the salience of environmental issues in parliamentary elections in several countries and the aggressive and persistent lobbying of NGOs, especially the Antarctic and Southern Oceans Coalition. The mining industry, which only had a possible future interest in Antarctica minerals, did not play much of a role in influencing governments. The ban was also facilitated by the Antarctic Treaty regime itself, in which a few parties have special veto powers, thus making it possible for Australia to lead an unlikely veto coalition in defeating the major powers' efforts on behalf of the regime. And the adoption of the ban was made easier by the fact that no country was in fact dependent on or planning to invest in mineral exploitation in Antarctica.

CLIMATE CHANGE

Global warming, or the greenhouse effect, is the prototype of the global commons issue. All nations are affected by the earth's climate system, and broad international cooperation is required to mitigate the threat of global warming. Although the impacts of global warming are expected to vary from one region to another, suggesting to some the possibility of winners and losers, that notion is based on the erroneous assumption that global warming will stop at a predictable point. In fact, unless states reduce their greenhouse gas emissions, there will not be any stabilization in the climate, and its capacity for adaptation could well be overwhelmed by continued warming.[81]

The negotiation of a regime to mitigate global climate change has been complicated by the multiple sources of emissions that contribute to global warming; by scientific uncertainties, especially the chemistry of the atmosphere; and by dependence on global climate modeling, which is far from an exact science.[82] Even more important, however, is the fact that energy is central to every nation's economy, and the policy changes required to reduce greenhouse gas emissions raise politically difficult political questions of who should bear the immediate costs. Even to stabilize the global concentrations of carbon dioxide (which would not reduce the warming to which earlier emissions have already committed the earth) would require reducing current emissions by roughly one-half. That would necessitate major gains in conservation and switching from coal and oil to natural gas and renewable sources, which would affect powerful economic and political interests in some of the most important emitters of greenhouse gases.

Greenhouse gas emissions from the burning of fossil fuels account for roughly 80 percent of the total, and deforestation and natural sources of methane contribute the rest. Fossil fuel burning has increased atmospheric concentrations of carbon dioxide by 30 percent since preindustrial times. (See Figure 3.2.) The main contributors to global greenhouse gas emissions are the United States (22 percent), China (14 percent), the Russian Federation (7 percent), Japan (5 percent), and India (4 percent). Ten other countries (Germany, United Kingdom, Canada, Republic of Korea, Italy, Ukraine, France, Poland, Mexico, and Australia) account for another 18 percent. Thus the top 15 emitters account for about 70 percent of the world's emissions of greenhouse gases. (See Table 3.1.)

The way in which key participants in the negotiations on climate change have defined their interests has been more closely correlated with their perceptions of the costs of the regime than their perceptions of vulnerability to the threat. The perceived costs of climate change, moreover, are related primarily to the country's "energy culture"—its historical experience with fossil fuels in relation to its economic growth. Since governments could not estimate eventual costs of mitigation measures in terms of overall economic growth without far more information than they had, perceptions of costs were usually shaped by their overall biases regarding energy policy in general.[83] Thus three groups of states can be distinguished.[84]

- Those states that are relatively dependent on imported energy and thus have learned to maintain high living standards while reducing their use of fossil fuel. This group includes Japan and most

FIGURE 3.2   Atmospheric Concentration of Carbon Dioxide, 1000–1997

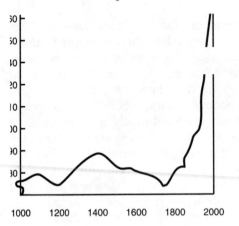

SOURCE: Lester Brown, et al. *State of the World 1999* (New York: W.W. Norton. 1999), p. 26.

Western European states, including Germany, Italy, France, the Netherlands, Denmark, Finland, and Sweden.
- Those states that have large supplies of cheap energy resources and that have had a culture of highly inefficient energy use. This group includes the United States, Russia, China, India, Brazil, and Mexico.
- Those states that have been highly dependent on fossil fuel exports for income, such as the Arab oil states, Australia, Norway, and the United Kingdom.

The "energy culture" of states has generally been a predictor of whether a state would be part of a lead state coalition or part of a veto state coalition on commitments to greenhouse gas emissions targets and timetables. The EU was the leader in pushing for targets and timetables during the 1990s, and the United States was the main veto state. And Russia, China, India, and Brazil have consistently played veto roles.

There have also been some exceptions: Norway and Australia were early lead states, mainly because domestic political pressures and an ini-

TABLE 3.1   Fifteen Countries with the Highest Fossil Fuel CO_2 Emissions

Country	1996 Total CO_2 Emissions (000 metric tons)	Percent of Global Total
United States	1,446,777	22.19
China	917,997	14.08
Russian Federation	431,090	6.61
Japan	318,686	4.89
India	272,212	4.17
Germany	235,050	3.61
United Kingdom	152,015	2.33
Canada	111,723	1.72
Republic of Korea	111,370	1.70
Italy	110,052	1.69
Ukraine	108,431	1.66
France	98,750	1.52
Poland	97,375	1.49
Mexico	95,007	1.46
Australia	83,688	1.29
Global Total	6,518,000	100

SOURCE: Marland, G., T. A. Boden, R. J. Andres, A. L. Brenkert, and C. Johnston. 1999. *Global, Regional, and National CO_2 Emissions. In Trends: A Compendium of Data on Global Change.* (Carbon Dioxide Information Analysis Center, Oak Ridge National Laboratory, U.S. Department of Energy, Oak Ridge, Tenn., U.S.A.)

tial focus on vulnerability drove their positions, but they later retreated to veto roles in negotiations over actual targets and timetables. The UK did not play a lead role but supported a strong climate regime early in the process, despite being a fossil fuel exporter, because its overall energy and industry policies were in transition to greater emphasis on energy efficiency and natural gas and less on coal. Japan was initially part of a veto coalition, but has been vacillating between roles since then.

It has long been known by scientists that the buildup of carbon dioxide in the atmosphere could cause climate change by means of the greenhouse effect. But the process of issue definition began to accelerate in 1985–1986. The World Meteorological Organization and UNEP took the first major step with a 1985 conference in Villach, Austria, that produced a new scientific consensus that global warming was a serious possibility.[85] And in 1986 WMO, the National Aeronautics and Space Administration (NASA), and several other agencies issued a three-volume report concluding that climate change was already taking place at a relatively rapid rate. The unusually hot summer of 1988 accelerated media and congressional attention and even thrust the climate issue into the presidential campaign. The testimony of prominent U.S. scientists suggesting that the climate was already changing irreversibly, primarily because of carbon dioxide emissions, further contributed to the definition of the climate change issue.[86]

The fact-finding process coincided with the issue definition stage. In an attempt to establish a common factual basis for negotiations that would focus on policy options, in 1988 WMO and UNEP organized the Intergovernmental Panel on Climate Change (IPCC). The IPCC is organized into three working groups: Working Group I concentrates on the climate system, Working Group II on impacts and response options, and Working Group III on economic and social dimensions. The First Assessment Report of the IPCC—approved by the participating states after long, grueling negotiations in August 1990—reaffirmed that global warming is a serious threat. The report predicted that if states continue to pursue "business as usual," the global average surface temperature will rise during the next century by an average of 0.3°C. per decade, a rate of change unprecedented in human history. However, despite the success of the IPCC in establishing a strong scientific consensus on climate change, it failed to establish a consensus on the economics of the problem, which was one of the key points of contention during the subsequent negotiations.

The international discussion of the actions that would be required to deal with climate change began when some states and NGOs called for specific targets and timetables for greenhouse gas emissions. A conference in Toronto, sponsored by the Canadian government in June 1988 and attended by government officials, scientists, and representatives of industry and environmental NGOs from 46 countries, was the first to call for a comprehensive global convention and protocols, a reduction in carbon dioxide emissions by about 20 percent of 1988 levels by the year 2005, and establishment of a world atmosphere fund financed partly by a tax on fossil fuel combustion. Regime development was given a boost when the G-7 meeting in Paris in 1989 endorsed the idea of a convention.

Throughout the process, targets and timetables were the central issue. At the Noordwijk conference in the Netherlands in 1989, the United States, the Soviet Union, China, and Japan, which together accounted for more than half the world's carbon dioxide emissions from fossil fuels, acted for the first time as a blocking coalition on global warming. The United States and Japan argued that further study of the goal of reducing carbon emissions was needed, and the Soviet Union rejected action on straightforward economic grounds.[87]

In the 18 months that followed, the initial coalition of lead states (Norway, Sweden, Finland, and the Netherlands) squared off with the United

States, as leader of the veto coalition, on whether the negotiations should produce a protocol with specific obligations on emissions. The lead states called for negotiation of a framework convention to be paralleled by negotiation of a protocol limiting emissions to be completed no later than a year after the convention. The United States insisted on a framework convention with no parallel negotiations on protocols, arguing that regulating carbon releases would require major changes in lifestyle and industrial structure. But in October 1990, Japan broke ranks with the United States on the issue by committing itself to stabilizing its greenhouse gas emissions at 1990 levels by the year 2000. That left the United States and the Soviet Union alone among industrialized countries rejecting a target and timetable for controlling emissions in a climate regime.[88]

The formal negotiation of a climate convention began officially in February 1991, under the auspices of the Intergovernmental Negotiating Committee (INC) for a Framework Convention on Climate Change, created by the UN General Assembly. The EC assumed a lead role in the negotiations by virtue of its commitment to returning its joint carbon dioxide emissions to 1990 levels by the year 2000. Germany, Denmark, Austria, Australia, the Netherlands, and New Zealand had committed themselves to reducing their emissions by 2000 or 2005.

Had binding commitments for controlling greenhouse emissions been included in the text, the developing countries' agreement would have been crucial to the regime. Although their share of such emissions, including carbon dioxide releases from deforestation, was estimated at around 45 percent of the worldwide total, they were expected to account for two-thirds of total emissions by 2025. The biggest rapidly industrializing countries (China, India, and Brazil), which already accounted for 21 percent of global emissions from all sources in 1989 (about the same as the United States), were a potential veto coalition.[89]

What was to have been the final round of negotiations in February 1992 ended without resolution of the issue of a stabilization target and timetable. With the deadline of the Earth Summit only weeks away, the negotiators agreed to one more session in April. German, British, Dutch, and other EC member states sent officials to Washington before the session in an unsuccessful effort to persuade the United States to go along with a commitment to stabilization of emissions at 1990 levels by the year 2000. But during the April session, President George Bush personally called German Prime Minister Helmut Kohl to ask him to drop his government's demand for the stabilization commitment in return for Bush's participation in the Earth Summit. Bush announced his decision to attend the Rio conference only after the final text of the climate change convention was adopted without reference to binding commitments to controlling greenhouse gases.[90]

The Framework Convention on Climate Change (FCCC) was signed by 154 countries in Rio in June 1992. It declares as its goal the restoration of greenhouse gas emissions in 2000 to "earlier levels"—a phrase interpreted by the EC to mean 1990 levels—but does not commit any government to hold emissions to a specific level by a certain date. Nor does it address a climate change goal after the year 2000. Of a lengthy list of commitments in the agreement, providing national reports is probably the only one that is enforceable. But the text does provide for regular review of the "adequacy" of the commitments.

The FCCC came into force in March 1994 after ratification by the minimum necessary 50 states.[91] The climate regime that resulted from the exercise of veto power by the United States was generally regarded as a weak one. However, a few states, led by Germany and strongly supported by a well-organized international network of NGOs, were determined to press the other parties to the convention to strengthen the climate regime significantly. The EU issued a statement upon signing the convention calling for an early start on negotiation of a protocol with binding targets and timetables.

The first COP of the FCCC in March–April 1995 agreed to negotiate by the end of 1997 quantitative limits on greenhouse gas emissions beyond the year 2000 but could not agree on whether those limits would be reductions or which countries would be subject to the new commitments. The EU supported a commitment to substantial reductions, but the JUSCANZ group (Japan, United States, Canada, Australia, and New Zealand) constituted a new veto coalition, opposing any negotiation of emissions reductions. To reduce emissions beyond the year 2000, it was widely recognized that the industrialized countries would have to adopt new economic measures that would help bring about fundamental changes in energy use. So COP-1 created the Ad Hoc Group on the Berlin Mandate (AGBM) to negotiate a binding agreement on actions to be taken after the year 2000.

The AGBM met eight times between August 1995 and December 1997. Halfway through the process, the Second Conference of the Parties met in July 1996 and adopted the IPCC's Second Assessment Report of December 1995. That report concluded that the earth's temperature had increased by 0.3 to 0.6 percent—nearly one temperature degree over the previous 100 years—and that there was a "discernible human influence" on climate. The report predicted an increase of another 2–6 degrees Fahrenheit over the next century if the trend in concentration of carbon dioxide in the atmosphere were not reversed.

During 1996 and 1997 major differences emerged among lead states and veto states over "quantified emission limitation and reduction objectives" (QELROs)—whether they should be equal or differentiated on the basis of particular characteristics of economies, whether they should apply only to developed countries, and how far QELROs should go. A further issue was how much flexibility should be allowed in the form of trading and borrowing from future targets.

By mid-1997, the EU had maintained its lead state role by tabling a proposal for reductions of the three main greenhouse gases (carbon dioxide, methane, and nitrous oxide) from 1990 levels of at least 7.5 percent by 2005 and of 15 percent by 2010. The EU proposal called for all EU member countries to be covered by the overall target, allowing some states, such as Germany, to undertake deeper emissions reductions and poorer EU member states to accept lower targets. In sharp contrast, the United States, leading the veto coalition, proposed the stabilization of all six greenhouse gases (including three whose impacts were less precisely quantifiable) at 1990 level by the years 2008 to 2010 for all industrialized country parties. The U.S. proposal also called for emissions trading among parties to begin at once without specified conditions for its application, and to include the emissions reductions to be assigned to Russia and former Soviet bloc states in Central and Eastern Europe. These emissions were called *hot air*, because they were already more than 30 percent below their 1990s level after shutting down so many obsolescent plants. Although the EU did not oppose carbon trading per se, it did strongly object to trading without adequate guidelines, and especially trading in "hot air," because it would allow the parties to meet any target on paper without taking any direct actions.

Finally, the United States wanted to be able to "borrow" from multiyear target periods. The proposal would allow a country to have a 2010–2020 emissions limit from which it could borrow during the near-term target period. Such borrowing would further obviate actual actions to reduce emissions in the shorter run.

Meanwhile, Australia had opened up yet another front in the diplomatic struggle, proposing that the QELROs be differentiated to take into account the greater economic burdens that equal QELROs would impose on certain states. It argued that because its economy was far more heavily dependent on exports of fossil fuels than the average Annex I party, it should not have to reduce as deeply as most such parties. This demand for differentiation represented another way for the veto coalition to weaken the targets and timetables agreement, by allowing some states to justify lower targets.

At the third Conference of the Parties in Kyoto the differences between lead and veto states widened rather than narrowed: The United States, which had previously supported equal reductions for all industrialized-country parties, also endorsed the concept of differentiation. The U.S.

Copyright *The Buffalo News*. Reprinted with permission.

delegation also took the position that it could not accept any QELROs unless developing countries also agreed formally to control their emissions—a condition that had been mandated by a unanimous vote in the U.S. Senate but was clearly unacceptable to developing countries. New Zealand similarly demanded that developing countries must specify by the year 2002 how much they would slow their emissions increases over the next 12 years. Australia insisted on an increase in emissions of greenhouse gases by 18 percent between 1990 and 2010, and Japan called for only a 2.5 percent cut in emissions by 2010.

Following a week and a half of intense, round-the-clock formal and informal negotiations, including a session that began on the final evening and lasted until 3:30 the following afternoon, the parties finally adopted the Kyoto Protocol.[92] The Protocol calls for the industrialized-country parties to reduce overall emissions of six greenhouse gases by at least 5.2 percent below their 1992 levels between the years 2008 and 2012. Although no formula for differentiation based on some objective characteristics of the party was adopted, the protocol does differentiate national targets, based on intense bargaining between and among veto states and the EU. The national targets vary from a 10 percent increase for Iceland and an 8 percent increase for Australia to 8 percent reductions for the EU and most of Eastern Europe. (See Table 3.2.)

The United States agreed to accept a target of a 7 percent reduction but did win a concession on the three newer greenhouse gases, which are to be calculated from a 1995 baseline rather than 1990, making the target

TABLE 3.2   Target Greenhouse Gas Emissions Reduction by 2012, Kyoto Protocol

Country	Kyoto Target
	(percent change from 1990 emissions)
Australia	8
Bulgaria	−8
Canada	−6
Croatia	−5
Estonia	−8
European Union	−8
Hungary	−6
Iceland	+10
Japan	−6
Latvia	−8
Liechtenstein	−8
Lithuania	−8
Monaco	−8
New Zealand	0
Norway	+1
Poland	−6
Romania	−8
Russian Federation	0
Slovakia	−8
Slovenia	−8
Switzerland	−8
Ukraine	0
United States	−7

SOURCE: United Nations, *Kyoto Protocol to the United Nations Framework Convention on Climate Change*, Article 3, Annex B. Reprinted with permission from the World Resources Institute, *World Resources 1998–99* (New York: Oxford University Press, 1998).

much less demanding. A more serious potential weakness in the protocol is the provision for trading of emissions credits, which could allow the United States and other states to accomplish much of their reductions by acquiring emissions credits from Russia, which, along with Ukraine, was not required to reduce emissions below 1990 levels.[93] The developing countries had opposed that provision but finally agreed to avoid a complete collapse of the negotiations. The emissions-trading loophole could be plugged by rules for monitoring and verifying trading that must be put in place before any trading starts, but it represents a serious threat to the integrity of the climate regime.

Another potential loophole was closed, however. The U.S. effort to get the right to borrow against future emissions levels was not accepted in the protocol, although "banking" excess reductions from the first commitment period to meet obligations from a subsequent commitment period was included.

The U.S. proposal for a formal commitment by developing countries to controlling and eventually reducing their emissions was finally deleted from the text after China, India, and other developing-country parties attacked it. Even an "opt-in" position that would have provided for voluntary adoption of an emissions target by non–Annex I states was vetoed by their delegations. But the issue was now on the agenda for future discussion in the COP.

Although the Climate Change Convention already had the GEF as a mechanism to provide assistance to non–Annex I Parties to the Convention, the Protocol also included a fund to provide money and technologies to carry out energy efficiency and renewable energy projects. Under what was called the Clean Development Mechanism, companies in industrialized countries could receive emissions credits for investing in such projects in developing countries. But the specifics of the fund still remained to be worked out.

The Kyoto Protocol would enter into force after it had received 55 instruments of ratification from developed-country Parties to the Convention, accounting for at least 55 percent of the carbon dioxide emissions of Annex I Parties in 1990. Thus, the Protocol could enter into force without the United States having ratified it, even though some countries are likely to wait to see if the world's largest emitter does join the regime.

Although it represented an effort to strengthen the climate regime by adding binding targets and timetables to the framework climate treaty, the Kyoto Protocol has a number of weaknesses. The Parties to the climate treaty will need to fix four major weaknesses or potential weaknesses in the Protocol, which two subsequent COPs in 1998 and 1999 left unresolved.

First, the Protocol must put in place a system of reporting, verifying, monitoring, and enforcement. The Protocol still needs to create a separate body to review compliance, as was done under the Montreal Protocol and the Second Sulfur Protocol to the LRTAP. The Parties need to agree on specific penalties and dispute resolution procedures for noncompliance. And a requirement for each Party to have national monitoring, compliance, and enforcement programs needs to be written into the treaty.

Second, the Parties must agree on much more stringent targets and timetables for greenhouse gas reductions. The reductions mandated by the Protocol fall far short of what was needed to have an impact on the threat of climate change. There is general agreement among scientists that, even if the reductions in the emissions of greenhouse gases required by the Protocol are fully implemented, the effect on global temperatures would be too small to be detectable.[94] Just to stabilize the concentration of greenhouse gases in the atmosphere would require roughly a 60 percent reduction in emissions worldwide. Although COP-4 and COP-5 agreed that existing commitments under the Protocol were inadequate, they still could not agree on what to do about it.

Third, the Parties must reach agreement on detailed rules for emissions trading that will put a cap on the percentage of total emissions reductions that can be obtained through trading. This loophole must be closed to avoid giving the United States, and possibly other countries, the option to avoid most of their obligations. The EU will insist that a cap be placed on international trading as a percentage of total reductions, and the United States still intends to oppose any such cap.

Fourth, the Parties must agree on a way to phase in commitments by the developing countries to control the growth of greenhouse gases. The very small cuts contemplated by the Protocol for developed countries will be swamped by increases in developing-country emissions over the next couple of decades unless those countries adopt effective controls on their emissions. Even if the developed world were to cut its emissions by 2 percent per annum throughout the next century, the anticipated growth in developing-country emissions would still bring about a doubling of preindustrial levels of carbon in the atmosphere before 2100.[95] But in order to have any credibility in bargaining with developing countries, the industrialized-country Parties will have to accept far more stringent reductions than they have thus far.

A strong climate regime is not likely to emerge in the coming years without the full participation and legal adherence to the Protocol by the United States. As long as the largest single emitting country remains the leading veto state in the process, the COP will not effectively address all these weaknesses, nor will it have the credibility to engage developing countries in negotiations to bring them fully under the Protocol. At COP-4 in November 1998, developing countries openly expressed doubts that the United States had any intention of actually reducing its emissions.[96]

Moreover, a failure by the United States to ratify the protocol would almost certainly mean that it will never enter into force. So domestic political opposition in the United States to assuming any emissions reductions obligations must be decisively overcome to allow the regime-strengthening process to succeed, or even for the climate regime to survive.

BIODIVERSITY LOSS

Biodiversity loss has been recognized by the scientific community as one of the most serious environmental threats facing humankind, but negotiation of a regime for conserving biodiversity has suffered from serious differences over the definition of the problem and from resistance to strong legal obligations by a veto coalition of developing states holding most of the world's biodiversity. Combined with a weak commitment on the part of the United States and other industrialized states, these problems have contributed to a relatively weak regime.

By the early 1980s a scientific consensus had begun to emerge that the rate of species extinction had increased alarmingly. The IUCN General Assembly requested the director-general of IUCN to set in motion a process aimed at producing a preliminary draft of a global agreement on conserving the world's genetic resources.[97] The United States took the lead in putting the issue of biodiversity loss on the international agenda in 1987, getting the UNEP Governing Council to create an ad hoc working group of experts to study an "umbrella convention" to rationalize activities in biodiversity conservation.[98] But it quickly became apparent to the experts that an umbrella convention would be an unworkable, and probably sterile, approach to the problem.

When the UNEP ad hoc working group began meeting in 1990, and issue definition got under way, the issue of a biodiversity convention became entangled in a North-South struggle over plant genetic resources and **intellectual property rights** (IPR), the rights of businesses, individuals, and states to legal protection of their discoveries and inventions. Up to that time, plant genetic resources had been regarded in international law as part of the "common heritage of mankind" and thus freely available to companies who wished to use them to create new commercial seeds. But developing-country states had long been dissatisfied with the fact that the hybrid seeds based on the genetic resources obtained from their countries were protected by intellectual property rights and thus were available to them only at much higher costs. In 1983, developing countries had tried to press for change in that system through the nonbinding FAO Undertaking on Plant Genetic Resources. That agreement applied the concept of the "common heritage of mankind" not only to the original genetic resources but also to the hybrid seeds created by the seed companies, which would have deprived the companies of intellectual property rights. But that maneuver ran into determined opposition from states in which seed companies were located (Canada, France, West Germany, Japan, the United Kingdom, and the United States), which refused to sign the Undertaking and boycotted the FAO's Commission on Plant Genetic Resources until it reassured them that the intellectual property rights of seed companies would be respected.

Having failed to change the IPR system through the FAO, some developing countries rejected in the UNEP working group the previously accepted notion that their genetic resources were part of the common heritage of humankind. They insisted instead that those resources belong to the states in which they are located, and that access to genetic resources should be on the basis of "mutual agreement between countries." They also asserted that provision for noncommercial access to biotechnologies based on plant genetic resources found in the South had to be a central element in any biodiversity convention. The industrialized countries, with the exception of the Nordics, initially opposed the inclusion of biotechnology in the convention, defining the scope of the regime to include only conservation of biodiversity in the wild and mechanisms to finance such efforts.[99]

The official negotiations on a biodiversity convention were completed in just five sessions over a relatively brief span of nine months from July 1991 to May 1992, with more than 100 states participating in the final session in Nairobi. The bargaining stage, polarized largely along North-South lines, was shaped largely by four factors: the veto power of developing countries over biodiversity conservation provisions, the veto power of industrialized countries over technology transfer and financing, the aggressive role played by UNEP executive director Mostafa Tolba, and the implicit deadline imposed by the Earth Summit in Rio in June 1992.

The resulting regime relies more on economic incentives than on legal obligations for biodiversity conservation, and it left key states in both North and South dissatisfied with provisions on technology transfer and financing. The convention puts access to genetic resources under the authority of the state in which they are found and calls for access to be granted on "mutually agreed terms." Thus companies interested in prospecting for genetic resources in a particular country have to negotiate with entities designated by the government of that country over the terms of that access, including royalties from any biotechnologies based on genetic resources transferred as the result of the agreement. Such deals are supposed to provide a new economic incentive for developing countries to conserve biological resources.

The scope of the conservation provisions was narrowed by the unwillingness of key actors to entertain the possibility of quantitative targets for percentage of land set aside for biodiversity conservation. That idea was raised informally by Germany early in the negotiations, but a veto coalition led by countries holding a large proportion of the world's biodiversity (Mexico, Brazil, and Indonesia) vociferously opposed such tough conservation provisions. And most European countries opposed such targets because they would embarrass countries that had already cut down most of their forests in past centuries.[100] They were never formally proposed in the negotiations.

Although the United States, sometimes supported by India, weakened the conservation provisions, the final text does obligate the parties to develop national strategies for conservation and sustainable use of biological diversity, to integrate conservation and sustainable use of biological diversity into relevant economic development policies and programs, to inventory and monitor biodiversity resources and processes that affect them adversely, and to preserve indigenous conservation practices.

The most contentious issues—transfer of technology and financing—could not be resolved at the final negotiating session to the satisfaction of all the key parties. On technology transfer, India, on behalf of the Group of 77, tried and failed to get language obligating the industrialized countries to compel biotechnology companies to turn over patented technologies to developing countries. The United States succeeded in getting a sentence clearly guaranteeing that any technology transfer under the agreement would be on terms that protected intellectual property rights. But India insisted that the same sentence had to be applied consistent with an ambiguous compromise paragraph calling on parties to ensure that intellectual property rights are "supportive of and do not run counter to" the convention's objectives. The United States objected that the ambiguous paragraph could be read as hostile to intellectual property rights.

The provisions on the convention's financial mechanism were equally divisive. The donor countries and most Latin American countries supported the Global Environment Facility (GEF), created by the donor countries and managed primarily by the World Bank, as the funding mechanism for the convention. But Asian and African states, led by India and Malaysia, were angry about the provision of the climate convention making the GEF the interim financial mechanism. They demanded the creation of a freestanding biodiversity fund having nothing to do with the World Bank, which they felt was controlled by the donor countries.[101]

During the final negotiating session in May 1992, UNEP executive director Mostafa Tolba, confronted with the possibility of a failure to reach agreement in time for the Rio conference, took over the negotiations personally. In an extraordinary intervention that was protested by both the United States and France, Tolba in effect suspended the rules, replaced the designated chair of the conference, and wrote his own text, which he submitted to the delegations as a fait accompli to be accepted or rejected shortly before the diplomatic conference that would formally adopt the convention.[102]

The text designated the GEF as the interim funding mechanism, with conditions relating to transparency and democracy, until the first Conference of the Parties but also had the GEF functioning under the authority of the Conference of the Parties—something the donor countries had rejected. It appeared to leave open the possibility that the COP could determine what levels of financial resources would be contributed by donor countries, something the United States declared to be unacceptable.

Other industrialized countries also had concerns, particularly on the financial mechanism, but felt that it was the best agreement that could be reached in time for the treaty to be opened for signature at the Earth Summit only 10 days later. They chose to issue their own interpretations of the text on financing and to sign the convention in Rio. One hundred and fifty-three countries signed the convention in Rio, but the United States refused to do so, citing the provisions on financing and intellectual property rights.

The United States reversed its position after the Clinton administration came into office and signed the convention in June 1993.[103] The convention entered into force on December 29, 1993, after ratification by 30 countries, 6 industrialized countries and 24 developing countries. As of January 2000, 176 countries had ratified the convention.

The process of regime strengthening for the biodiversity convention has been less focused and effective than those for other major environmental regimes. The sluggishness of the process reflects the more diffuse nature of the regime's rules and norms, the absence of a strong lead state coalition, and the general lack of political will to adopt a tougher regime. The three major problems for strengthening the regime are to tighten up the language of key articles, to develop protocols on conservation and/or sustainable use in particular sectors, and to strengthen the regime's system of monitoring compliance.

Most of the convention's key provisions, including Articles 7 through 11, covering identification and monitoring, in situ and ex situ conservation, sustainable use, and incentive measures, qualify their respective obligations with the phrase "as far as possible and as appropriate," which gives Parties wide latitude to implement the articles as little or as much as they wish. Removing the ambiguity of the legal obligation would be an important step toward holding Parties accountable for their compliance. But the obligations themselves are also vague and lack any standards or criteria for measuring compliance. Article 9 on in situ conservation, for example, merely requires the establishment of "a system of protected areas or areas where special measures need to be taken to conserve biological diversity." More concrete criteria for an effective protected-area system are needed to make it an action-forcing mechanism. The same thing applies to the obligation to "integrate consideration of the conservation and sustainable use of biological resources into national decision-making" in Article 10 on sustainable use. But the COP has not discussed tightening up the language of these articles through amendments to the treaty. Even more important would be to add to Article 6 on national plans a requirement to include measurable targets and timetables for conservation and sustainable use of biodiversity.

A second major task facing the Parties is to focus on priority areas for development of protocols detailing obligations on particular biodiversity issues. The greatest wealth of biodiversity is found in tropical forests and coastal marine ecosystems, and working on protocols in those two areas would have had the greatest payoff for regime strengthening. For example, sectoral protocols on forest and marine biodiversity could include concrete obligations on effective protected-area systems, as well as commitments of resources by donor institutions to support their implementation. Most protected-area systems in the world are now "paper parks," in which overexploitation of biological resources are carried on with little or no interference. Many are too small and fragmented to provide meaningful protection, and most are grossly underfunded and understaffed.

But the COP deliberately avoided binding obligations on forests, deferring instead to the UN Commission on Sustainable Development's Intergovernmental Panel on Forests (IPF), which was never intended to create new international norms for forest conservation and sustainable use. Major forest-products-exporting countries, including Brazil, Canada, and Malaysia, ensured that the Convention would not take the lead on forests. On marine biodiversity, COP-2 adopted a nonbinding agenda for action outlining important issues (the "Jakarta Mandate") in 1995, which could be the basis for a future protocol but lacks the concreteness needed to be an action-forcing mechanism.

Instead of focusing on the highest-priority biodiversity problems, the Parties agreed at COP-2 to negotiate a protocol on **biosafety**, and that work has taken much of the time and energy of the Parties since then. Biosafety refers to a set of precautionary practices to ensure the safe transfer, handling, use, and disposal of living modified organisms derived from modern **biotechnology**. Many countries with biotechnology industries have domestic biosafety legislation in place, but there are no binding international agreements on the problem of genetically modified organisms (GMOs) that cross national borders. Several European governments joined some European environmental NGOs, including Friends of the

Earth (UK), in calling for a moratorium on the import of genetically modified foods, provoking a conflict between the United States and the EU.

The biosafety protocol was negotiated during a series of five meetings from 1996 to 1998. In February 1999 delegates convened in Cartagena, Colombia, to complete negotiations in a sixth session and to adopt the protocol at an extraordinary session of the COP. But a veto coalition consisting of the world's major grain exporters minus the EU (Argentina, Australia, Canada, Chile, the United States, and Uruguay), called the Miami Group, successfully thwarted efforts to complete the protocol on schedule. The veto coalition was concerned that the draft protocol—particularly the requirement to obtain the advanced informed consent from the importer prior to exporting GMOs or GMO-related foodstuffs—would harm the multi-billion-dollar agricultural export business.

It took another year of informal consultations before the protocol was finally adopted. The president of the extraordinary Conference of the Parties, Colombian environment minister Juan Mayr, held three sets of informal consultations to facilitate discussion on key outstanding issues and enable the major coalitions to forge an agreement. The major coalitions that emerged from Cartagena were the Miami Group, the Central and Eastern European countries, the Compromise Group (Japan, Mexico, Norway, South Korea, and Switzerland), the European Union, and the Like-Minded Group (the majority of developing countries). The consultations focused on the issues of commodities, the protocol's relationship with other international agreements, the protocol's scope, and the application of the advance informed-agreement procedure. After a week of formal negotiations in Montreal in January 2000, the major coalitions, with a lot of prodding from Mayr, were able to reach agreement and adopt the Cartagena Protocol on Biosafety.[104]

A third challenge to regime strengthening is to create a more effective mechanism for monitoring compliance with the convention. Article 26 gives no details on national reporting on implementation, but COP-2 established general guidelines for their contents, calling for them to focus primarily on Article 6, which requires the development of "national strategies plans or programmes" for conservation and sustainable use of biodiversity. The COP-2 decision also provided "suggested guidelines" for national reports, including identification of specific targets for the protection of biodiversity, a timetable for implementing various tasks, and indicators for tracking results of national action plans. The Secretariat was asked to issue a synthesis of the information contained in the national reports.

By the end of 1998, 107 of 108 parties had submitted at least interim reports, but reliance on nonbinding guidelines and a general synthesis report does not provide adequate accountability with regard to treaty compliance. Reporting on specified issues in a common format is not required, and there is no public review of compliance by each Party. The Secretariat's synthesis document concluded that implementation had been initiated in most countries, but it did not even provide information on how many countries had adopted targets and indicators, suggesting that few had done so.[105]

To hold parties accountable for their compliance with the agreement, the COP will have to adopt a system of reporting on the key obligations that is mandatory and that either the Secretariat or a committee of the COP reviews and analyzes country by country. The voluntary guidelines on targets and timetables in national plans could also be made mandatory. The combination of required targets and timetables and public reports on the extent of compliance by each Party would make Article 6 into an effective action-forcing mechanism.

Action to strengthen the biodiversity regime will depend on greater commitment by lead states. Although a few parties, including Sweden, Australia, New Zealand, and Germany, have been active in trying to strengthen the regime, the lead state coalition needs to have greater political and financial clout. That means that the United States must play a lead role. But its role has been constrained by the fact that the United States has not even been able to ratify the Convention, because of the opposition of the Republican-controlled Senate. Any major progress in regime strengthening on biodiversity probably would also require a broader North-South accommodation, probably involving a range of issues, including trade and financial concessions to developing-country interests.

DESERTIFICATION

The Convention to Combat Desertification is one of only two international regimes that were established on the initiative of the developing countries despite the resistance of industrialized countries. Desertification, which affects the lives of 1 billion people in many regions of the world, had been the subject of international cooperation for nearly three decades, since the first major drought in sub-Saharan Africa, but was put on the UNCED agenda in 1992 only because of the persistence of African countries. As the first treaty to be negotiated after UNCED, it was looked upon by some as a test of whether governments had the political will to follow up on Agenda 21 commitments.

The stage of issue definition was plagued by complexity, vagueness and disagreement on whether desertification was indeed a "global" problem. Desertification was defined by UNEP and by most specialists as sustained land degradation in arid, semiarid, and dry subhumid areas result-

Eucalyptus saplings planted to prevent soil erosion. Lompoul, Senegal, 1984 (Photo by J. Isaac, UN/DPI.).

ing mainly from adverse human impact.[106] But the term *desertification* evokes images of deserts advancing and destroying productive land, whereas scientists have found no evidence to support claims that the Sahara is expanding at an alarming rate. Foes of a convention exploited that fact: At one point in the UNCED negotiations, the United States dismissed the term *desertification* and suggested substituting *land degradation*.[107] Some donor countries objected to the designation *global* because that might imply that treaty implementation efforts would be eligible for funding from the Global Environment Facility.[108]

African countries encountered other problems in defining desertification. First, desertification does not involve resources or life support systems of global interest, as do other environmental issues on which regimes have been negotiated. It affects countries not suffering from desertification only because it threatens the economies and societies of a large number of countries. Second, a bewildering array of natural and social factors appears to affect land degradation in drylands, including overpopulation, climatic cycles, social and economic structures, poor pastoral or agricultural practices, bad policies on the part of governments and donors, and North-South economic relations. So it was difficult to articulate simply and clearly either the nature of the problem or the international actions needed to address it.

Indeed, for many African countries, there is a strong link between poverty alleviation and desertification control. The African countries' definition of the problem emphasized the need for additional funding for as yet unidentified activities. These countries hoped that a desertification convention would help them gain access to additional funding through the Global Environment Facility, which had rejected desertification as one of the global environmental problems it could finance.[109]

Finally, the African countries' attempt to define the desertification issue was hampered by the fact that the earlier Plan of Action to Combat Desertification (PACD), launched in 1977, was generally acknowledged to have been a failure. A UNEP evaluation of the plan had blamed the failure on both African governments and the donor community for not giving the issue priority. UNEP had also found that only $1 billion of the $9 billion provided by donor agencies from 1978 to 1983 was spent on direct field projects.[110]

So when the issue of a desertification convention was first raised in UNCED, only France, with its special ties with Africa, expressed support for the idea. Most industrialized countries and the World Bank argued that the primary problems were with the structure and macroeconomic policies of African governments (such as excessive taxes on agriculture and failing to grant enforceable property rights) and that policy reforms, better planning, and more popular participation would achieve better results than a new international program or formal agreement.[111] Moreover, the G-77 failed to endorse the African call for a desertification convention in the communiqué of the 1992 Kuala Lumpur ministerial meeting, dominated by host government Malaysia.

Despite these problems in the definition of the issue of desertification, UNCED put it on the global agenda because of African persistence and because the United States unexpectedly supported the African position. At the Earth Summit in Rio, the United States, after opposing a desertification convention throughout the UNCED negotiations, shifted to backing such a convention in the hope of getting African support on forests and on the remaining issues in the Rio Declaration.[112] Other industrialized countries then followed suit, but the EC initially resisted the U.S. proposal. Finally the EC relented, and the call for a desertification convention became part of Agenda 21.[113]

Negotiations by the Intergovernmental Negotiating Committee on the International Convention to Combat Desertification began in May 1993 and were completed in a brief 15 months. The formal fact-finding process, carried out in an "information sharing segment" at the first session of the INC, focused primarily on socioeconomic strategies for slowing and reversing desertification and on reports from individual countries rather than on scientific understanding of the problem. That process produced general agreement on the importance of such strategies as integrating arid and semiarid areas into national economies, popular participation in anti-desertification efforts, and land tenure reform.[114] As a result, the convention would be the first to call for affected countries to provide for effective participation by grassroots organizations, NGOs, and local populations, both men and women, in the preparation of national action programs.[115]

The bargaining stage revolved not around commitments to environmental conservation actions but around financial, trade, institutional, and symbolic issues. The African countries were the lead states. The Organization of African Unity (OAU) had detailed draft sections for every section of the convention, some of which were accepted as the basis for negotiation.

Whether debt and trade issues should be included within the scope of the convention was a central issue, affecting the obligations, action programs, and regional annexes as well as sections on scope, objectives, and principles. The OAU and other developing countries asserted that external debt burdens and commodity prices, among other international economic policy issues, affected their ability to combat desertification. The industrialized countries argued that those North-South economic issues could be negotiated only in other international forums. They did agree to general obligations to "give due attention" to the trade and debt problems of affected countries in order to create an "enabling international economic environment" for those countries.

Differences over financial resources and the financial mechanism nearly caused the negotiations to collapse. Some members of the G-77 and China demanded commitments to "new and additional" financial resources and creation of a special fund for desertification as the center-piece of the convention. The industrialized countries were a united veto coalition in rejecting any provision for new and additional financing, agreeing only to ensure "adequate" financial resources for antidesertification programs. The developed countries felt they bore no responsibility for the problem of desertification worldwide, unlike the issues of ozone depletion and climate change, and were therefore unwilling to incur any obligation to increase their financial assistance to affected countries.[116] They insisted that the overhead associated with a special fund would reduce the resources needed in the field and that existing resources could be used more effectively. They also vetoed the use of GEF funds unless the project contributed either to prevention of climate change or to biodiversity conservation.

The deadlock on a funding mechanism was broken only after the United States proposed a "global mechanism" under the authority of the conference of the parties, to be housed within an existing organization, which would improve monitoring and assessment of existing aid flows and increase coordination among donors. Developing countries remained dissatisfied because such a mechanism would not increase development assistance to African and other countries suffering desertification. But they ultimately accepted it as the only compromise acceptable to the donor countries.[117]

The problem of how to reflect the priority to be given to Africa, called for in the UNGA resolution on the convention, while meeting demands from other regions for equitable treatment, arose in negotiating regional annexes to the convention. The original intention of African and industrialized countries' delegations was to negotiate a regional implementation annex only for Africa by the deadline of July 1994, but other developing-country delegations demanded that implementation annexes for their own regions be negotiated simultaneously with the one for Africa. In the end, each regional grouping got its own annex, but the priority for Africa was ensured by a special resolution that encouraged donor countries to provide financial support of national action programs in Africa without waiting for the convention to come into force.

The Convention to Combat Desertification was opened for signature in October 1994 and entered into force on December 26, 1996. As of March 2000, 165 countries had ratified or acceded to the Convention. The Convention recognizes the physical, biological, and socioeconomic aspects of desertification, the importance of redirecting technology transfer so that it is demand-driven, and the importance of the involvement of local populations in any efforts to combat desertification. The core of the Convention is the development of national and subregional/regional action programs by national governments in cooperation with donors, local populations, and NGOs.

The regime-strengthening stage began at the first meeting of the Conference of the Parties in Rome in October 1997. At both COP-1 and COP-2, which was held in Dakar, Senegal, in December 1998, delegates began the difficult process of translating the words of the Convention into practice. Challenges have included the definition, establishment, and operationalization of the "Global Mechanism," a financial mechanism created by and loosely defined in the Convention. Another challenge has been reconciling the Convention's emphasis on "bottom-up" approaches and involvement at all levels by all relevant actors, while remaining an international coordinating body. At the national level, the challenge is for affected countries to develop effective action programs, in conjunction with donor countries and organizations as well as local communities and NGOs.[118]

STRADDLING AND
HIGHLY MIGRATORY FISH STOCKS

For many centuries, the ocean's bounties have been viewed as limitless. But for the past three decades, the world's marine fisheries have been in crisis, as they have been overexploited to the point that the most valuable fish stocks have been depleted and, in some cases, virtually eliminated. By the mid-1990s, about 70 percent of the world's marine fish stocks were already depleted, slowly recovering from depletion, overexploited, or fully exploited.[119] Because fishing fleets could overexploit one fishery and then move on to another, and because fleets continued to catch high levels of lower-value fish even after depleting the most desirable stocks, the fisheries crisis was disguised by a constant increase in global catch figures from 20 million tons annually in 1950 to nearly 90 million tons in 1989 before leveling off.[120]

The primary reason for the worsening depletion of fishery resources is the uncontrolled growth in the number of fishing vessels and the introduction of increasingly effective fishing technologies, such as electronic fish-finding equipment, bigger nets, larger storage capacity, more powerful engines, and mechanized hauling gear, all of which gave fleets far more catching power than fisheries could support. By the early 1990s, the global fishing fleet had as much as two and a half times more capacity than could be used sustainably.[121] Inadequate regulations on catch and enforcement also contributed to the crisis.

The politics of the formation of a regime governing the global over-fishing problem is complicated by the fact that fishery resources are found both under national jurisdiction and in international waters, and often in some combination of the two. Although global fish catch is not as concentrated as whaling, greenhouse gas emissions, or consumption of ozone-destroying chemicals, the six biggest fishing states (China, Peru, Chile, Japan, the United States, and the Russian Federation) and the European Union account for 56 percent of the catch. The six countries with "distant-water" fishing fleets (Russia, Japan, Spain, Poland, the Republic of Korea, and Taiwan) are responsible for 90 percent of the catch in international waters.[122] Those 10 countries and the EU thus had the greatest potential for vetoing an international agreement to address the overfishing problem.

Ninety-five percent of the fish catch worldwide is taken within the 200-mile exclusive economic zones (EEZs) under national jurisdiction. But some important fish stocks, such as cod and pollack, occur both within the EEZs of coastal states and in the adjacent high seas. And some highly migratory stocks, especially tuna and swordfish, move long distances through the high seas and through the EEZs of coastal states. Straddling and highly migratory fish stocks are particularly important on the Challenger Plateau off the coast of New Zealand, off Argentina's Patagonian Shelf, off the coasts of Chile and Peru, in the Barents Sea off the coast of Norway, in the Bering Sea, the Sea of Okhotsk, and the South Pacific Ocean and on the Grand Banks of Newfoundland outside Canada's 200-mile nautical zone. As straddling stocks and highly migratory fish stocks have dwindled and been depleted, both coastal and distant-water states have blamed overfishing on the other.

The first binding global agreement to address overfishing, the United Nations Agreement for the Implementation of the Provisions of the United Nations Convention on the Law of the Sea of 10 December 1982 Relating to the Conservation and Management of Straddling Fish Stocks and Highly Migratory Fish Stocks, came about mainly because of these conflicts over straddling stocks and highly migratory stocks. Canada was the main actor in getting the issue of a new global management regime for these stocks on the political agenda for action, but although it tried to define the issue, it did not put forward a definition that could form the basis for a successful conservation regime.

Canada was motivated to push for formal agreement limiting the freedom of distant-water fishing fleets to exploit these stocks because of a dispute with the EU, and especially Spain, over the Spanish fleet's overfishing of the stocks on the Grand Banks outside Canada's EEZ. The regional fisheries management organization responsible for regulating fishing in the Grand Banks area, both within Canada's EEZ and on the high seas, is

FIGURE 3.3   Commercial Harvests in the Northwest Atlantic of Some Important Fish Stocks, 1950–1995

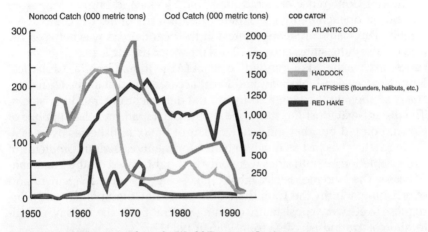

Reprinted with permission from the World Resources Institute, *World Resources 1998–99* (New York: Oxford University Press, 1998).

the Northwest Atlantic Fisheries Organization (NAFO), founded in 1979. From 1986 to 1990, the NAFO had failed to enforce high-seas catch limits agreed to by the organization on most of the straddling stocks, because the EU had exercised its right to opt out of the regional quotas. (See Figure 3.3.) Therefore, Canada appealed to the broader international community to adopt a global policy governing the problem.

At the UNCED negotiations that began in 1991 on what would become the nonbinding Agenda 21 document, a paper from coastal states proposed that new conservation rules should be established for high-seas fisheries, but not for fisheries under national jurisdiction. Canada proposed language calling for the recognizing the special interests of coastal states in highly migratory stocks and stocks that straddle national EEZs and international waters. The EU disagreed, producing a diplomatic deadlock on the issue. The issue remained unresolved until the Rio Conference, when UNCED Main Committee Chairman Tommy Koh asked the United States to broker a compromise between Canada and the EU. The result was an agreement to hold an intergovernmental conference under UN auspices "with a view to promoting effective implementation of the provisions of the Law of the Sea on straddling and highly migratory fish stocks." The EU agreed to that formula because its diplomats believed the Convention on the Law of the Sea guaranteed the sovereign right of states to fish on the high seas. Canada, however, hoped that the need for conservation would trump that traditional sovereign right.

The UN Conference on Straddling Fish Stocks and Highly Migratory Fish Stocks opened in July 1993 under the authority of the UN General Assembly. The main conflict of interest in the negotiations was between the 70 coastal fishing states and the 10 distant-water fishing states. The coastal states, led by the "like-minded" caucus (Argentina, Canada, Chile, Iceland, New Zealand, Norway, and Peru) accused the distant-water fishing states of abusing their right to fish to the detriment of straddling stocks. The distant-water fishing states, led by the EU, Japan, and the Republic of Korea, pointed out that mismanagement of national fisheries by coastal fishing states was just as much to blame for the most serious problems of stock depletion.[123] Both sides were only half right, based on the Canadian-EU case: The evidence is clear that there was gross mismanagement and overfishing within the Canadian EEZ, and that the Spanish and Portuguese fleets were consistently catching several times the EU's NAFO allocation of groundfish catch from 1986 to 1989.[124]

As they had during the UNCED negotiations, the "like-minded" caucus proposed a legally binding agreement that would prescribe conservation rules for high-seas fishing that affected straddling stocks and migratory stocks. But the coastal states resisted international rules that would limit their freedom to manage their EEZs. Distant-water states called for nonbinding conservation guidelines that would apply equally to both coastal state fisheries and the high seas. They had long argued that the regulation of fishing practices on the high seas should be left to regional or subregional organizations. While the UN conference was going on, consultations were also being held on a nonbinding FAO Code of Conduct for Responsible Fisheries, and the two groups of fishing states took opposite positions about that process: Coastal states insisted that the entire text be bracketed until the UN agreement on straddling stocks and highly migratory stocks was adopted, whereas the distant-water fishing states favored the FAO process because it was voluntary.

Both groups of states were thus separate veto coalitions who were prepared, at least initially, to block agreement on needed measures to conserve stocks effectively. The United States, which is both a coastal fishing state and a distant-water fishing state, was in a pivotal position to play the role of lead state in negotiating the regime. Initially, however, the United States was ready to join with the distant-water states to oppose a binding convention, because of its close historic ties with the EU and Japan on Law of the Sea issues. The United States had clashed with Canada and other coastal states during the negotiations on the Law of the Sea Treaty. But in 1994, White House and National Oceans and Atmospheric Administration officials with a strong commitment to conservation intervened in the issue, after being lobbied by NGOs. As a result, the United States decided to come out for a binding agreement and began playing the lead state role.

One of the U.S. contributions to the text was a proposal that the "precautionary approach" to fishing be applied by requiring the adoption of "reference points" (target levels of fishing effort aimed at conserving fish stocks) and measures for rebuilding the stock, including reduced fishing effort, if the reference points are exceeded. Canada resisted the application of precautionary reference points within fisheries under national jurisdiction, along with other conservation requirements, as a violation of national sovereignty. The United States pushed Canada and the like-minded caucus to accept certain basic conservation principles and guidelines for their application to straddling stocks both on the high seas and within areas under national jurisdiction, but the issue remained unresolved even after the fourth session in April 1995.

Another issue pressed by the "like-minded" caucus was the right of a coastal state to board and inspect fishing vessels in international waters. It argued that such a right was necessary to ensure compliance with international conservation measures. Traditionally the enforcement of legal obligations on the high seas was in the hands of the "flag state" (the state in which the vessel was registered) and distant-water fishing states wanted to maintain the status quo. The United States again sided with the like-minded caucus in supporting wider latitude for high-seas inspection by states other than the flag state under certain circumstances, but the distant-water states continued to resist until the last session.

Before the negotiations could be completed, tensions between Canada and the EU escalated to the use of force over Spanish fishing for turbot, allegedly in violation of NAFO quotas. In September 1994, the 13 members of NAFO voted to reduce the annual total allowable catch of rapidly declining stocks of turbot by 38 percent and reallocated much of the EU share of the quota to Canada. The EU again used its right to opt out of the quota and set its own, much higher, unilateral quota. In response, in February 1995, the Canadian fisheries minister warned that Canada would not let EU vessels "devastate turbot the way it devastated other ground fish stocks."[125] In March 1995, Canadian ships aggressively pursued and seized or cut the nets of Spanish trawlers outside the Canadian EEZ.

The Canadian actions angered the EU and temporarily polarized the conference. The March-April 1995 round of negotiations was still deadlocked on the issue of the right of coastal states to board ships on the high seas when they are suspected of having violated a regional fisheries conservation measure. The chairman's draft allowed wider latitude for such high-seas boarding and inspection than the distant-water states were prepared to accept.

But a new Canadian-EU agreement reached immediately after that round may have contributed to a successful conclusion of the negotiations. Canada compromised on the 1995 quota and agreed to give the EU the same amount as Canada, rather than the one-fifth of the Canadian quota that had been authorized by NAFO. Canada also dropped charges against the Spanish trawler it had seized and repealed legislation authorizing such actions in international waters. In return, the EU agreed to a new regime of independent inspectors onboard every EU ship in the NAFO area. to ensure that conservation rules were being followed.[126]

In the fifth and final negotiating session in August 1995, both high-seas boarding and the "precautionary approach" to fisheries management were still being resisted by distant-water states. On the issue of boarding and inspecting on the high seas, the distant-water states had agreed on boarding and inspecting in principle, but there were still differences over whether the regional fisheries organization had to reach agreement on procedures governing such boarding and procedures: Canada insisted that it would not require prior agreement on procedures by the organization, whereas Japan and South Korea both insisted on regional agreement as a precondition for such boarding and inspection. The compromise that was ultimately adopted was that states that are parties to regional fishing organizations could board and inspect vessels on the high seas of parties to the straddling stocks convention suspected of violating regional conservation measures without prior regional agreement, but only if the regional organization had failed to adopt procedures for such boarding and inspection for two years prior to the boarding.

The precautionary approach requires that scientific uncertainty not be used as a reason for postponing or failing to take effective conservation and management measures.[127] Japan was concerned that the coastal states would use the precautionary approach as an open license to adopt moratoria on fishing as a new management norm and was very reluctant to see it enter into a binding international agreement. But Japan finally accepted the precautionary approach, perhaps because it did not want to be blamed for the collapse of the negotiations and considered nonratification as an option.

The straddling-stocks agreement is to come into force when ratified by 30 signatories. But as of 2000, only 4 of the top 20 fishing states (Norway, Russia, the United States, and Iceland) had ratified the convention, although the EU had already agreed to do so. And many of the most important fishing states, including Peru, Chile, India, Thailand, Mexico, Malaysia, and Vietnam, had not even signed the agreement. Mexico has probably hesitated to sign because the agreement requires that states join or comply with the conservation measures of relevant regional fisheries organizations. Mexico has avoided joining the Inter-American Tropical

Tuna Commission because it does not want to be bound by regionally agreed-on catch quotas and capacity limits. The failure of Peru and Chile to sign the agreement may reflect their concern about having to comply with the convention's requirements for precautionary targets for limits on fishing.

The straddling stocks agreement does not apply to all fish stocks under national jurisdiction but only to those referred to in the title—approximately 20 percent of the global fish catch. Although the agreement represents a major step forward in global cooperation for conservation of fish stocks, it failed to fix two primary global management issues. The first is the fact that regional fisheries organizations that make decisions on management measures such as catch quotas normally allow member states to simply opt out of the decision if they don't like it—the weakness that prompted Canada's original push for a new regime.

The second problem is overcapacity in the global fishing fleet. Although the agreement calls for states to take measures to "prevent or eliminate excess fishing capacity," it does not spell out this obligation or set up any mechanism for implementation. The problem of excess fishing capacity was only addressed by the international community in 1998–1999, when the FAO Committee on Fisheries negotiated and adopted the International Plan of Action for the Management of Fishing Capacity.[128]

The regime formation process for the UN agreement on straddling stocks and highly migratory stocks is one in which not one veto coalition but two—the "like-minded" caucus of coastal states and the major distant-water states—initially opposed key provisions of the regime. The original impetus for the agreement does not appear to have been a broad demand for conservation of straddling stocks as much as Canada's desire to overcome the EU's ability to determine its own catch levels in the Grand Banks fishery.

The shift of the United States from veto state to lead state was undoubtedly a major factor in overcoming the resistance of the two veto coalitions and gave greater impetus to the adoption of innovative conservation measures in the convention. And the willingness of Canada to use physical force on the high seas in its dispute with the EU, with the result that the EU agreed to onboard inspectors on the high seas, probably helped to put the issue of boarding and inspecting in a different light for a key veto state.

CONCLUSION

These cases of environmental regime formation show that the negotiation of a strong global environmental regime almost always depends on inducing one or more key states in a veto coalition to go along with one or more of the core proposed provisions of the regime. By a strong or effective regime, we mean an agreement that includes obligations or norms that are sufficiently clear that parties can be held accountable for implementing them, and that calls for actions that can reasonably be expected to have an impact on the problem if they are implemented. Whether a regime actually succeeds in addressing an environmental threat depends, of course, both on how strong the regime is in the above sense and on the degree to which parties comply with its core provisions. When veto power has been successfully overcome, and when vital proposed norms or actions have been agreed to, it has been for one of four possible reasons:

- A veto state changed its own understanding of the problem because of new scientific evidence;
- A veto state had a change of government, and the new government had a different policy toward the issue;
- A veto state came under effective domestic political pressure to change its policy; or
- A veto state feared negative reactions from other governments or adverse international opinion, which it regarded as more important than its interest in vetoing a specific provision of the regime.

As Table 3.3 shows, in some of these cases, one or more veto states either agreed to the central obligation proposed by the lead state coalition or accepted the regime in general despite earlier rejection.

New scientific evidence has helped move veto states on some issues (acid rain, ozone depletion, and climate change) but has been secondary or irrelevant in other issues (whaling, hazardous waste trade, Antarctic minerals, and African elephants). International considerations were primary in several cases: Japan's concern with economic and diplomatic ties with other major trading nations and its international image helped tilt its stand on the ivory ban. French and British desires to maintain close relations with former colonies were a factor conditioning their views on the hazardous waste trade issue. The United States bowed to the views of other governments and dropped its opposition to the 50-year moratorium on mineral exploitation in Antarctica. Canada and the leading distant-water fishing states dropped their resistance to key provisions in the agreement on straddling fish stocks and highly migratory fish stocks at least in part because they did not want to appear to be blocking the first major global agreement on sustainable fishing.

In all cases, domestic political developments played a key role in facilitating agreement. On Antarctica, the United States softened its opposition to a mining ban only after Congress voted to support such a ban. Australia and France shifted from supporters of a mining regime to supporters of the world park concept because of clear signals from the public.

Regime formation also requires leadership by one or more states committed to defining the issue and proposing a detailed policy approach as the basis for the regime. Sometimes that lead role is played by states that are motivated by particular vulnerability (Sweden, Finland, and Norway on acid rain; the African countries on hazardous waste trade and desertification; the small island states on climate change) and sometimes by a state that has an advantageous legal or other status (Australia in the regime for Antarctica).

But as these cases show, the United States has greater diplomatic influence on other state actors and IOs than any other state. When the United States has taken the lead, as it did on the Montreal Protocol on ozone de-

TABLE 3.3 Veto States and Regime Creation or Strengthening

Issue	Key Veto States	Basis of Veto Power	Veto State Concession
Acid rain (sulfur dioxide)	Germany, Belgium, and Denmark	Export of sulfur dioxide	Joining the "30 Percent Club"
Ozone depletion	EC Commission	Percent of CFC production	Agreeing to 50 percent cut; agreeing to phaseout
African elephant ivory	Japan	Percent of imports	No reservation to CITES uplist
Whaling	Japan and Norway	Percent of catch	Acceptance of ban on whaling against depleted populations
Toxic waste trade	United States, EU, Japan	Percent of exports	Agreeing to ban exports
Antarctic environment	United States, United Kingdom, Japan	Potential for mineral exploitation	Agreeing to world park
Straddling and highly migratory fish stocks	EC Commission, Japan, and the like-minded caucus	Percentage of global catch of straddling and highly migratory stocks	Agreement to precautionary reference points and new enforcement measures

pletion, whaling, or the African elephant, the result has been a much stronger regime than would otherwise have been established. In the case of the fishing regime, the leadership role of the United States was crucial to agreement on conservation norms applying both on the high seas and within EEZs. But when the United States has been a veto state, as in the sulfur dioxide protocol to the acid rain convention, the hazardous waste trade convention, the biodiversity convention, and the climate convention, the result is a significantly weaker regime. Only in the case of the Antarctic negotiations has a U.S. veto role not contributed to seriously undermining the regime, at least initially. And that may be in large part because of the peculiar rules of the Antarctic Treaty's requiring consensus, which permitted Australia and France to nullify U.S. influence.

In the cases of the climate change and biodiversity regimes, veto power wielded by key states has not so far been overcome either in the initial negotiations on regime formation or in subsequent negotiations on regime strengthening. The result is regimes that are notably weak in terms of the expected impact of the norms and regulations adopted on the threats in question. In the negotiations on strengthening the climate change regime, the key veto states have been the United States, China, India, and Brazil, which together account for well over half of global greenhouse gas emissions. The United States, hobbled by strong domestic political opposition to any meaningful commitment to emissions reduction, regardless of which party is in the White House or in control of Congress, has consistently opposed ambitious targets for reducing greenhouse gas emissions and has the single greatest impact on the effectiveness of the resulting targets (although the resistance of a number of other countries has also contributed to the result). But the insistence of major developing countries whose emissions already account for a large proportion of global emissions that no obligations for controlling emissions be placed on them has relegated the existing regime to even greater ineffectiveness.

The biodiversity convention has similarly been shown to be a relatively weak regime, in part because of the veto power wielded at the outset by key states and never seriously challenged since the initial negotiations on regime formation. Megadiversity states (Mexico, Brazil, and Indonesia) vetoed the use of quantitative targets for the protection of forest biodiversity as an instrument of change, and they have vetoed any serious effort to negotiate a protocol with tougher forest conservation obligations in the years since the convention went into effect.

But the absence of an effective lead state coalition has also contributed to the biodiversity regime's ineffectiveness thus far. The fact that the language of the main conservation provisions of the biodiversity treaty remains for the most part more advisory than binding is not the result of a few veto states but of the absence of any lead state coalition effort to strengthen the regime. For several different reasons (greater complexity, lack of high levels of press interest, and less domestic lobbying by environmental NGOs), the biodiversity convention has not gotten as much high-level political attention in major states as the climate change convention. So no bold proposals for strengthening the regime in biodiversity have yet been forthcoming.

As these cases of environmental regimes established or strengthened during the 1979–2000 period indicate, the international community has been able to reach an impressively large number of agreements to reduce environmental threats. This could be interpreted as an indicator of the paradigm shift toward sustainable development. Many of these agreements were believed impossible to achieve only a few months before they were successfully completed. Moreover, they have been negotiated more rapidly than were previous treaties dealing with environment and natural resources, indicating a process of international learning about how to reach agreement on complex and contentious environmental issues. The Law of the Sea Convention took nine years to negotiate, and the Antarctic minerals treaty took seven (without being completed), but the biodiversity convention took only nine months to negotiate, and desertification and climate conventions were completed in 15 and 16 months, respectively.

Global environmental regimes also have evolved from agreements that originally had limited membership (whaling, Antarctic, acid rain) to conventions that have achieved nearly universal adherence. The FCCC had 154 signatories and the biodiversity convention 167. Finally, some of the new regimes (climate, biodiversity, hazardous waste trade, and desertification) have the potential for affecting fundamental economic development strategies, production technologies, and even domestic political processes.

FOUR

□ □ □

Implementing and Financing Environmental Regimes

The last 25 years have seen an unprecedented explosion of international negotiations and cooperation on global environmental issues. By 1992, when countries gathered in Rio de Janeiro for the Earth Summit, there were more than 900 international legal instruments (binding and non-binding) that were either fully directed to environmental protection or had more than one important provision addressing the issue.[1] Yet, despite the successful negotiation of agreements that address environmental concerns, international agreements are only as effective as the parties make them.

The effectiveness of an environmental regime is a function of how strong the regime is in terms of the key provisions aimed at addressing an environmental threat, how seriously states implement those provisions, and how amenable to pressure the states are. This chapter examines implementation of environmental agreements by states (the formal legislation or regulations that countries adopt to comply with the agreement) and their compliance with agreements (the degree to which states' implementation is in conformity with the explicit rules and norms of the agreement). A treaty's effectiveness is the result not only of how governments implement agreements, the formal legislation or regulations that countries adopt to comply with the agreement, but also of compliance, the observance of these regulations and the commitments contained in the international agreement.[2] The first section of this chapter will look at the issue of compliance at the national level and examine those variables that influence levels of compliance with an environmental agreement and then present some recommendations on how to improve compliance. The second section of this chapter will discuss the financing of global environmental regimes. For some countries, the major obstacle to effective compliance with environmental treaties is the lack of adequate financial resources to fulfill treaty obligations. The question of financial resources has been at the center of global environmental policy negotiations and discussions for many years and will continue to be for the foreseeable future.

IMPROVING COMPLIANCE
WITH ENVIRONMENTAL CONVENTIONS

Compliance refers to whether countries have adhered to the provisions of an environmental convention and to the implementing measures that they have instituted. Compliance has several dimensions. Treaties contain specific obligations, some of which are procedural, such as the requirement to report. There are also substantive obligations, such as the obligation to cease or control an activity, such as the production of CFCs. Measuring compliance involves assessing the extent to which governments follow through on the steps they have taken to implement international treaties.[3]

Countries that sign and ratify international conventions usually do so with the intention of complying fully with their provisions, and most do comply to the best of their ability.[4] But compliance may turn out to be more politically or technically difficult or more costly than anticipated. And some countries may sign and comply with an environmental convention primarily in order to avoid international opprobrium rather than because they are convinced that it is in their best interest.

The states of the former Soviet Union are a special case in this regard. The Soviet Union signed a number of global environmental conventions but failed to implement them. Since the collapse of the Soviet state, a number of cases of treaty violations and false reporting, including ocean dumping of nuclear wastes and whaling, has been disclosed.[5] However, since the Russian economy has had so many problems, a side effect has been that the Russians are not polluting nearly as much. With regard to atmospheric treaties, such as those on climate, ozone, and acid rain, the former Soviet Union and its successor states, preoccupied with dire political and economic crises, have not been prepared to make the investments needed to comply with treaties they have signed and ratified.

To ensure maximum compliance with environmental regimes, therefore, a range of mechanisms is available, including regular reporting by the parties, independent evaluation and public availability of such reports, review of implementation at regular meetings of the parties, the readiness of some parties to call noncomplying parties to account publicly, monitoring of compliance by NGOs, and international assistance for building administrative and financial capacity to implement environmental agreements.[6] In some cases one or more determined governments and a technically and politically sophisticated NGO can pressure states effectively by publicizing evidence of their noncompliance. In the United States, for example, environmental groups have been an important complement to the government's enforcement efforts, in particular, when they serve as watchdogs reporting violations to the appropriate authorities. Within the context of the Montreal Protocol, NGOs such as Environmental Defense have been critical to ensure that the U.S. government has developed regulations to phase out CFCs and other controlled substances.

Most global environmental conventions rely on the parties to monitor and verify their own compliance. These conventions generally require the parties to submit data on their compliance to their respective secretariats, which is then made available to the public. However, not all countries submit reports and those that are submitted vary greatly in quality and timeliness. For example, CITES requires that countries provide annual reports, which include export and import permit data. Countries must also file biennial reports on legislative, regulative, and administrative measures undertaken to improve implementation and enforcement. The Secretariat repeatedly expressed frustration with the quality and quantity of reports received. In 1991, the parties adopted a resolution that failure to file the required annual report on time is an infraction of the treaty. A list of countries committing infractions was compiled and circulated to the parties. In April 1993, for the first time, the Secretariat sent a letter to countries indicating that if they did not file reports, that failure would be considered a "major implementation problem" under the Convention. The letter further offered the assistance of the Secretariat in preparing and filing the reports. As a result of these measures, the number of timely reports and the quality of the reports increased.[7]

OECD countries face a different but less serious obstacle to reporting consistent data: harmonization of national methods. Typically, international data-reporting systems stem from already existing national systems, which aggregate and estimate data in different ways. These differences in reporting systems serve to reduce both compliance with data-reporting requirements and the secretariat's ability to analyze the data. This has been the case with the Long-Range Transboundary Air Pollution regime in Europe.[8]

To complicate matters even further, even when parties submit their reports, the secretariats of the conventions often lack the authority and/or personnel to evaluate and verify information submitted by the parties, eliminating one of the sources of pressure on governments to comply fully with the agreement. The secretariats of environmental conventions often lack the staff and funding needed to fulfill the functions they are assigned and countries that do not want close supervision do not approve the secretariats' requests for increased budgets and staff. The total combined professional staff of five agreements (Montreal Protocol, CITES, Convention to Combat Desertification, Framework Convention on Climate Change, and Convention on Biological Diversity) in 1999 was only 100 people, and their combined 1999 budget was estimated at $43.5 million.[9] To make matters worse, one of the biggest problems faced by the secretariats is funding shortfalls caused by the failure of parties to approve adequate budgets or to pay their contributions.[10] On the positive side, secretariats do get a lot of volunteer assistance by interested parties, including governments, NGOs, and academics.

Obstacles to Compliance

A growing literature on international environmental law has analyzed the obstacles to effective implementation of international environmental agreements.[11] Although each one approaches treaty compliance from a different perspective, there are some areas where there seems to be a basis for consensus. There is general agreement that rarely do governments deliberately fail to comply with an international treaty to which they are a party. Instead noncompliance is due to a number of different factors, including: inadequate translation into domestic law; lack of respect for rule of law within the country; high relative costs of compliance; inability to monitor compliance; and low administrative capacity.

Inadequate Translation into Domestic Law. Many countries that are parties to international environmental agreements fail to adopt implementing legislation that is needed to implement the agreement properly. For instance, Peter Sand has noted that "the main constraint on the implementation of CITES in each Party has been the need to create national legislation. Although this is an obligation under [CITES], several countries have not complied. . . . Others have only incomplete legislation, lacking . . . means for sanctions against offenders."[12]

In democracies with nonintegrated federal structures, the federal government may not have the jurisdiction to implement international environmental agreements at the state or provincial level. For example, in Belgium, each of the autonomous regions must separately adopt environmental legislation. In Canada, the provinces control environmental policy, not the federal government.[13] Federal systems typically leave policing and enforcement to the regional authorities, many of whose administrative capacities are extremely limited and must be divided among a number of tasks. In India, for example, guerrilla insurgents keep their bases in some of the largest tropical forests and wildlife sanctuaries and have developed close relations with poachers. For regional authorities compliance with international treaties takes a distant back seat to the problem of political instability.[14]

A second constraint on compliance is domestic political opposition. Depending upon the internal political system of the individual state, treaties can be held hostage by lawmakers as leverage to achieve other political ends, or they can be bogged down in debates over economic resource allocation.[15] For example, in the United States in the latter half of the 1990s, Senator Jesse Helms, a Republican from North Carolina, as chairman of the Foreign Relations Committee, refused to allow the Senate to vote on key environmental treaties, such as the Convention on Biological Diversity, the Convention to Combat Desertification, and the Kyoto Protocol.

Lack of Respect for the Rule of Law Within the Country. The lack of respect for the rule of law can also become an impediment to the effective implementation of environmental agreements. This problem tends to arise more often in developing countries where governments have trouble enforcing international environmental agreements because the general public or particular socioeconomic groups have little respect for the law. Merely passing implementing legislation has no practical effect because it is simply ignored by the public. For example, Kenya has been ruled since the 1970s by the dictator Daniel arap Moi. Because there is no meaningful democratic process in Kenya, the people do not feel that they participate in the lawmaking apparatus. This lack of participation undermines a respect for the law, including regulations on wildlife conservation.[16]

Similarly, in Indonesia, especially since the financial crisis in 1998, there has been an epidemic of illegal logging in national parks. This is largely due to a combination of breakdown of law and order and economic pressures. The illegal logging is often financed by large international wood products companies who are trying to obtain cheap timber. This makes it even more difficult, if not impossible, for the Indonesian government to protect the biodiversity in its protected-area system.[17]

High Relative Costs of Compliance. Domestic enforcement of international environmental agreements is likely to be affected by the relationship between the costs of compliance and a country's wealth or level of prosperity.[18] Sometimes affluent countries experiencing relatively high economic growth rates are often more willing to comply with relatively costly environmental regulations than are poorer states or states whose economies are growing slowly or not at all. For example, developing countries pushed for and received special treatment under the Montreal Protocol and the Climate Change Convention because of the perceived high cost of compliance. If the costs of compliance are relatively modest, or if compliance produces a net economic gain, a state's level of economic well-being may be less critical.

Domestic compliance with international environmental agreements is affected by the costs of such compliance relative to the country's wealth per capita and general economic health. States that have low per capita income are generally reluctant to commit significant new funds to actions to comply with commitments to reduce global threats, even if it is in the country's long-term interest, because such investments must compete with investments for short-term economic growth. Thus some key developing countries (including India and China) insisted on a commitment from donor countries to financing the additional costs they would incur by phasing out the production of CFCs and shifting to safer alternatives as the price for their participation in the Montreal Protocol (although it must be noted that some of the "poorest" states spend a high percentage of their national budgets on the military). And developing countries often limit their additional spending on expanding protected areas to projects that are financed primarily by the Global Environment Facility. Countries that are experiencing economic and financial crisis are likely to refuse to comply fully with global environmental agreements, or to suspend such compliance. This has been compounded in some cases by structural adjustment programs, which have actually cut environmental budgets in many debtor countries. The Russian Federation, for example, reported to the Montreal Protocol that it could not meet the 1996 target for compliance with the CFC phase-out because of its critical economic situation.

Inability to Monitor Compliance. Two major factors affect national monitoring capacity: first, whether states have adequate feedback mechanisms, such as on-site monitoring by inspectors, reporting requirements, complaint mechanisms, or close working relationships with NGOs, and second, the number and size of the potential violators whose conduct the government is responsible for monitoring.[19]

Some agreements are dependent on cooperation between states, NGOs, IOs, or industry to monitor and enhance compliance. For example, governments, the major industries in the private sector, and NGOs monitor compliance with the Montreal Protocol. International NGOs also work closely with the CITES Secretariat to monitor wildlife trade. TRAFFIC—the wildlife trade monitoring program of the WWF and IUCN—helps ensure that wildlife trade is at sustainable levels and in accordance with domestic and international laws and agreements. Established in 1976, TRAFFIC is now a network of 21 offices organized in seven regional programs. TRAFFIC assists in official investigations and enforcement actions; provides expertise for formulation, review, and amendment of wildlife trade legislation; and liaises with key wildlife consumers, producers, and managers to determine how best to dissuade unsustainable and illegal trade and to advocate to stakeholders solutions to any problems identified.[20]

There appears to be a relatively high level of compliance with the Montreal Protocol, in part because the science is clear to all and the agreement places manageable limits on the number of sources or sites that require monitoring. Compliance with the Kyoto Protocol, however, may prove to be more difficult because of the large number of sources of greenhouse gas emissions. Similarly, compliance with CITES appears to be much more problematic, in part because the number of potential violators is so large.

Low Administrative Capacity. Another reason for inadequate compliance, especially in developing countries, is low capacity. Skills, knowledge, and technical know-how at the individual and institutional levels are necessary if a country is to comply with the provisions of international environmental agreements. For example, CITES has provisions for trade measures to enforce its controls on wildlife trade, but many countries lack the budgets or trained personnel needed to comply.[21] Compliance with the Convention on Biological Diversity is hindered by a lack of capacity to manage protected-area systems and to analyze the impacts of development projects on biodiversity. And the Basel Convention contains no provision for monitoring the accuracy of hazardous waste labels or spot-checking shipments in receiving-country ports. The developing countries, whose inability to monitor and regulate the trade led them to call for a ban on international waste shipments, are left to enforce the agreement themselves.[22]

Financial resources for implementation are often inadequate at the national level, especially in developing countries. This not only limits the number of staff involved in the implementation of agreements, but they also may not have easy access to the scientific data they need for effective implementation. Technical problems, such as lack of adequate training, however, affect developed and developing countries alike. In an experiment conducted by WWF, volunteers declared or displayed a cactus to customs officials in several countries, including the United Kingdom, Switzerland, Germany, Sweden, Denmark, and the United States. Despite the fact that virtually all cacti are protected under the CITES agreement, no questions were asked by officials in any of these countries about the species of the plant or its origins.[23]

Options for Strengthening Compliance

Several options are available to strengthen compliance with environmental agreements. Whether these options or incentives can actually lead a government to comply depends on how willing and able other actors are to manipulate incentives to make compliance both possible and preferable.[24]

Increased Funding for Secretariats. Secretariats of environmental conventions tend to be small and their budgets are minuscule in comparison with the budgets of formal international organizations. Yet, they have the potential to be powerful actors because their staffs may be the only people with comprehensive knowledge of whether states and other actors are complying with a treaty and of the problems that have arisen at the national level.[25] However, the modest budgets and the continuing problem of late payment and nonpayment of pledges decrease the effectiveness of the secretariats in monitoring compliance. One current trend is the increasing use of short-term contracts (one to six months) for staff positions in secretariats. This development reflects budget uncertainties and funding constraints and, over the long term, will harm the quality of the secretariat staffs and their productivity.[26] The use of consultants means there is no institutional memory and none of the working relationships that are so important to implementation. One way to resolve this problem is that donor countries can negotiate a new joint commitment to increase funding for secretariats of global environmental conventions and to end the practices of late payment and nonpayment of pledges to them.

New Monitoring and Assessment Power to the Secretariat. A convention's provisions for compliance can be amended to give new monitoring and assessment power to the secretariat. The United States has resisted such proposals in the past on the ground that monitoring authority should not be given to international civil servants.[27] But that attitude simply gives parties to environmental treaties greater opportunities to be global environmental "free riders." Depending on the treaty, formal enforcement officers could be included in the secretariat or links with Interpol may be made (particularly in the case of CITES or other wildlife-related treaties, or even with regard to CFC smuggling in violation of the Montreal Protocol). In the early 1990s, CITES had an enforcement officer formally attached to its Secretariat who could conduct on-site investigations. Under the CITES Lusaka Agreement, CITES enforcement officers in member countries could link directly with Interpol. Another option would be to have consultants or NGOs, rather than the secretariat, reporting to the parties and secretariats serving indirectly to assist compliance by detecting violations and corrupt behavior.[28]

Increasing Donor Support for Strengthening Developing Countries' Capacity. Donor countries and multilateral agencies could increase funding for programs that strengthen developing countries' capacity to implement conventions. The Global Environment Facility and UNDP's Capacity 21 program have strengthened developing-country capacity largely through funding for the implementation of projects, where individuals and institutions gain critical technical, financial/business, and regulatory skills. All GEF projects on biodiversity and climate change are either focused entirely on capacity building or integrate capacity-building components into investment projects. Of 252 regular GEF biodiversity projects in the first operational phase, 6 were stand-alone capacity-building projects, and the rest all had capacity-building components. Climate change projects included 18 stand-alone capacity-building projects and 315 with capacity-building components. In addition, the GEF provides "enabling activity" grants to help recipient countries to prepare national plans and strategies and to meet their national reporting requirements under the biodiversity and climate change conventions. Although this may be a good start, it is too soon to determine if these projects will make a difference in the long-term capacity of the recipient countries.

Other capacity-building activities include the CITES training strategy, which "trains the trainers" in-country, by holding seminars and providing training materials.[29] Countries are asked to contribute to the training program, so that they become engaged in its success. UNDP is also assisting developing countries in this regard with its Capacity 21 program. Growing awareness of noncompliance due to incapacity has also led nations to establish mechanisms to finance compliance, as in the London Amendments to the Montreal Protocol, the Framework Convention on Climate Change, and the Convention on Biological Diversity.

Trade Sanctions. In some cases, trade sanctions against those parties found in violation could be used as a central mechanism for enforcement. Although there is generally little support for trade sanctions as a remedy for treaty violations, they would make sense in situations such as overfishing, where trade sanctions (in this case, curbs on fishing rights or imports) can be directly related to the failure to comply with the treaty. To be effective, trade sanctions must be both credible and potent. States that are consciously violating a treaty or measures adopted by a multilateral environmental agreement, such as a regional fisheries management organization, must be convinced not only that they will face penalties for the violation, but that the costs of the violation will exceed the gains expected from it.[30] Trade sanctions could raise that cost to the necessary level in some cases, but the larger the economy of the violating country, the less likely it is that sanctions will bite hard enough.

Negative Publicity. Because fear of negative publicity has proven to be a strong deterrent to treaty violations, an appropriate mechanism could be created by which the secretariats or COPs of treaties would address complaints about states' compliance brought by interest groups, including NGOs, in each country.[31] With the use of the Internet, global television networks such as CNN, and improved telecommunications, it is getting easier, cheaper, and faster to collect and distribute information. Norway lost money and public support when the European Union boycotted Norwegian fish products because of Norway's position on whaling. Likewise, the U.S. agricultural industry is finding that it has to respond to European boycotts and negative publicity with regard to genetically modified crops. This could be particularly important for conventions whose implementation involves complex social and economic policies, such as the biodiversity and desertification conventions.

FINANCING GLOBAL ENVIRONMENTAL REGIMES AND AGENDA 21

Lack of financial resources is often cited as the primary reason that developing countries are unable or unwilling to comply with global environmental regimes, including the soft-law regime on sustainable development, Agenda 21. Providing countries with financial assistance to help them comply with their obligations under environmental treaties can be crucial for advancing compliance.[32] However, not all treaties have mechanisms for providing financial assistance. Although no environmental convention negotiated prior to the Montreal Protocol included provisions for providing financial assistance to developing countries and countries with economies in transition for compliance with the treaty, both the biodiversity and climate change treaties include some mechanism for such assistance. But ever since, the United States and other donors have tried not to have a specific funding mechanism for each treaty.

The implementation of the new generation of global environmental regimes, including those for climate, biodiversity, and desertification, require transitions to environmentally sound technologies and new natural resource management strategies. Such transitions require difficult political decisions that are likely to meet resistance from powerful interests, as well as investments to ease the transitions. The question of external financing for developing-country implementation has therefore been a key issue in each one of these agreements. The Montreal Protocol demonstrated that donor countries and recipient countries participating in a global environmental regime can devise a regime that equitably distributes power over the financial mechanism and that can link financial assistance effectively with compliance. The Global Environment Facility, which the biodiversity and climate regimes have used as their financing mechanism, has a somewhat similar governance structure but faces more difficult issues in trying to link assistance with global environmental benefits. However, based on its first six years of operations, the Global Environment Facility cannot be expected to provide sufficient funds to assist developing countries in achieving compliance with the biodiversity and climate change conventions. And the donor countries do not seem to have the political will to provide adequate bilateral funding in support of global environmental objectives.

The Financial Context:
Slower Growth, Declining Aid Flows

This section first examines the context of declining aid flows that directly affects the financing available for the implementation of global environmental regimes. Second, it examines the UNCED negotiations on finance, which clearly illustrate the unequal bargaining power of the North and the South when it comes to financial resources. The rest of the section describes two different examples of financing mechanisms for the global environment: the Montreal Protocol Fund and the Global Environment Facility.

External assistance for developing countries in general has been declining since the Earth Summit, and that decline has been accelerated by the recession in Japan, the East Asian financial crisis, and the Russian economic crisis. By 1998 the rate of growth of the world economy had declined considerably.[33] This has had a direct effect on both national spending on the environment in developing countries and bilateral and multilateral assistance.

Moreover, in many developing countries, the debt situation remains a major constraint on achieving sustainable development. Although the debt situation of some middle-income countries has improved, there is a need to continue to address the heavily indebted poor countries, which continue to face unsustainable external debt burdens. Heavy indebtedness often forces countries to mine their natural resources for export. It also diverts budgetary resources from sustainable development programs. The overall foreign debt of developing countries reached an all-time high in 1997 estimated at $2,171 billion, compared to $603 billion in 1980.[34] Over 50 countries in the world, mostly in Africa, have debts that will never be paid back but continue to be paid daily with people's lives. The debt burden of the poorest countries is 93 percent of their income. In Zambia, every citizen now owes the country's creditors $790—more than twice the average annual income.[35] Servicing debt requires most of the foreign earnings in some countries. As a result, the most highly indebted poor countries can barely afford to provide basic services for their people, including health care, education, and food, much less provide funds for the implementation of global environmental treaties.

Developing countries insist that financing for the global environment should be *new and additional funding*, meaning that resources for global environmental measures should be provided beyond those allocated to traditional development cooperation rather than coming at the expense of development assistance flows. However, neither the Rio Declaration nor Agenda 21, which adopted this principle, provided an operational definition of the concept of *new and additional funding*. Such a definition would require a clear statement of what flows are to be included in the yardstick for determining "new and additional": only grant assistance? grants and concessional loans? all grant and grantlike flows? Should bilateral debt relief be included? What about contributions to multilateral agencies and development banks? The result would be different depending on which data are used for comparison. However, no international body or conference has ever defined what *new and additional* means in practice. It remains a principle that can be used in whatever way a government wishes.

Since 1992, official development assistance (ODA), including both bilateral and multilateral foreign aid, which increased modestly in real terms during the 1981–1991 decade, began to fall off substantially. Aggregate ODA from OECD countries in 1997 was 20 percent lower than it was in 1992 and represented just 0.39 percent of their combined GNPs.[36] (See Figure 4.1.) The largest aid donor, Japan, which contributes about one-fifth of all ODA worldwide, increased its ODA to a high of $14.49 billion in 1995 but has since decreased its contribution by 35 percent, to $9.36 billion in 1997, as a result of the Japanese recession. With the exception of a few countries, most donor states have either reduced or frozen their ODA.[37] The only countries that have reached the UN target of 0.7 percent of GNP for ODA are Denmark, the Netherlands, Norway, and Sweden.[38] The United States gives less of its GNP for ODA than many small European countries, including Finland.

There are several reasons for the decrease in ODA, most of which are likely to persist in the immediate future. In donor countries, the political commitment to aid is being challenged by chronic budgetary pressures, the end of Cold War rationales for aid, the perception of aid dependence among the poorest countries, a decreasing need for aid among middle-income countries, and skepticism about the historical effectiveness of aid in promoting development and reducing poverty.[39]

However, although ODA flows have declined overall, the share of ODA going to the conservation and management of natural resources has

FIGURE 4.1   Net ODA Flows, 1977–1997*

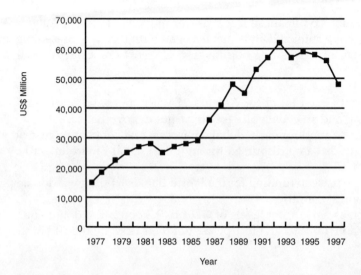

*ODA flows include both bilateral and multilateral assistance. Multilateral assistance includes contributions to UN-related funds, EC funds, the World Bank, IMF, WTO, and other organizations and funds, including conventions and the GEF.
SOURCE: OECD/DAC Statistical Reporting Systems (8 February 1999).

been rising. The share of funds committed to conservation and management of resources (including protection of the atmosphere, land resources, combating deforestation, sustainable agriculture, conservation of biological diversity, protection of oceans and seas, and management of hazardous and solid wastes) has risen from roughly 18.76 percent in 1983 to 24.69 percent in 1996. In nominal terms, the allocation of commitments to the protection of freshwater resources has doubled.[40] Slower growth worldwide, deeper indebtedness in the poorest developing countries, and the decline of concessional aid flows put greater pressure on national budgets for conservation and other environmental problems. The financing of activities by developing countries that benefit the global environment was already a politically explosive issue in North-South relations by the early 1990s, and tensions over the issue have not subsided. The creation and operation of effective funding mechanisms for the global environment, in a setting of North-South conflict over financial relations, has been one of the major challenges facing the global political system in the environmental arena.

The UNCED Negotiations on Finance

The negotiations on financial resources for implementation of Agenda 21 and global environmental agreements began with the G-77 presenting an ambitious set of negotiating objectives at UNCED PrepCom IV (March-April 1992):

- a special Green Fund for Agenda 21 with "new and additional" funding and an equal voice for all parties in governance;
- a separate fund for each global environmental convention instead of all funds being disbursed through the Global Environment Facility (GEF);
- a real increase in funding for the World Bank's lending window for the poorest countries;
- an increase in current levels of ODA to 0.7 percent of donor countries' GNP by 1995 and to 1 percent of their GNP by the end of the century.

But donor countries insisted that the GEF must be the only funding mechanism on global environmental issues and offered no new ODA commitments.[41] The G-77 then compromised on or abandoned all of its demands except its opposition to the GEF as the only mechanism for global environmental funding. And when the EC was inflexible on that issue, the G-77 decided to terminate the financial negotiations until the Rio conference, hoping to enhance its bargaining leverage on the issue of ODA targets and timetables.[42]

In Rio, the G-77 accepted the GEF and focused instead on a commitment by all OECD countries, including the United States, to achieving the target of 0.7 percent of GNP going to ODA by the year 2000. It also asked for a "substantial initial financial commitment" to Agenda 21 by the OECD countries and a pledging conference at the next UN General Assembly session. Those demands left plenty of room for a last-minute compromise on increased financial commitments. But in the end all the G-77 got was a reaffirmation that those countries that supported the ODA target would implement it and others would not. The United States maintained its decades-long rejection of any target for future ODA levels in relation to GNP; the EC was divided on the issue.[43]

The failure of the G-77 to win any significant concession on financial resources set the tone and agenda for all subsequent North-South debates. It reflected both the veto power of the OECD countries on the issue and the unequal bargaining power of the North and South at the end of the negotiations. Some OECD delegations, including the United States, had been worried at PrepCom IV that failure to come up with an acceptable financial chapter to Agenda 21 could cause the UNCED to "crash," that is, collapse without agreements.[44] But by the opening of the Earth Summit itself, it was clear that the G-77 did not intend to walk out of the conference over financial resources, and the United States and other donor countries relaxed. But it was probably responsible for part of the developing countries' stubbornness on other issues, including climate change. When asked in Rio whether the G-77 would accept a text that lacked even a provision for a pledging conference, a U.S. official responded, "They won't have any choice."[45]

The Montreal Protocol Fund

Most treaties have no separate funding mechanism; the ozone regime is the exception. The Montreal Protocol is the first regime in which the financing mechanism was a central issue in negotiations on regime formation. It was symptomatic of the birth pains of this new phenomenon in global environmental politics that in 1989–1990 the most important donor country, the United States, very nearly vetoed the whole idea of a special financing mechanism for a global environmental regime. Under the influence of conservative advisers John Sununu and Richard Darman, the Bush administration did not want every regime to have its own funding mechanism and feared that a Montreal Protocol Fund would establish the precedent. The United States wanted to turn the problem over to the World Bank, where the United States and other donor countries could count on their dominant votes to maintain control. But no other donor country was ready to support the U.S. position, and British prime minister Margaret Thatcher warned President Bush that the United States would face international isolation and be blamed for the breakdown of negotiations. The United States finally gave in and supported the fund in principle.

During the negotiations in 1989–1990, several political issues over financing of a global regime surfaced that would reappear again in other global environmental negotiations: Who would control the fund? What kind of governance structure should it have? How should the funds be mobilized? And how should decisions be made on allocating the funds?

With regard to the question of control over the mechanism, developing countries demanded that a new organization be set up with a governance structure that would give them at least equal power over funding decisions. Donor countries, on the other hand, wanted to rely on existing institutions, especially the World Bank, to provide the administration of the funds. After heated debate, the South accepted a compromise: shared control of the fund by the World Bank, UNDP, UNIDO, and UNEP, which they hoped would at least dilute the World Bank's control. But the World Bank was clearly designated as administrator of the fund, reflecting the supremacy of the donors' veto power.

Negotiations over the governance structure produced another, more innovative, idea: a combination of voting by region or constituencies and a double majority system that gave both donors and recipient countries veto power. The Executive Committee created to guide the new institution has 14 members, with equal representation by donors and recipients, with representatives chosen for defined regions or groups of countries, and with the United States granted a permanent seat. Voting is by a two-thirds majority that includes simple majorities of both donor countries and recipient countries.

The Montreal Protocol Fund[46] was inaugurated in 1990 for three years as an interim fund (the Interim Multilateral [Ozone] Fund, or IMOF). It was made permanent at the Fourth Meeting of the Conference of Parties in November 1992, despite the insistence of European donor countries that the IMOF cede responsibility for funding to the GEF, which had been established for its pilot phase by then. They argued that only one body should deal with all different global problems, for the sake of efficiency, and that IMOF wasn't working well enough. The South resisted this, fearing the GEF would be less friendly to Southern influence and more under the Bank's thumb because of the Bank's weighted voting system.

The reason that the donor countries gave in to recipient country demands on this issue was that the Montreal Protocol, for all its political problems, had one major virtue: It was a mechanism that involved real commitments by developing countries to formulating strategies for phasing out CFC production that existed in no other institution. Each country makes its own country ozone-depleting-substances (ODS) phase-out strategy, then presents it to the Executive Committee for approval. For example, China's ODS phase-out strategy involved 10 components, including a permit and quota system to manage production, an import restriction policy, a pricing policy, a taxation policy, and "green labels" on ODS-substitute or non-ODS goods. Country programs are the basis for development of a work program with the consent of recipient countries. The work program covers funding for activities that are on the Fund's list of activities that it will support, including the costs of production of substitutes for ODS, converting existing facilities, establishing new ones, and retiring the obsolete ones.

The Montreal Protocol Fund has been replenished three times: $240 million (1991–1993), $455 million (1994–1996), and $266 million (1997–1999). As of March 31, 2000, 32 industrialized countries had contributed $1.05 billion to the Fund. These funds have been used to support 3,300 projects and activities in 121 developing countries, resulting in the phase-out of the consumption of more than 131,334 tons of ozone-depleting substances.[47] Although there have been complaints by both donor countries and recipient countries about its operation, the Fund has demonstrated that a funding mechanism jointly run by donors and recipients can effectively link the provision of financial resources with measures that make significant contributions to reducing the global environmental threat.

The Global Environment Facility

As financial assistance has assumed greater importance in environmental regimes, control over the use of that assistance emerged as an issue in global environmental politics. Nowhere is this better reflected than in the struggle over the GEF. The GEF is a financial mechanism that promotes international cooperation and fosters actions to protect the global environment. The grants and concessional funds disbursed complement traditional development assistance by covering the additional costs (also known as *agreed incremental costs*) incurred when a national, regional, or global development project also targets global environmental objectives, for example, not for their local pollution clean-up but for climate, oceans, biodiversity, and ozone depletions, from which other countries would benefit as well. The GEF not only is a direct provider of grant and concessional resources but also serves as an instrument for leveraging resources from other donors, governments, and the private sector. GEF projects cover four focal areas: biodiversity, climate change, ozone-depleting substances, and international waters. (See Figure 4.2.)

The GEF began in 1991 essentially as an arm of the World Bank, with UNEP and UNDP providing technical and scientific advice. At that time, most of the donor countries wished primarily to avoid a separate fund for each global environmental convention and to keep control of other funds out of the hands of developing-country majorities and of UNEP executive director Mostafa Tolba, whom they distrusted. So the donor countries insisted on putting control over project planning and financing decisions in the World Bank, in which they had most of the votes on the governing board.

The Group of 77 developing countries firmly opposed the GEF as the sole funding mechanism for environmental agreements on the grounds that a few industrialized countries had set it up without consultation with the developing countries themselves, and that the World Bank, which was controlled by industrialized countries, would run it. They charged that it would focus only on environmental issues of interest to the North, such as

FIGURE 4.2   Distribution of GEF Funding by Project Type

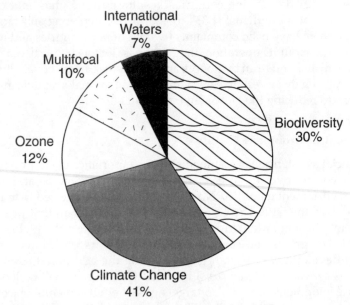

SOURCE: GEF Secretariat, Quarterly Operational Report, June 1997.

climate and biodiversity, rather than on those of concern to the South, such as soil erosion, freshwater, and wastes.[48] And developing countries could participate in GEF governance only by contributing $2 million to the GEF, a sum that discouraged most of them from participating.

Most NGOs in both North and South, meanwhile, found the central role of the Bank in the administration of the GEF unacceptable. They were especially incensed at the fact that most GEF projects were actually attached to larger World Bank projects, suggesting that the Bank was simply doing more of its traditional and not necessarily sustainable practices through the GEF. U.S.-based NGOs also criticized the GEF's lack of openness and accountability and its failure to consult with grassroots groups in the recipient countries and permit NGOs to attend the meetings of GEF participants as observers.

Whether the GEF would be accepted by developing countries as the funding mechanism for global environmental conventions ultimately depended on reaching agreement on a governing structure. Donor countries wanted a governing structure based on the World Bank model, with weighted voting according to financial contribution and decisions made by a qualified majority. Developing countries demanded a governing structure based on full equality for all participants, as in the UN General Assembly, with decisions made by a simple majority.

In May 1992 the climate and biodiversity conventions both accepted the GEF as the "interim" funding mechanism in return for the promise that the GEF would have "equitable and balanced representation" (climate convention) and be "democratic" (biodiversity convention), suggesting that the donor countries had given up their insistence on the World Bank model for governance of the GEF.

It took three years of acrimonious debate to work out the details of a system of governance that would satisfy both donor and developing countries. In the end, the two groups of countries agreed to a voting system requiring both a 60 percent majority of the members of the governing body (one state, one vote) and a 60 percent majority of states making the contributions for a decision. They also agreed that in addition to a GEF "council," in which a smaller number of countries would represent the entire membership of the GEF, there would also be a participants' assembly with universal membership that would meet less frequently.[49]

The portfolio of GEF projects for biodiversity and climate has reflected, to varying degrees, the GEF's own Operational Strategy, the decisions of the climate change and biodiversity conventions, and the priorities of recipient countries and implementing agencies.[50] Almost all biodiversity projects funded in the GEF's first operational phase were primarily for creating or strengthening the management of protected areas, although several of these projects also included components promoting the sustainable use of biodiversity. Although recipient countries are particularly eager to have funding for projects that promote the sustainable use of wildlife or other biological resources rather than its protection, shifting from unsustainable to sustainable exploitation of forests, for example, would not be an activity that represents additional costs for the recipient country's economy, as would protected-area projects. So there are unresolved questions about what kinds of sustainable-use projects are appropriate for GEF funding.

The original GEF Operational Strategy for climate calls for funding of projects that remove barriers to energy efficiency or energy conservation, promote renewable energy, or promote other low-greenhouse-gas-emitting technologies. In 1997, reducing emissions in the transport sector and reducing emissions through carbon sequestration were added to the list of objectives. The GEF climate portfolio is more consciously focused on priority countries than is the biodiversity portfolio: the top 10 greenhouse-gas-emitting countries received 87 percent of the climate funding during the first operational phase. Most of the GEF's climate projects have been aimed at removing various administrative, technical, policy-related, and other barriers to market penetration by climate-friendly technologies, including those for energy efficiency. Such projects clearly involve benefits to the national economies of the recipient countries as well as to the global environment. But the GEF Council finally decided that, without GEF financing, such "win-win" solutions would not be implemented.[51]

Since the GEF's restructuring, there have been two replenishments, of $2 billion and $2.75 billion, which is insufficient to achieve environmental benefits. The replenishment for its operational phase translated into an average of $140 million annually for biodiversity and about $166 million annually for climate change during the first three years. These levels of funding are clearly only the smallest fraction of the resources that will be needed to address the threats to biodiversity and climate effectively. One estimate of the cost of conserving critical biodiversity globally would be about $20 billion annually, based on extrapolations of data provided in UNEP's Biodiversity Country Studies. And the costs of investments in greenhouse-gas-emissions-reduction options that would not reduce economic growth are far higher: The Asian Development Bank estimated in 1994 that it would require $135 billion for India alone.[52]

The GEF was never intended to invest that level of financial resources in assisting developing countries in reducing global environmental threat. Instead, the GEF was expected to leverage additional investments by mobilizing cofinancing for its projects and, more important, by demonstrating approaches that are successful and replicable. The GEF has had some success in leveraging cofinancing from other sources, but it appears to be far more modest than the three dollars it claimed were leveraged for every dollar invested during GEF 1.[53]

Even if it were successful in mobilizing three dollars for every dollar invested, however, the resources leveraged would be minuscule by comparison with the challenges faced. The GEF represents a symbolic international response to the need for financial assistance to address global environmental issues, based on resources that donor governments are able to commit from national budgets.

The GEF has become, in effect, the permanent financial mechanism for both the climate change and biodiversity conventions and the main, although tiny, source of financing for global environmental measures by developing countries. But North-South conflicts over donor country domination of GEF policies and decisions on allocation of resources continue. Even after seven years of the operation of the GEF, developing countries are still not comfortable enough to accept the principle of incremental cost funding, which they feel discriminates against their interests. But donor veto power leaves the developing countries little choice but to go along with it.

Generating Additional Financial Support for Global Environmental Regimes

For the foreseeable future, any significant increase in financial resources for global environmental regimes and sustainable development worldwide will have to come from reorienting existing bilateral and multilateral ODA, canceling debt of the poorest countries, adopting innovative international approaches to financing, and adopting new priorities for national spending that reflect social and environmental concerns. The main options for generating additional financial support for global environmental conventions and sustainable development include refocusing multilateral and bilateral assistance, carbon sequestration, international taxes, debt relief, and elimination of subsidies.

Refocusing Multilateral and Bilateral Assistance on Projects That Will Be Supportive of Environmental Regimes and Agenda 21 Goals. ODA programs could devote more resources to promoting the social bases of sustainable development, including basic health and nutrition, family planning, and education—especially for women. Better health and education contribute to smaller families, more productive agriculture, higher incomes, and less stress on the environment and natural resources. According to the OECD, in 1996, only 16.8 percent of total ODA was allocated to education, health, and population concerns.[54]

Since the early 1990s, UNDP and UNICEF have advocated a plan under which bilateral and multilateral ODA agencies and the developing countries themselves would make commitments to parallel budgetary shifts to give greater priority to human resource development (health, nutrition, and basic education). In the proposed 20/20 Global Compact, developing countries would agree to increase the percentage of their own national budgets allotted for human resource development programs, from the current 13 percent on average to a minimum of 20 percent, in return for a commitment by donor agencies to increase their investments in the same social sectors from the current 10 percent on average to 20 percent of their total ODA. UNDP calculated that such a compact would generate $30 to $40 billion in additional investment in human development programs annually.[55] Most developing countries are sympathetic to the idea that more ODA should be focused on human resources development; a few, notably China and Pakistan, have opposed it, citing the nonviability of developing a mathematical formula for human development.[56] Although most states are sympathetic to establishment of a 20 percent basic floor of support for social development, the 1995 World Summit for Social Development endorsed the 20–20 concept only as a nonbinding goal.[57]

Carbon Sequestration. A source of financing that holds significant potential for supporting forest conservation is private funding for carbon sequestration projects by which private companies could receive credits for offsetting their carbon emissions under the Clean Development Mechanism (CDM) created by the Kyoto Protocol. (See Chapter 3.) Deforestation is estimated to contribute 20–25 percent of all net greenhouse gas emissions, and protecting forests that would otherwise be cut down thus contributes both to reducing overall carbon emissions and to conservation goals. The ability to measure and quantify changes in forest biomass, moreover, is well understood by scientists, so it is possible to calculate how much carbon emissions are saved by protecting a given amount of forest.

If such credits were provided for in the CDM, it could draw hundreds of millions or even billions of dollars of private financing into forest conservation projects. But the Conference of the Parties to the Climate Change Convention will have to approve the inclusion of forests in the CDM, and this inclusion is by no means assured. The European Union and a number of NGOs have expressed some major concerns about allowing forest conservation projects to be credited under the Kyoto Protocol. One is that it will prove very difficult to determine whether a given forest area would actually have been cut down in the absence of the project. Another is that it will prove impossible to protect forests in the long run from illegal logging or burning. And a third is the fear that industrialized states will rely on such projects as an alternative to reducing their fossil fuel consumption at home. Although each of these concerns could be addressed in the rules for operation of the CDM, the U.S. opposition to any cap on carbon credit trading as a means of fulfilling national obligations has made this a red flag issue for the European Union, which feels the commitments accepted are already too little, even if fully implemented domestically.

Tax International Currency Transactions, Air Travel, or the Trade in Arms to Generate Funds for Support of Sustainable Development. Many ideas for international taxes are on the table for raising new revenue for sustainable development. They are based on the notion that the earth's oceans and atmosphere are common resources, and that all citizens of the planet have rights and responsibilities concerning them. It is already accepted that if you take your garbage to a landfill site, you will be charged a tipping fee. Therefore, if a country uses the atmosphere for waste disposal, should it not pay a global environmental tax?

The European Union is currently studying a proposal for an air fuel tax to raise funds for environmental projects. The revenue from such a tax, which could generate over $1 billion,[58] could go directly to UNEP, which urgently needs new sources of funding. Another proposal is for a tax on currency trading, an idea which won the support of François Mitterrand when he was president of France. And a tax of just 0.005 percent on international movements of speculative capital, the ease and speed of which present a threat to the stability of currencies, could generate $15 billion a year.[59] That would be far more than would be needed to pay for all the UN peacekeeping efforts and thus could also be a major source of funding for global environmental protection efforts.[60] A global energy tax of $1 per barrel of oil or its coal equivalent could raise $66 billion annually.

Many practical issues concerning the accountability and administration of global taxes need to be resolved, and there are some national governments that fear losing revenues or are concerned that such taxes will become slush funds and the money will be wasted. In the United States, for example, Congress has passed legislation that makes it illegal for the United States to participate in any global taxes. Although there is strong opposition, in principle the concept of a global environmental tax would finally recognize in international law that dumping toxic materials in the oceans or greenhouse gases in the atmosphere is not "free" and that there are real long-term costs that our children will have to pay.[61]

Forgiving the Debt Obligations of the Poorest Developing Countries and of Lower-Middle-Income Countries in Return for Sustainable Development Policy Reforms and Investments. As mentioned above, debt obligations place often huge burdens on developing countries, which force them to mine their natural resources for export and do not give them any budgetary resources to implement environmental conventions or sustainable development programs. Instead, the option is available to the international community to link debt reduction with the allocation of budgetary resources for sustainable development. This could be a way to fund some of the programs that are needed to combat desertification in Africa, for example.

Under pressure from poor countries and NGOs in September 1996, the World Bank and the IMF launched the Initiative for Heavily Indebted Poor Countries (HIPC). The HIPC Initiative is an agreement among official creditors designed to help the poorest, most heavily indebted countries escape from unsustainable debt. It enables poor countries to focus their energies on building the policy and institutional foundation for sustainable development and poverty reduction. The initiative is designed to reduce debts to sustainable levels for poor countries that pursue economic and social policy reforms and is used specifically in cases where traditional debt relief mechanisms will not be enough to help countries exit from the rescheduling process. Unlike earlier debt relief mechanisms, it deals with debt in a comprehensive way and involves all creditors, including multilateral financial institutions.

As of November 1999, eligibility has been reviewed for 14 countries. Relief has been agreed on under the original framework for seven countries (Bolivia, Burkina Faso, Côte d'Ivoire, Guyana, Mali, Mozambique, and Uganda) yielding debt relief of $3.4 billion in net present value. Four countries (Bolivia, Uganda, Guyana, and Mozambique) have already received debt relief amounting to $2.8 billion in net present value. Five more countries (Ethiopia, Guinea-Bissau, Nicaragua, Mauritania, and Tanzania) have completed their preliminary review and could qualify for billions of dollars debt relief.[62]

The Jubilee 2000, an international movement of religious, charitable, environmental, and labor groups in over 40 countries advocating a debt-free start to the millennium for a billion people, is calling for a cancellation of the unpayable debts of the world's poorest countries, under a fair and transparent process. Although Jubilee 2000 recognizes the importance of the HIPC initiative, organizers argue that there has been resistance by an old guard in the IMF, World Bank, and finance ministries of many of the industrialized countries that has made the HIPC unworkable. According to Jubilee 2000, secretive negotiations and unworkable criteria now provide too little debt relief too late. Uganda gained debt relief a year later than predicted; it will pay the same in debt service after the HIPC completion point as it paid before. After a year of infighting among creditors, a deal has been reached for Mozambique to pay more after HIPC completion than it does now; it will defer the implementation of universal primary education because money must be diverted to debt service, after HIPC. Furthermore, HIPC defines *sustainability* in terms of how much a country can pay, rather than in terms of how much it needs to sustainably develop. According to Jubilee 2000, HIPC does represents a fundamental break with the past and points a way forward. The challenge now is to accept the implications of HIPC and to quickly grant deep debt relief based on genuine debtor participation and on development instead of accounting criteria, and to ensure that debt relief will be conditioned on either allocations of greater resources to conservation and sustainable management of resources or basic policy reforms.[63]

Eliminating Subsidies in Industrialized Countries for Use of Natural Resources (Water and Energy) and for Environmentally Harmful Activities (Such as Using Pesticides and Fertilizers) in Order to Set an Example for Developing Countries. One very direct method of increasing the sustainability of agriculture, forestry, and fisheries is to eliminate subsidies that contribute to more production in the subsidized sector and to overexploitation of land, forests, and fish. The period from the 1960s through the 1980s saw a rapid expansion of subsidies to natural resource production worldwide. Although there is evidence of some reductions in subsidies to agriculture and fisheries in the 1990s, the scale of environmentally harmful subsidies is still staggering.[64] Estimates of such subsidies in the mid-1990s ranged from $700 billion to $870 billion annually, of which roughly 90–95 percent was accounted for by energy, road transport, water use, and agriculture. Developing countries had already reduced their energy subsidies by half in the 1990s, but there are still an estimated $58 billion that could be saved by subsidy elimination, while making energy more efficient and reducing carbon emissions.[65]

Subsidies to the fisheries sector, as of 1996, were estimated by the FAO at $7–14 billion worldwide annually, and it is increasingly recognized that they contribute to fishing-fleet overcapacity.[66] The next round of multilateral trade negotiations could include for the first time an agreement on eliminating such perverse fisheries subsidies, which would increase the resources available for sustainable development by billions of dollars, while easing one kind of upward pressure on fleet capacity.

Despite the financial and environmental advantages of ending such subsidies, however, governments are usually reluctant to end policies that benefit powerful economic elites. The largest category of environmentally harmful subsidies in the industrialized world is subsidies for agricultural exports, which cost consumers and taxpayers in OECD countries $335 billion in 1995, depress prices, and discourage producers from developing countries.[67] Because of the resistance of powerful agricultural lobbies in the United States and Europe, governments were unwilling to agree to phase them out during the Uruguay Round negotiations, even in the face of heavy pressure from the United States. As budgets continue to get tighter in the OECD countries, however, pressures to cut such subsidies are growing, increasing the chances for international agreement on the issue.

CONCLUSION

The regime-building process does not end with the signing and ratification of a global environmental convention but continues through the implementation of the convention, which is considered by some to be the most important part of the process. Usually that process involves steady efforts to strengthen the regime. Two primary issues that affect the implementation and effectiveness of an international environmental agreement were addressed in this chapter: national-level compliance and the availability of financial resources.

National-level compliance with an environmental treaty is affected by a number of different factors, including adequate translation into domestic law, lack of respect for the rule of law within the country, high relative costs of compliance, inability to monitor compliance, and low administrative capacity. There are several options available to strengthen compliance with environmental agreements, including increased funding for secretariats, new monitoring and assessment power to the secretariat, strengthening developing countries' capacity, imposition of trade sanctions, and negative publicity. All of these factors are strongly affected by the level of a government's self-interest, which is why countries negotiated a treaty in the first place.

Lack of financial resources is often cited as the primary reason why countries are unable to effectively implement global environmental regimes. Providing countries with financial assistance can promote greater compliance. External financing for environmental agreements is closely linked to the economies of industrialized countries. While at one time there were relatively strong financial flows in terms of official development assistance, support for multilateral funding agencies, and foreign direct investment. However, during times of recession, the flows dry up considerably, as has been the case in the latter half of the 1990s. Yet even as economies in some developed countries, such as the United States, have rebounded, it is unlikely that foreign assistance funding will follow suit, largely because of domestic political pressures.

This chapter outlined several ways to increase funding for global environmental regimes, including refocusing the current multilateral bank programs as well as bilateral assistance and current developing-country spending on projects that will be supportive of environmental regimes and Agenda 21 goals; carbon sequestration; international taxes; forgiving the debt obligations of the poorest developing countries in return for sustainable development policy reforms and investments; and eliminating subsidies in industrialized countries for use of natural resources and environmentally harmful activities.

In spite of daunting obstacles preventing effective implementation of international environmental agreements, it is something of a wonder that they are, in fact, mostly observed and slowly strengthened. Although we have presented a number of policy prescriptions that could help to solve these problems, the most important factor needed to meet the challenge is political will in both rich and poor countries. In many cases, political will hinges on domestic economic policies or interests. A few more environmental crises may be required to do the trick. Many of these interests, as represented by finance or trade ministries, business and industry, unions, the defense establishment, and others, still subscribe to the dominant social paradigm that justifies unlimited exploitation of nature and places certain economic and political interests above the environment. The worsening of environmental trends is not currently matched by necessary international solutions. Progress will have to be faster and more comprehensive to sustain the planet's resources for future generations.

FIVE

□   □   □

Economics, Development, and the Future of Global Environmental Politics

Global environmental politics have become increasingly intertwined with the politics of the global economy in recent years as environmental issues begin to impinge on core economic concerns of countries. Trade and environment, the financing of sustainable development, and consumption patterns were not on the international political agenda a decade ago. But several developments converged to change all that: the emergence of environmental problems and regimes requiring major social and economic transitions in all societies, and the recognition of these issues during the first global negotiations encompassing both environmental and economic policies—the 1992 United Nations Conference on Environment and Development, and the growing influence of environmental consciousness on trade policies.

Inequitable economic relations between North and South have proven to be a crucial element of the political context of global environmental politics, as on other issues. The developing states' perceptions of the global economic structure as fundamentally inequitable often shape their policy responses to global environmental issues and their strategies for negotiating on issues as different as elephants and climate. Moreover, unfavorable trends in North-South economic relations since the mid-1970s have not only sharpened the inequalities between North and South but weakened the bargaining position of the South in issues involving North-South economic relations, including environmental issues.

As linkages with economic relations and development have multiplied, the boundaries of global environmental politics have broadened. In this chapter, after a review of North-South economic relations and the environment, we analyze two political issues and processes involving both global environmental issues and the political dynamics of trade and economic growth that have emerged since the UNCED negotiations: the clash between the drive for free trade and the drive to protect the environment and efforts to craft an international forest regime. The politics of global forests show how the fears over loss of markets can block progress toward international agreement on norms for sustainable resource management. The politics of trade and environment, on the other hand, show how difficult it is to insert environmental considerations into the global trade regime.

NORTH-SOUTH ECONOMIC RELATIONS AND THE ENVIRONMENT

In 1974, encouraged by a surge in commodity prices and the Organization of Petroleum Exporting Countries' (OPEC) successful manipulation of oil supplies in the early 1970s, developing countries attempted to restructure the whole global economic system. The South called for a bold but largely unrealistic plan, the **New International Economic Order** (NIEO), a list of demands for redistribution of wealth, which would include a new system of international commodity agreements, a unilateral reduction of barriers to imports from developing states in industrialized countries, enhancement of developing countries' capabilities in science and technology, increased Northern financing of technology transfer, and changes in patent laws to lower the cost of such transfers.[1] It was a strong bid for equality.

From the late 1970s onward, however, the NIEO faded from the global political agenda as economic trends turned against the South and the North consequently felt even more strongly it could disregard such Southern demands for change. Falling commodity prices devastated the economies of those countries that were heavily dependent on commodity exports. Between 1980 and 1991, the weighted index for 33 primary commodities exported by developing countries, not including energy, declined by 46 percent.[2] And heavy debt burdens, taken on at a time when commodity prices were high and Northern banks were freely lending dollars from Arab oil revenues, siphoned off much of the foreign exchange of many developing countries. By 1995, total external debt of the least developed countries was $136 billion, which represented 112.7 percent of their GNP that year.[3]

During the early 1990s, trade barriers erected by industrialized countries against imports of manufactured and processed goods from the developing countries continued to increase even as most developing countries (under pressure from international financial institutions) were lowering their own barriers to imports.[4] Industrialized-country tariffs on textiles and clothing and other products of particular importance to developing countries' exports tended to be the highest tariff rates in industrialized countries, which often increase tariff rates on goods in proportion to the degree of processing involved, a process called tariff escalation. New kinds of **nontariff barriers** to trade (such as antidumping and countervailing duty actions), export-restraint agreements (such as the Multi-Fibre Arrangement), and direct subsidies have been used to protect industries in the industrialized countries against imports from developing countries. These have made developing countries suspicious to this day of anything called a nontariff barrier.

The negotiations on liberalization of world trade, known as the Uruguay Round, began in 1985 under the auspices of the Global Agreement on Tariffs and Trade (GATT) and were concluded in April 1994. The Uruguay Round was supposed to reduce some of these barriers, but the overall impact appears to have been slight. Although the average level of protection in the industrial countries is relatively low, there are serious barriers to entry in certain sectors of particular interest to developing countries, including agriculture, textiles, clothing, and fish and fish products. Developing countries continue to express concern about preference erosion, tariff escalation, and the risks in being left out of the proliferating free trade areas and customs unions.[5]

There has been growing discontent among developing countries toward developed countries' agricultural policies. Several developing countries have complained that they have liberalized their agricultural markets only to face domestic competition from subsidized agricultural imports from developed economies, especially the EU and Japan. At the same time they say developed countries' markets remain relatively closed to agricultural exports from developing countries via a number of nontariff barriers to trade such as sanitary measures and country-of-origin labeling. Exacerbating the situation, developing countries' attempts to modernize agriculture infrastructure have been hampered by depressed commodity prices and a subsequent decline in investment in agriculture.[6]

Despite the rapid growth in a number of East Asian economies in the 1980s, the income gap between the industrialized world and the developing world continued to grow. Whereas the richest 20 percent of the world controlled 70 percent of global gross domestic product (GDP) in 1960, the richest 20 percent controlled 80 percent of global GDP by 1997.[7]

Existing patterns of North-South economic relations have contributed to the degradation and depletion of natural resources. Sudden increased demand in the North for certain commodities has increased their price and stimulated increased exploitation of the resource. When Japan began major imports of tropical timber in the 1960s and 1970s, for example, it raised tropical timber prices and impelled the Philippines and Indonesia to step up their exports of raw logs and processed timber products, regardless of long-range environmental and development implications.[8]

But the pressure on natural resources also increases when falling commodity prices are combined with debt burdens and protectionism. Countries that are indebted and heavily dependent on commodity exports often have adjusted to falling prices by increasing the volume of commodity exports, thus depleting agricultural land, forests, and other natural resources. For example, several of the Sahelian countries increased their cotton production by 20 percent in the 1980s even as world cotton prices fell by 30 percent. The expansion of cotton production forced grain farmers off their land, encouraged heavy use of pesticides, and exacerbated the problem of soil depletion and desertification.[9]

Northern protectionism also forces developing countries to exploit their natural resources more heavily. Subsidies to agricultural exporters in the United States and other OECD countries deprive developing-country producers of markets and depress world prices for those goods, exacerbating trade imbalances and developing-country indebtedness. European beef exporters undercut African producers by massive subsidies, for example, and thus dominate African markets.[10] Often poor countries adjust to this loss by expanding acreage for export crops or livestock. Depressed food prices discourage marginal farmers in food-exporting developing countries from making the investments in soil conservation and water management necessary for sustainable agricultural development. Meanwhile, subsidized prices for exportable agricultural commodities provide powerful incentives for the agricultural sector in developed countries to use more fertilizers, pesticides, and water, polluting groundwater supplies and depleting underground aquifers.[11]

Northern and Southern Perspectives
on the Global Environment

Historically, the developing countries' views on global environmental issues have been shaped to a considerable extent by their preoccupation with economic growth, their fears of high costs of environmental protection, and their general distrust of the policies of industrialized states. Developing countries have generally regarded the negotiation of global regimes on ozone depletion, climate change, biodiversity loss, and conservation of endangered species as a Northern agenda. Their own environmental priorities have been urban air and water pollution, the erosion and salinization of agricultural land, and toxic chemical contamination; but for most developing countries, economic growth, employment, and overcoming poverty have been the dominant concerns. Although developing countries are now active participants in many of these "Northern" regimes, their main concern is usually to ensure that their economic interests are protected.

Although many officials of developing countries, particularly in environment ministries, recognize the seriousness of local and global environmental degradation for their own economic future, many of them regard environmental regimes for ozone and climate, for example, as a means by which industrialized countries will maintain their control over resources and technology or even gain control over resources now located in the South. One developing-country delegate to the second meeting of the parties to the Montreal Protocol in 1990 declared that for "some countries," the protocol was a "pretext to place new obstacles in the way of efforts by developing countries to develop their economies."[12] And some officials of developing countries viewed the efforts of industrialized countries to bring them into a global climate change convention as a ploy to constrain economic development in the South so that the developed countries could dominate the world's remaining oil resources.[13]

Developing countries, many of which were already subject to macroeconomic policy conditions on loans from multilateral banks, reacted strongly to any suggestion that industrialized countries would also impose environmental conditions on economic assistance or restrict their exports on environmental grounds. The Conference of the Nonaligned Movement (NAM) held in September 1998, although subscribing to the values of environmental protection, labor standards, intellectual property protection, sound macroeconomic management, and promotion and protection of human rights, rejected all attempts to use these issues as conditionalities and pretexts for restricting market access or aid and technology flows to developing countries.[14]

Despite growing disparities among the developing countries between rapidly industrializing countries, such as China, India, Malaysia, and Brazil, and debt-ridden countries that have experienced little or no growth since the 1980s, such as most of sub-Saharan Africa, Vietnam, Myanmar, and Nicaragua, developing countries share a common view of the relationship between global environmental issues and North-South economic relations. They insist that the industrialized countries, because of their historical dominance in the production and consumption of CFCs and combustion of fossil fuels, are responsible for the thinning of the ozone layer and global warming. More generally, they identify wasteful Northern patterns of excessive consumption as a key cause of global environmental degradation. According to UNDP's 1998 *Human Development Report*, the 20 percent of the world's people in the highest-income countries account for 86 percent of total private consumption expenditures—the poorest 20 percent for a minuscule 1.3 percent. More specifically, the richest fifth:

- Consume 45 percent of all meat and fish; the poorest fifth, 5 percent.
- Consume 58 percent of total energy; the poorest fifth, less than 4 percent.
- Have 74 percent of all telephone lines; the poorest fifth, 1.5 percent.
- Consume 84 percent of all paper; the poorest fifth, 1.1 percent.
- Own 87 percent of the world's vehicle fleet; the poorest fifth, less than 1 percent.[15]

Based on such comparisons, developing-country officials as well as NGOs began to demand in the early 1990s that industrialized countries reduce their share of what they call "environmental space"—the use of the earth's limited natural resources and environmental services—and permit developing countries to use more of that environmental space in order to raise their living standards.[16]

Developing countries also believe that the North should bear the financial burden of measures to reverse ecological damage. In the climate change and biodiversity negotiations, as well as in the UNCED negotiations, demands from the South for "new and additional" funding for de-

"And may we continue to be worthy of consuming a disproportionate share of this planet's resources."

Drawing by Lorenz; © 1992 The New Yorker Magazine, Inc.

veloping countries' implementation of the agreement have been a central issue. A sharp reduction in ODA below even the 1992 level and the failure of wealthy countries to amend trade policies that harm the interests of poor countries has increasingly irritated the developing countries. In the latter half of the 1990s, they started to use the threat of retreating from previous consensus agreements on global environmental issues as leverage on the donor countries. At the Earth Summit +5 (the 1997 Special Session of the UN General Assembly to review the implementation of Agenda 21 and the other Rio agreements), the G-77 and China refused to oppose proposals by oil-exporting states to delete all references to reducing consumption of fossil fuels. This tactic failed, however, to shake the veto exercised by donor countries on targets for ODA.[17]

Another consistent theme in developing-country views of global environmental issues is the inequality in governing structures of international organizations such as the World Bank, which allows a minority of donor countries to outvote the rest of the world. Developing countries have demanded that institutions making decisions on how to spend funds on the global environment should have a "democratic" structure, that is, one in which each country is equally represented. Thus developing countries did some of their toughest bargaining in negotiations relating to the environment when they resisted the donor countries' proposed governance structure for the Global Environment Facility. (See Chapter 4.)

The South also has demanded that transfer of environmental technologies on concessional or preferential terms be part of the agreements on recent conventions and on UNCED's Agenda 21. In the Montreal Protocol negotiations, for instance, developing states demanded a guarantee from the industrialized countries that corporations would provide them with patents and technical knowledge on substitutes for CFCs. In 1990 India tried unsuccessfully to get language into the amended protocol that would make the obligations of developing states to phase out CFCs subject to the private transfer of technology.

A few European states and numerous Northern NGOs have supported the South's view on environmental space and its demands for resource transfers. And most industrialized countries accepted the South's argument in the UNCED negotiations that Northern consumption patterns were responsible for much global environmental degradation. The willingness of Northern countries to permit developing countries to have a relatively long grace period before having to comply with the ozone and climate change conventions reflects the general acceptance that poor countries had relatively little responsibility for those problems. But the North generally emphasizes the responsibility of all countries to contribute to solving global environmental problems, which implies a need for developing countries to avoid duplicating the unsustainable historical development patterns of the industrialized world.

These incompatible perspectives have continued to clash in negotiations on strengthening the climate change regime, as developing countries have become increasingly articulate about the case for industrialized-country responsibility for the problem and the implications for commitments to emissions reductions. During the negotiations of the Kyoto Protocol, Brazil presented an analysis that compared the relative responsibility of Annex I (industrialized) countries and of non–Annex I (developing) countries for climate change, not just in terms of carbon dioxide emissions in a given year, but in terms of carbon dioxide concentrations because of historical emissions. It showed that the responsibility of non–Annex I countries for accumulated emissions would not equal that of Annex I countries until the middle of the 22nd century.[18]

The effectiveness of the climate change convention as well as the biodiversity convention is in doubt, in part because developing countries adopt the fundamental stance that they should not be asked to bear the same degree of responsibility or the same level of obligations for reversing these global threats as advanced industrialized countries. That attitude is clearly related to convictions that the global economic system has always been and continues to be skewed in favor of the advanced industrialized countries. Using the global inequality argument is obviously a useful tactic for developing countries to keep as much of the burden of emissions reductions in the climate regime on the Annex I countries for as long as possible, and a strong argument for the Annex I countries to take the first major steps and firmly lead the way.

TRADE AND THE ENVIRONMENT

The effects of trade policy on the environment have often been an element in global environmental politics. However, the global trade system has evolved for decades without any thought about its impact on the environment. When the GATT, the central pillar of the international trading system, was negotiated just after World War II, there was no mention of the word *environment*. At that time no one saw much connection between trade liberalization and environmental protection. In fact, for the next 40 years, trade and environmental policymakers pursued their respective agendas on parallel tracks that rarely, if ever, intersected. The wake-up call for environmentalists was the U.S. ban on tuna from Mexico and Venezuela on the ground that their fleets did not meet U.S. standards for minimizing dolphin kills in tuna fishing. In 1991 the GATT declared that the U.S. ban was illegal under the rules of international trade. U.S. environmentalists were alarmed that a national environmental law could be overturned by the GATT and began to take seriously the environmental implications of trade.[19]

But it was not until the United States began to negotiate a free trade agreement with Mexico that U.S. environmentalists saw a way to influence the process. Suddenly, by 1992 trade and environment became a high-profile international political issue. The North American Free Trade Agreement (NAFTA) was seen as a symbol of economic integration between countries at different stages of economic development. There was a concern among environmentalists and organized labor that a trade agreement with Mexico might trigger a downward spiral in environmental and labor standards on both sides of the border as industry claims of competitive disadvantage induced governments to relax their environmental and labor regulations.[20] U.S. environmentalists worked closer than ever before with organized labor in the United States and with Mexican environmental groups and workers' organizations. It marked the beginning of a broader, mutual understanding among labor, environmentalists, and consumers that is still growing today.

The result was the first international trade agreement that included supplemental agreements on labor and environmental issues.

The GATT and the World Trade Organization (WTO) constitute a regime that seeks to promote a common set of international trade rules, a reduction in tariffs and other trade barriers, and the elimination of discriminatory treatment in international trade relations.[21] The WTO, which was created in 1995 pursuant to the Uruguay Round trade agreement, has the mandate to rule on a very large spectrum of issues, from trade in goods and services to intellectual property rights including issues affecting human health, the use of natural resources, and the protection of the environment.

In the preamble to the 1994 treaty under which the WTO was established, it was recognized that the organization should ensure "the optimal use of the world's resources in accordance with the objective of sustainable development."[22] This was a last-minute victory for environmentalists, although the statement is nonbinding. With this in mind, and with a desire to coordinate the policies in the field of trade and environment, when trade ministers approved the results of the Uruguay Round negotiations in Marrakesh in April 1994, they also decided to begin a work program on trade and environment in the WTO. Their decision, which established the WTO's Committee on Trade and Environment (CTE), ensured that the subject would be given a place on the WTO agenda. But although the CTE has been the main arena for discussing trade-environment policy linkages since 1994, it has been unable to make any decisions on policy issues, even in the form of referring an issue to another WTO committee for action.[23]

Relationship Between Multilateral
Environmental Agreements and the GATT/WTO

Some multilateral environmental agreements (MEAs) use ETMs to promote cooperation through the use of a variety of incentives related directly to the environmental problem at issue. For example, an MEA may use trade measures to regulate trade among parties and nonparties of the product that is considered a major contributor to the environmental degradation the agreement seeks to curtail. By a WTO staff reckoning, only 18 out of a total of approximately 180 MEAs currently in effect contain trade measures. For instance, the main treaties with trade measures are CITES, the Montreal Protocol, and the Basel Convention. Under all three treaties, trade in the specified products (endangered species, controlled ozone depleting substances, and hazardous wastes) is banned between parties and nonparties.

CITES, which was negotiated in the early 1970s, before trade became an issue for environmentalists, uses a number of different trade measures to promote compliance. It invokes trade restrictions against parties and nonparties to protect listed species of animals and plants threatened with extinction and endangerment. CITES also utilizes a permit and listing system to prohibit the import or export of listed wildlife and wildlife products unless a scientific finding is made that the trade in question will not threaten the existence of the species. These trade provisions are designed to severely constrict the market demand for wildlife and wildlife products and, hopefully, reduce the international market demand for the products and thereby discourage the initial taking of the wildlife.

The Montreal Protocol prohibits trade in ozone-depleting substances with nonparties unless the nonparty has demonstrated its full compliance with the control measures under the Protocol. The Montreal Protocol seeks to restrict the global market in consumption and production of ozone-depleting substances and uses trade provisions to encourage the phase-out of these substances and to discourage the establishment of "pollution havens" where parties shift their manufacturing capabilities to nonparties. In reducing market demand, the Protocol reduces the release of these substances into the atmosphere and provides an incentive for the development of benign substitutes.

The Basel Convention uses trade measures to limit the market for the transboundary movement and disposal of hazardous waste between OECD and non-OECD countries. The agreement's trade provisions encourage the management of waste in an environmentally sound manner and with prior informed consent. The convention also provides that a party shall not permit hazardous waste or other wastes to be traded with a nonparty unless that party enters into a bilateral, multilateral, or regional agreement.[24]

No GATT or WTO trade dispute has arisen so far over the use of trade measures applied to achieve an agreed-on environmental purpose, primarily because in these cases the trade itself is a threat to the environment and attempts to reduce it are logical. Furthermore, we must remember that trade agreements do not have automatic precedence over MEAs. Nevertheless, doubts have been expressed by some WTO members about the WTO consistency of certain trade measures applied pursuant to some MEAs, in particular discriminatory trade restrictions applied by MEA parties against nonparties that involve extrajurisdictional action. The CTE worked intensively on this issue in 1995–1996 in preparation for a report to the WTO Ministerial Conference in December 1996. It debated whether there was a need to clarify the scope for such measures under GATT provisions, and especially whether Article XX, which details exceptions to the rest of the GATT principles, should be amended to do so.

Three major positions emerged within the CTE on this issue.[25] Yet all of these positions, in essence, elevated trade agreements to a higher plane in international law than environmental law. The European Community took the most proenvironmental position by arguing that the GATT Article XX should be clarified so that it is clearly understood that environmental objectives of an MEA are valid exceptions to GATT principles. The European Community proposal called for development of an "understanding" that the provisions of Article XX do in fact cover trade measures by a state pursuant to an MEA. If a trade measure taken under an MEA was subsequently challenged by a nonparty, the WTO dispute panel could then review the issue of whether the measure had been taken pursuant to the specific provisions of a valid MEA. It could determine whether the environmental objective was legitimate but not whether the trade measure was necessary. However, under the European Community's proposal, a unilateral trade measure could be examined by a WTO panel in terms of its necessity as well as the validity of the objective.

The European Community's position had very little international support in the CTE. Only the United States and two or three other OECD countries were even willing to discuss it. The developing countries rejected it out of hand, arguing that it would allow the industrialized countries to do whatever they want on trade in MEAs. Both Canada and Japan were also very critical of it.

New Zealand outlined an approach to the problem of trade measures in MEAs that would be more oriented toward free trade and less toward accommodation of MEAs. In this proposal, the WTO would set out guidelines for MEAs' use of trade measures that would include not only procedural principles in terms of what constitutes a valid MEA, but also substantive criteria for trade measures, such as whether they apply to unrelated products and whether they are no more trade-restrictive than necessary. This has been called the *ex-post approach*, because it would mean that each MEA would be reviewed after it adopts trade measures and that the WTO would clearly have authority to pass judgment on every MEA's use of trade measures in substantive terms.

The developing countries, led by India, have taken the position that trade measures in MEAs are unnecessary and that even if they were necessary, they are already covered by existing WTO provisions. The developing countries are concerned that spelling out exceptions for the environment in Article XX would risk the conversion of those exceptions into new WTO provisions. So they call for the status quo.

The United States, which has been the most active state in using trade measures unilaterally for international environmental objectives, did not play a lead role on the issue of MEAs in the CTE. The Clinton administration was internally divided between officials in the National Oceanic and Atmospheric Administration (NOAA), who wanted to aggressively advocate amending Article XX to clarify the legitimacy of trade measures in MEAs, mainly in order to advance trade measures in regional fisheries organizations, and State Department officials who felt that environmental interests would be better served by simply proceeding to build trade into MEAs without consulting the WTO. In the end, the United States submitted a paper to the CTE that was broadly supportive of the EU position.

The CTE was unable to agree on any course regarding trade measures in MEAs, so the WTO has made no move to amend Article XX. There is still a danger that some WTO members will resort to the WTO dispute settlement to undermine trade measures taken pursuant to MEAs. In 1998 Brazil raised the issue of the GATT compatibility of trade sanctions adopted by the International Convention for the Conservation of Atlantic Tuna, arguing that quotas adopted did not adequately involve the participation of developing-country fishing states. But some U.S. officials who once supported an aggressive approach in the CTE have concluded that the United States can better advance the cause of using trade measures in MEAs by going ahead with initiatives in regional fisheries organizations than by trying to amend or clarify Article XX in the WTO. They argue that trying to revise the language of the GATT Article XX would take too long, and that trade lawyers can always find a way to justify a country's position, regardless of the language of the GATT articles.

Environmental Trade Measures and Dispute Resolution

Many environmental laws authorize restrictions on trade for a variety of policy objectives related to the environment, both domestic and international. Such laws have been called *environmental trade measures* (ETMs) and include import prohibitions, product standards, standards governing production of natural resource exports, and mandatory ecolabeling schemes.[26] But exporters that are disadvantaged by such environmental measures sometimes charge that they are intended to protect domestic producers from foreign competition, and in a few cases, the governments of the exporting countries have brought such complaints to WTO's dispute resolution panels.

The United States has taken the lead in defending the right to use ETMs for both domestic and international environmental objectives, and it is no accident that it has been the target of a number of cases brought before GATT/WTO dispute panels. As the largest single market in world trade, the United States has a unique capability to exert pressure on the environmental and trade policies of other countries, and it has been pressured by U.S. environmental NGOs to do so, at least in marine conservation issues. The United States used trade restrictions in conjunction with its leadership role to end commercial whaling and to protect dolphins from excessive killing by tuna fishermen and marine mammals generally from the use of destructive drift nets. The U.S. threat to ban Korean fish products from the U.S. market and to prohibit Korean fishing operations in U.S. waters persuaded South Korea to give up whaling as well as drift-net operations in the Pacific Ocean.[27] The United States also banned wildlife-related exports from Taiwan in 1994 after finding that that country had violated CITES by failing to control trade in rhino horn and tiger bone. Although environmentalists see these as justifiable protections, one can understand how it looks to much less powerful countries that the United States is throwing its weight around.

Developing countries are concerned about the use of ETMs by industrialized countries, even for domestic environmental purposes, because they view them as potential barriers to their exports. Rapidly industrializing countries fear that the United States in particular will use ETMs to protect its domestic industries, just as it used antidumping legislation for that objective in the past. In negotiations on the UNCED Rio Declaration and in the Uruguay Round, developing countries clashed with the United States over ETMs related to extrajurisdictional issues. During UNCED, India and South Korea proposed that unilateral actions to deal with environmental problems outside the jurisdiction of the importing country "should be avoided," a proposal that became Principle 12 in the draft Rio Declaration. The U.S. delegation objected but bowed to the consensus on the declaration in Rio, although it submitted an interpretative statement on Principle 12 that "in certain situations," such ETMs might be "effective and appropriate means" of addressing environmental concerns beyond the jurisdiction of the importing country and specifically referred to forest management as an example.[28]

Environmental NGOs also have argued that basic trade rules and institutions have been systematically biased against the environment. The GATT was created in the 1940s when the environment was not an issue domestically or internationally. Trade rules and mechanisms that are used to handle disputes between trading partners have long been geared primarily to removing barriers to free trade. Moreover, the deliberations of GATT dispute panels are carried out in secret with no opportunity for nongovernmental testimony or briefs. There is a profound lack of environmental expertise represented on the panel. All of this adds up to a secret trial (for that is what these deliberations are) with no expert witnesses, no observers, and the full weight of its authority, since there is no appeal. It may be the only international agent that can tell even the mighty United States what to do.

NGOs demanded changes in GATT rules to guarantee a country's right to set environmental domestic standards as high as it wished, to allow NGO participation and greater transparency in the GATT's deliberations, and to reform the dispute resolution process to ensure that environmental experts are included in cases involving the environment. Many NGOs opposed the GATT Uruguay Round agreement in 1994, based on the absence of any environmental provisions. In 1994 the fear that the WTO, operating in secret, without even the requirement that they justify decisions, could threaten U.S. laws became a major theme of domestic political opposition to the Uruguay Round agreement in the United States, as labor leaders picked up on it, although their fears were over competition from low-paid workers.

Trade officials of most countries as well as the WTO secretariat have great faith that increased trade liberalization will lead to economic growth, which will in turn lead to greater investment in environmental protection. They argue that trade-restricting measures usually only stunt economic growth and are generally ineffective in accomplishing environmental objectives. They also fear that domestic economic interests will use the environment as a cover for protectionist aims. Free-trade advocates have been particularly vociferous in opposing ETMs aimed at influencing environmental issues beyond the boundaries of the importing country.

GATT/WTO dispute resolution panels have the authority to determine whether a particular trade measure is compatible with the GATT articles based on a complaint by a state alleging that its market access has been unfairly restricted by the measure. These panels consist of trade specialists from three or five contracting parties with no stake in the case or issue who have been agreed to by both parties to the dispute. Dispute panel rulings are normally submitted to the WTO Council (which includes all parties to the agreement) for approval. Under the old GATT dispute resolution rules, a ruling could be vetoed by a single member of the GATT Council. However, the Uruguay Round agreement provides for automatic acceptance of a dispute panel ruling by the WTO Council within 60 days unless there is a consensus within the Council to reject it. Decisions carry real weight. If a country fails to bring its law into conformity with the decision, its trade partners could take retaliatory trade measures against it, such as a consideration that is more threatening to small countries than large trading countries like the United States, or the EU, although it is doubtful that smaller countries will risk taking such measures against the United States or the EU.[29]

The GATT/WTO dispute resolution panels have been a focal point of political contention over the legitimacy of specific ETMs. In several cases it was an action by the United States, mandated by national law to protect the environment, that was challenged.

The first such dispute panel report, the 1991 panel decision on the U.S.-Mexican tuna-dolphin dispute, was a major factor in shaping the politics of trade and environment issues in subsequent years. As a result of the dispute, developing countries became even more determined to create international rules against what they regarded as unfair trade pressures. Meanwhile the GATT panel decision prompted many environmental NGOs in the United States to press even harder for changes in the GATT, including provision for ETMs covering issues beyond the jurisdiction of the importing country.[30]

Mexico had filed a complaint with the GATT charging that the U.S. embargo against Mexican yellowfin tuna—imposed under an amendment to the 1972 Marine Mammal Protection Act (MMPA) because of the Mexican fleet's killing dolphins at twice the rate of the U.S. fleet in catching tuna—was a protectionist measure on behalf of the U.S. tuna industry. Mexico and Venezuela asked why they should forgo export earnings and a low-cost source of protein for their own people to reduce the incidental impact on a marine mammal that was not an endangered species.[31]

The GATT panel found that the U.S. ban was a violation of the GATT because it was concerned only with the process of tuna fishing rather than with the product. It also ruled that GATT Article XX, which allows trade restrictions for human health or the conservation of animal or plant life, cannot justify an exception to that rule because the article does not apply beyond U.S. jurisdiction. This was a historic decision. The GATT panel's ruling on the tuna-dolphin issue reflects the tendency of most trade specialists to view any restrictions on trade for environmental purposes as setting a dangerous precedent that could destroy the entire world trade system. It may also have been influenced by the fact that eight governments or agencies spoke against the U.S. tuna ban before the panel and that not a single party spoke for it.[32]

The decision came at an embarrassing moment, when the United States and Mexico were negotiating NAFTA. Because both governments really wanted the agreement, the United States was able to work out an agreement with Mexico that prevented the GATT panel decision from being presented to the GATT Council. But in 1994 the European Union brought a second complaint on the U.S. tuna ban to a GATT dispute panel to get resolution on the principle of extraterritorial unilateral actions. The EU charged that its exports of tuna were adversely affected by the MMPA's "secondary embargo" against imports of tuna from intermediary nations that fail to certify that they do not buy tuna from nations embargoed under the law.

The GATT panel found the U.S. ban incompatible with the GATT articles, but it accepted two key contentions of environmental critics of the GATT. It rejected the EU's arguments that dolphins are not an exhaustible natural resource and that Article XX applies only to the protection of resources located within the territory of the country applying the trade measure in question. But it held that such measures could be used only to conserve those resources directly and not to change the policy of another state—a distinction that is difficult, if not impossible, for policymakers to apply in practice—and thus found the U.S. MMPA incompatible with the GATT.[33]

In two other cases the EU challenged U.S. laws meant to increase fuel efficiency in automobiles sold in the U.S.—the 1978 "gas guzzler" tax and the CAFE (Corporate Average Fuel Economy) standards.[34] The "gas guzzler" tax levied taxes on auto models whose fuel efficiency falls below 22.5 miles per gallon, with the size of the tax depending on how far the model's rate was from the minimum. The EU argued that treatment of its cars under the measure was discriminatory, since the tax fell disproportionately on cars of European origin, and that it was not effective in conserving fuel because only a small proportion of cars in the U.S. market were subject to the tax. The GATT panel found that the gas guzzler tax did not unfairly protect U.S. auto manufacturers and that although the measure may not be as effective in fuel conservation as a fuel tax, it has had the desired effect. So here we have a GATT panel with no environmental expertise whatsoever making a judgment about what is the best strategy.

On the CAFE standards, the GATT panel ruled slightly differently. The CAFE legislation, passed in 1975, was aimed at doubling the average fuel efficiency of the automobiles sold in the U.S. market within 10 years. It requires that automakers' domestic fleets average at least 27.5 miles per gallon of gasoline and that the total fleet of foreign-made automobiles sold in the U.S. market must meet the same average. Failure to meet the fleet average results in a fine of $5 for every tenth of a mile per gallon below that average multiplied by the number of automobiles in the manufacturer's fleet. U.S. manufacturers can average their large fuel-consuming vehicles with smaller, more fuel-efficient models; European manufacturers, who sell almost entirely larger luxury automobiles in the U.S. market, cannot. The EU argued that the law worked to the disadvantage of limited-line car producers concentrating on the top of the car market and that individual foreign cars are treated differently from domestic cars. The United States insisted that the CAFE legislation is based on objective criteria and was not aimed at affording protection to domestic production.

The panel found that CAFE was intended to promote fuel efficiency. But the requirement that foreign fleets must be accounted for separately, based on ownership and control relationships rather than characteristics of the products themselves, was found to give foreign cars less favorable conditions of competition than domestically produced cars. The panel also found that the requirement was not aimed at conserving fuel. It concluded that the separate foreign fleet accounting could not be justified under the exceptions in Article XX(g) and recommended that the United States be requested to amend the CAFE regulation to eliminate that requirement, which it did.[35]

Two other complaints over environmental trade measures have been brought under WTO dispute settlement rules operating since 1995. In each case, the complainant state challenged national or EU environmental protection measures, and in each case, the WTO ruled against those measures. In the Venezuela Reformulated Gasoline Case, Venezuela and Brazil claimed to be discriminated against by a U.S. EPA rule under the Clean Air Act that required all refineries to make cleaner gasoline using the 1990 U.S. industry standard as a baseline. Since fuel from foreign refineries was not as "clean" in 1990 as that from U.S. refineries, the importing countries were starting their clean-up efforts from a different starting point. The WTO panel ruled in 1997 for Venezuela and Brazil, and EPA set about revising its rules.[36]

In a second case, in January 1997, India, Pakistan, Malaysia, and Thailand charged that a U.S. ban on the importation of shrimp caught by vessels that kill endangered migratory sea turtles violates WTO rules that no nation can use trade restrictions to influence (fishing) rules of other countries. The U.S. argued that relatively simple and inexpensive turtle excluder devices (TEDs) can be placed on shrimp trawlers to save the turtles. To implement the U.S. Endangered Species Act, the U.S. Court of International Trade, in response to a lawsuit brought forth by an NGO, the Earth Island Institute, ruled in December 1995 that in order to export mechanically caught marine shrimp into the United States, countries who trawl for shrimp in waters where marine turtles occur must, as of June 1996, be certified by the U.S. government to have equipped their vessels with TEDs. TEDs have been mandatory on all U.S. shrimp trawlers since December 1994. If properly installed and operated, TEDs permit most sea turtles to escape from shrimp trawling nets before they are drowned, while minimizing loss of the shrimp catch. The United States argued the trade measure was necessary because sea turtles were threatened with extinction and the use of TEDs on shrimp nets was the only way to effectively protect them from drowning in shrimp nets.

In April 1998, the WTO dispute settlement panel held that the U.S. import ban on shrimp was "clearly a threat to the multilateral trading system" and consequently was "not within the scope of measures permitted under the chapeau of Article XX." The United States appealed the decision, and in October 1998 the appellate body found that the U.S. ban legitimately related to the "protection of exhaustible natural resources" and thus qualified for provisional justification under Article XX(g). This decision represented a step forward for the use of unilateral trade measures for environmental purposes. But the decision also found that the U.S. import ban was applied in an unjustifiably or arbitrarily discriminatory manner, citing seven distinct flaws in the legislation. It found, for example, that the requirement that all exporters adopt "essentially the same policy" as that applied by the United States had an unjustifiably "coercive effect" on foreign countries. It also found that the United States had not seriously attempted to reach a multilateral solution with the four complaining countries,[37] and that the process for certification of turtle protection programs was not "transparent" or "predictable."

The ruling thus left open the possibility that a unilaterally imposed trade ban in response to foreign environmental practices, and based on non-product-related issues, could be implemented in compliance with the GATT. But some trade law experts believed the procedural criteria in the ruling were unrealistic, and the case underlined once again the problem of a WTO panel, which lacks either environmental expertise or mandate, passing judgment on trade measures for environmental purposes.

In response to the appellate body decision, the United States issued new guidelines on the issue in July 1999. The new guidelines still prohibited the import of shrimp that was harvested with technology adversely affecting the relevant sea turtle species. But instead of requiring the use of TEDs by the exporting country, it allowed the exporting country to present evidence that its program to protect sea turtles in the course of shrimp trawling was comparable in effectiveness to the U.S. program. The guidelines noted, however, that the Department of State was not aware of any technology that was as effective as the TED.[38]

Ecolabeling

Ecolabels are labels indicating that certain products are better for the environment to help consumers exercise preferences for environmentally sound production methods for products, for example, wood harvested from sustainably managed forests, not clear-cutting. Although some eco-labels are conferred by firms on themselves and others by trade associations on their members, the ones that have credibility with consumers are "third-party" ecolabels awarded by independent entities. The ecolabels that are important to the environment are those that use criteria based on "process and production methods" (PPMs); that is, they make judgments on the ecological efficacy of the methods by which a product is made/grown/caught—not on the product itself—such as tuna-fishing practices that kill large numbers of dolphins or unsustainable logging practices. A number of governments have sponsored their own ecolabels, but some of the most important are private, voluntary schemes. Third-party ecolabels have already demonstrated their potential for getting the attention of producers where international policymaking has failed, as shown by the case of the Forest Stewardship Council and timber products (see the section on forests later in this chapter). But they can in some circumstances be unfairly discriminatory. So they have become a focus of international conflicts and of debate in the WTO since 1994 on whether and how that body should address ecolabeling schemes.

Both OECD countries and developing countries have expressed justifiable concerns about some government-sponsored ecolabeling schemes that are skewed in favor of domestic producers and against foreign competitors. An ecolabeling scheme may convey an advantage to a domestic industry by virtually mandating a particular technology or production process, ignoring the fact that another technology or process may be equally or more environmentally sound and more suitable in the country of origin. In the case of a proposed private German labeling scheme for textiles, for example, natural dyes that are used more in developing countries are excluded by the criteria for environmentally friendly chemicals. Several countries that export paper products, including the United States, Canada, and Brazil, have complained about an official EU ecolabel regarding paper, fearing it would create disadvantages for their producers in the European market. For example, the ecolabel's stress on the use of recycled paper in papermaking is seen by Brazil as discriminating against its pulp and paper industry, because the availability of fast-growing eucalyptus plantation fiber and the relatively low consumption of paper within Brazil make the use of recycled paper in papermaking an uneconomical choice for the industry, which obtains much of its comparative advantage from its plantations.[39]

Some countries are also hostile to private ecolabeling schemes simply because they threaten to reduce markets for a domestic industry that is guilty of unsustainable practices. The transparency of official and private voluntary ecolabeling schemes and the ability of affected exporters to participate in their development thus emerged as an issue in the WTO. Canada proposed that the WTO consider both official and private ecolabeling schemes as falling under the disciplines of the WTO Technical Barriers to Trade (TBT) Agreement. The TBT requires that government-sponsored technical regulations and standards treat domestic and foreign products equally ("national treatment") and treat products from different WTO members equally ("most favored nations"), that standards and regulations not constitute unnecessary obstacles to trade, and that governments take steps to ensure that standardizing bodies improve transparency and involve interested parties in standard setting. The Canadian proposal would force a private ecolabeling scheme to allow exporters affected by it to have input into its development.

The CTE has recognized that well-designed ecolabeling programs could be effective instruments of environmental policy, but at the same time concerns have been expressed about their possible trade effect: the multiplication of ecolabeling schemes with different criteria and requirements, or the fact that they could reflect the environmental conditions, preferences, and priorities prevailing in a country's domestic market, which might have the effect of limiting market access for overseas suppliers. The CTE also noted that increased transparency could help deal with trade concerns regarding ecolabeling schemes and stressed the importance of WTO members' respecting the provisions of the TBT Agreement.[40]

However, there was strong disagreement over whether the TBT Agreement should be considered as covering ecolabels based on PPMs. Many members, including the entire South-East Asian bloc, were afraid that agreeing that ecolabels incorporating PPMs would compromise the WTO principle that no trade measures based on PPMs are legitimate. The EU also took the view that ecolabeling incorporating PPMs are not covered by the TBT Agreement and proposed either extending the transparency obligations of the TBT Agreement to ecolabels or creating a separate legal instrument on transparency in ecolabeling. The United States, on the other hand, opposed the EU view because it implied that there was no right to challenge ecolabels on transparency grounds. The United States insisted that the TBT did cover ecolabels incorporating PPMs, but that transparency provisions should be further strengthened to allow exporters the right to have input into the decision on what products will be selected for the development of ecolabels.[41]

Protecting private ecolabeling schemes from government interference has become one of the primary trade and environment concerns of environmental NGOs. They argue that the voluntary private ecolabeling schemes cannot be considered to be in violation of WTO principles and have called on the WTO to refrain from limiting their development.[42] Legal analyses have concluded that private ecolabels based on PPMs do not fall under the TBT Agreement and are free of the disciplines of the GATT/WTO system, regardless of their impacts on trade.[43] Although no moves have been made in the WTO to regulate the development and operation of ecolabels that incorporate PPMs, some governments expressed opposition to the appearance of a new private ecolabeling scheme for fisheries. After the formation of the Marine Stewardship Council in 1996 by WWF and Unilever, the largest seafood-processing company in the world, the governments of Brazil, Japan, and Norway, as well as the delegation of the EU, all complained at a meeting of the FAO Committee on Fisheries that it had the potential to have adverse impacts on seafood trade. NGOs and business formed the Marine Stewardship Council to get around WTO restrictions in a political response to frustration about the lack of progress within the WTO on environmental considerations.

The conflict between governments and private ecolabeling schemes now seems unlikely to result in far-reaching moves to restrict their freedom. But the issue of official ecolabels that discriminate against foreign exporters could still be the subject of a complaint within the WTO dispute resolution process, if not of international agreement on new rules governing them.

Subsidies and the Environment

Another new issue on the trade and environment agenda in the latter half of the 1990s was what the CTE called "the environmental benefits of removing trade restrictions and distortions"—a lengthy trade euphemism for subsidy elimination and the environment. A subsidy may be defined as a government-directed intervention, whether through budgeted programs or other means, that transfer resources to a particular economic group. Subsidies distort markets by sending signals to producers and consumers that fail to reflect the true costs of production, thus misallocating financial and natural resources. And subsidies to goods traded internationally give unfair advantages to exports that are subsidized over others.

Subsidies also have negative impacts on the environment, especially in the commodity sectors (agriculture, forests, and fisheries). They draw a higher level of investment into these sectors and exacerbate the overexploitation of land, forests, and fish, and they make technologies that exploit natural resources more intensively cheaper to acquire, such as flood irrigation or excessive use of pesticides.[44] Thus eliminating subsidies to these sectors represents a rare case of a clear-cut win-win solution in which trade liberalization benefits the environment. The Uruguay Round Agreement of 1994 represented the first substantial step toward subsidy removal in agriculture, as the United States and the "Cairns Group" of industrialized and developing countries supportive of agricultural trade liberalization got the EU to agree to a 20 percent reduction in total support compared to a 1986–1988 base period. But subsidies to fisheries and forests remained outside the agreement.

During a series of debates on subsidies and the environment during 1996, a clear international cleavage emerged between antisubsidy and prosubsidy members. The Cairns Group of agricultural exporting countries[45] argued that the environmental costs of agricultural subsidies justified further liberalization of trade in that sector. And a new lead state coalition emerged on the issue of fisheries subsidies that included the United States, New Zealand, and Iceland. New Zealand and Iceland had already acted to eliminate subsidies, but the United States assumed a lead role despite the fact that its industry is still subsidized, because of NGO pressures and the concern of the U.S. fishing industry that other fleets are being subsidized even more heavily.

The lead states advocated a WTO agreement on eliminating subsidies to fisheries that contribute to fishing fleet overcapacity. But a veto coalition consisting of heavily subsidizing members (EU, Japan, and South Korea) argued that empirical evidence that subsidy elimination would benefit the environment was still weak, and that support for agricultural subsidies benefited the environment in various ways, such as flood control and maintenance of rural landscapes. The WTO Secretariat contributed an analysis that documented the environmental benefits of subsidy removal in each natural resource sector, leaving no doubt about which side of the debate it was on.

In the maneuvering in 1999 over the "Millennium Round" of trade negotiations, subsidy elimination was one of the most hotly contested issues. A group of states calling itself the "Friends of Fish," including the United States, Iceland, New Zealand, Norway, Peru, the Philippines, and Indonesia, pushed for inclusion of a paragraph in the draft ministerial declaration for the Seattle WTO summit calling for a working group on fisheries subsidies. And a disputed paragraph in the draft called for "further substantial reductions in export subsidies, including commitments resulting in the elimination of such subsidies."

At the December 1999 Seattle WTO Ministerial Conference, which was supposed to be the beginning of the Millennium Round, the issue of agricultural subsidies was one of the major stumbling blocks to agreement on a framework for the trade negotiations. While protestors were stealing the headlines, the EU and Japan agreed with the United States on language endorsing the aim of ending agricultural subsidies, in return for U.S. concessions on other trade issues of interest to those two actors, but the two sides could not agree on a timetable for eliminating subsidies before the talks collapsed in bitterness.

On fisheries subsidies, an issue that was a lower priority for the United States, the question that remained to be resolved was whether the text would commit WTO members to begin negotiations on the issue immediately or only to study the issue, deferring a decision on actual negotiations until the midpoint in the round. With the unsuccessful end of the ministerial conference, the future of negotiations on subsidy elimination in the fisheries sector was left highly uncertain. But the lead state coalition for such subsidy elimination was growing rapidly just before and during the Seattle ministerial, picking up the support of a number of key developing countries, including Indonesia, Morocco, Malaysia, Venezuela, and Thailand.

The Future of Trade and Environment After Seattle

The protests against the WTO and its policies by tens of thousands of activists, combined with the collapse of the Seattle Ministerial Conference of the WTO in December 1999, left the future of the WTO and global trade liberalization in doubt. On one hand, the unpopularity of the organization in many quarters throughout the industrialized world left an indelible impression on the entire world, overshadowing the substantive issues at stake in the conference. On the other hand, the inability of the organization to agree on an agenda for a new round of trade liberalization negotiations raised the question of whether new progress was possible in the direction of reducing trade barriers.

As the world's trade officials retreated to figure out how to put trade liberalization back on track, a central issue facing the organization was whether it had sufficient legitimacy with civil society in the major democratic member countries to successfully negotiate trade agreements. The protests reflected a range of complaints about the WTO and globalization of the economy, but one common theme was that the world's trade officials had long reached agreements without sufficient transparency and participation by civil society.

Environmental NGOs had been advocating greater transparency of WTO processes, including dispute panels, since the early 1990s, but with little success. They called for meetings open to the press and the public, NGO input in the selection of experts on the dispute panels, and more NGO input into WTO decisions, but these calls fell on deaf ears. The United States, under pressure from its own NGOs, has pushed for greater transparency in the WTO, proposing in 1994 that NGOs be permitted to observe WTO proceedings. But WTO delegations from developing countries and other industrialized countries alike rejected the participation of environmental NGOs generally, because they perceived the worldwide

NGO movement as dominated by U.S. NGOs. They also rejected any breaching of the confidentiality of the dispute resolution process.

The NGO campaign for greater transparency in the WTO was bolstered by the successful campaign to stop negotiations on a Multilateral Agreement on Investment (MAI) under the auspices of the OECD in December 1998. Negotiations on this proposed international economic agreement began in 1995 at the OECD. The MAI was designed to make it easier for individual and corporate investors to move assets—whether money or production facilities—across international borders. Environmental NGOs expressed opposition to the MAI on several grounds, including these: The MAI would prevent governments from screening out companies with poor environmental records, and the MAI would pressure countries to reduce environmental protections as they compete to attract capital in the global economy.

Although the choice of the OECD as a venue was controversial because it includes no developing country members, proponents argued that since its members represented 85 percent of foreign direct investment outflows, having them negotiate among themselves would produce a better agreement. In practice this meant shutting out the developing countries.[46]

Proponents of the MAI claimed that the agreement would provide needed protections for U.S. and other international investors against discrimination and expropriation, open new markets to U.S. investors on favorable terms, and help businesses, consumers, and workers in the long run by improving the efficiency of the global economy.[47] In other words, the MAI would help the economies of many industrialized nations by facilitating international investment. Opponents of the MAI argued that the proposed agreement would accelerate an economic and environmental "race to the bottom" as countries feel new pressure to compete for increasingly mobile investment capital by lowering wages and environmental safeguards.[48] Thus it could be said that the MAI would help rich nations and rich investors become richer at the expense of the environment and labor.

In February 1997 an early draft of the treaty, replete with numerous contradictions, was leaked to Public Citizen, a Washington-based public interest group founded by Ralph Nader, and then immediately published on the Internet. Up to that point, negotiations had been conducted among the 29 countries of the OECD in secrecy. Suddenly, OECD representatives became targets of unprecedented scrutiny. The MAI was denounced as a major and immediate threat to democracy, sovereignty, the environment, human rights, and economic development.[49] Three years of negotiation came to a halt in April 1998 when the OECD announced that talks would be delayed for six months. Negotiators called for a time-out to allow for consultation among the parties and with civil society. In December 1998, NGOs celebrated when the OECD announced that it had ceased negotiations on the MAI.

The "Battle of Seattle" and the failure of the MAI may have helped to convince officials of many countries that they must make more accommodations with civil society, especially environmental and developmental NGOs, in order to function successfully in the twenty-first century. For the first time, public opposition to the WTO not only in the United States but in other industrialized countries is perceived as a serious threat. It is not an accident that the WTO's Secretary-General, Mike Moore, was quoting approvingly the work of the World Wildlife Fund in advocating subsidy removal, during the turmoil in Seattle. That could be the first indication that the organization will be forced to open up its processes, including dispute resolution panels, and show more concern for nontrade issues such as the environment than it has in the past, to shed its present image of an isolated and arrogant organization. The Battle of Seattle may therefore open up some new opportunities for changing how the environment is treated in the world trade system.

THE POLITICS AND ECONOMICS
OF GLOBAL FOREST LOSS

Although the global economy and the world trade system affect many environmental issues, one issue continues to defy the creation of a single comprehensive regime; yet it is one that has been pushed to the forefront, not by governments but by NGOs through the market. This issue is protection of the world's forests.

Forests cover nearly 3.5 million hectares, or more than one-fourth of the total land area of the world (not including Greenland and Antarctica). However, only about 40 percent of the earth's forests are in relatively undisturbed tracts ("frontier forests") that are large enough to provide habitats for large wildlife species of mammals. Half of those undisturbed forest tracts are **boreal** forests (those slow-growing forests lying between arctic tundra to the north and warmer temperate forests to the south) in Canada, Russia, and Alaska. Forty-four percent of the remaining frontier forests are tropical forests, those located in warm regions within 30 degrees of the equator, whereas only about three percent of the remaining "frontier forests" are temperate forests, which extend through Europe, the United States, parts of Canada, Australia, New Zealand, Chile, and Argentina. The Russian Federation (26 percent), Canada (25 percent), and Brazil (17 percent) account for two-thirds of the world's frontier forests.

Peru, Indonesia, Venezuela, and Colombia account for another 14 percent. When boreal forests are excluded, 75 percent of the world's remaining frontier forests are under serious threat.[50]

Although public awareness of the impact of global deforestation has increased in the last 15 years, it has not slowed the rate of deforestation appreciably. Although the rate of deforestation (forests converted permanently to nonforest uses such as agriculture, highways, or urban settlement) slowed slightly in the 1990s, there is no dispute that deforestation rates remain high in many countries.[51] Between 1980 and 1995, the extent of the world's forests decreased by some 180 million hectares. There was a net increase of 20 million hectares in developed countries, but a net loss of 200 million hectares—an area larger than Mexico—in developing nations.[52] (See Figure 5.1.)

The many causes of forest degradation include overharvesting of industrial wood and fuelwood, overgrazing, fire, insect pests and diseases, storms, and air pollution. Most forests are being cleared to provide land

FIGURE 5.1   Forest Area in 1995 as Compared with 1980

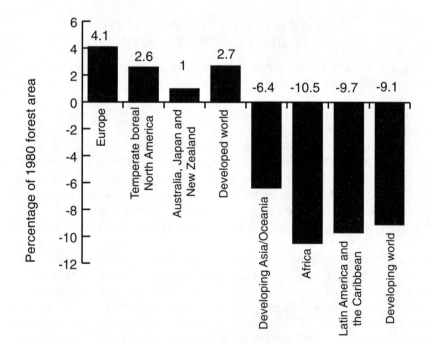

NOTE: Data exclude the countries of the former Soviet Union
SOURCE: FAO, *State of the World's Forests, 1999* (Rome: FAO, 1999)

"And see this ring right here, Jimmy? . . . That's another time when the old fellow miraculously survived some big forest fire."

for food and cash crops. Fuelwood is also the main cooking fuel of nearly half the world's people, the poorest of them. Wood is essential for building construction and a host of other uses. Timber exports are a source of foreign exchange for many countries. Although cutting trees and clearing forests make perfect sense to those who are doing it, as the trees disappear there are also losers. Forest dwellers, often the poorest and most vulnerable members of society, are deprived of their homes and livelihoods. Fuelwood and other forest products become harder to obtain. Flooding results, land is eroded, and lakes and dams are filled with silt. With fewer trees to soak up carbon dioxide from the atmosphere, the risk of global warming is increased. As plant and wildlife species become extinct, biological diversity is reduced.[53]

Forest fires were one of the most visible causes of forest degradation in 1997–1998. These were the worst two years for wildfires and forest fires in recent times. Millions of hectares of forest burned in Brazil, Indonesia, Mexico, and the Russian Federation; all regions of the world were affected; and nearly all types of forests burned. National disasters were declared, and national and international resources were mobilized to fight the fires. Although droughts associated with the unusually strong El Niño weather pattern contributed to the increased number, size, intensity, and duration of fires, land use practices, mainly in agriculture and forestry, were clearly major causes of many fires. For example, in Indonesia, devastating forest fires raged over an estimated area of more than 5 million hectares—an area larger than the Netherlands. A large number of these fires were started to speed up the "conversion" of tropical forests to palm oil plantations.[54]

Commercial logging is largely responsible for tropical forest degradation worldwide. Although loggers rarely clear cut tropical forests, they are the most important factor triggering the process of deforestation. They selectively cut the largest and most valuable trees from primary forests. The number of species extracted may be as low as 1 (where there is a specialty wood, such as mahogany) or as high as 80 to 90 (where there is demand for a wide variety). Logging companies generally show little concern for the condition of residual stands and make no investment in regeneration. They leave debris and open spaces that make the remaining forests more susceptible to fires. Logging roads provide migration routes for the poor, and the removal of the largest trees opens the way for alternative land uses for forests, including small-scale agriculture, export cash crops, and ranching.[55]

Forests have been shrinking in large part because of growth in consumer demand for wood and wood-based products. In the last 35 years, wood consumption has doubled and paper use has more than tripled. Less than one-fifth of the world's population living in Europe, the United States, and Japan consumes over half the world's industrial timber and more than two-thirds of its paper. Japan alone consumes almost as much paper as the entire nation of China, a country with nearly 10 times as many people. Prior to the economic crisis, demand in Asia has been growing faster than anywhere else, with growth rates in the consumption of wood panels more than three times the world average. Having depleted their domestic forests, many Asian timber companies are now moving elsewhere, including Papua New Guinea and the Solomon Islands.[56] The amount of Amazon forest under concession to Asian companies quadrupled in 1996 to more than 12 million hectares.[57]

On the positive side, innovative ways of satisfying the need for forest products less wastefully are also being pursued, from reducing waste in the forest and in processing, to more efficient use of building material, to expanding paper recycling. Over 40 percent of the world's paper is now recovered and recycled; in many countries the proportion is even higher. Recycling worldwide is so successful that today over one-third of the fiber used to make paper comes from recovered paper, up from just under one-quarter in 1970.[58] But recycling alone will not meet the rising demand for paper. Reducing wasteful consumption and shifting to more sustainable forest management are also required.

Forests must be managed sustainably in order to ensure both continuing production of wood products and the continued provision of vital services, such as watershed protection, wildlife habitats, and climate and water regulation. Sustaining the world's forests through the next century and beyond will require reforming domestic forest management policies, recognizing communities' rights to the sustainable use of their forests, and ensuring that forest regulations are effective and are adequately enforced.

Governments have been discussing these issues in international forums for more than a decade. But little progress has been made in building an international regime for the world's forests by establishing meaningful rules or norms for conserving and managing forests sustainably.

North-South Polarization
and the "Forest Principles"

Forests were among the most contentious issues considered at the Earth Summit. Many had hoped that a world forest treaty would be adopted in Rio, along with the climate change and biodiversity conventions. At the July 1990 summit of the G-7 countries in Houston, the United States had proposed a framework convention—one that would have required no binding commitments to forest conservation. Mistakenly thinking such an agreement would be easy to achieve and would help mute environmental criticism at home, where tropical deforestation was a hot topic, the Bush administration viewed such a forest convention as its main UNCED initiative. But at PrepCom II in February 1991, the G-77 rejected the negotiation of a binding agreement before Rio and agreed only to negotiation of a nonbinding Authoritative Statement of Principles on the World's Forests.[59]

Negotiations on the forest principles quickly became polarized between the "global responsibility" approach of the United States and Canada and the "sovereign discretion" approach of Malaysia and India.[60] The United States and Canada tried to link the principle of the sovereignty of countries over their own forest resources with the principles of national responsibility and global concern for forests. Canada, with huge forest resources under rapid development, proposed to establish the principle that forests are of interest to the international community, that international standards should be implemented in forest management, and that targets and time frames should be included in national forestry plans.

But Malaysia and India saw these formulations as an effort to establish the legal principle that forests are "global commons" or part of the "common heritage of mankind," thus giving industrialized countries some right to interfere in the management of the tropical forest countries' resources.[61] Malaysia, as the world's largest exporter of tropical timber, had a particularly intense interest in the issue. It was determined to become a "fully developed country" by 2020, using export earnings from timber and other export crops grown on land converted from forests.[62]

The final version of the forest principles document only hints at the fact that forests are a global environmental issue and drops both the idea of international guidelines for forest management and any reference to trade in "sustainably managed" forest products. It also gives blanket approval to conversion of natural forests to other uses. The agreement was widely regarded by OECD countries as worse than no declaration at all because it appeared to legitimize unsustainable forest management policies.[63] The Forest Principles and Chapter 11 of Agenda 21 reaffirmed the rights of sovereign nations to utilize their forests in accordance with their national priorities and policy objectives. The Rio agreements also stress the cross-sectoral nature of forests and the fact that forests simultaneously provide a wide range of socioeconomic benefits as well as environmental values and services.

New Alliances and Cleavages

The forest principles agreement and the North-South confrontation over the issue seemed to shut the door on global negotiations on forests. Between 1992 and 1995, however, a series of international meetings and ongoing initiatives, including several joint North-South collaborations, began a new process of maneuvering over sustainable forest management. These initiatives included the Conference on Global Partnerships on Forests organized by Indonesia, the India-UK initiative to establish reporting guidelines for forests to the Commission on Sustainable Development (CSD), and Intergovernmental Working Group on Global Forests, convened jointly by Malaysia and Canada, which met twice in 1994, to prepare for the review of the Forest Principles and Chapter 11 of Agenda 21 by the Commission on Sustainable Development in 1995.

These initiatives helped some key forest countries identify areas of common interest and develop a common international agenda on forests.[64] One of the products of the Malaysia-Canada initiative was agreement on what became the Intergovernmental Panel on Forests (IPF). With Canada and Malaysia in the lead, the CSD established the IPF with a two-year mandate to build consensus on 11 priority issues under five interrelated categories of issues: implementation of UNCED decisions related to forests at the national and international level; international cooperation in financial assistance and technology transfer; scientific research, forest assessment, and development of criteria and indicators for sustainable forest management; trade and environment relating to forest products and services; and international organizations and instruments, including the possibility of a forests convention.

It was evident at the outset that the Panel would not be able to deal with all the complex issues on its work program in four sessions, lasting a total of seven working weeks. Consequently, a number of governments, international organizations, and NGOs convened special meetings of experts and workshops and commissioned studies on various aspects of management, conservation, and sustainable development of forests. The outcome of these initiatives had a significant bearing on the IPF's conclusions and proposals for action.[65]

By the time the IPF had completed its work in February 1997, it had developed over 100 proposals for action on issues related to sustainable forest management, including national forest programs; forest assessment; criteria and indicators; traditional forest-related knowledge; and underlying causes of deforestation.[66] These recommendations, most of which related to national forest programs, did not effectively leverage changes in forest management policies and practices. Many involved lengthy texts that did not identify key issues and actions to be taken; others did not clearly indicate whether action should be taken at the national or international level. Relatively few suggested any regulatory measures. And implementation was left to the discretion of the country. No mechanism for reporting or follow-up on the recommendations was created by the IPF, further limiting the recommendations' impact on policy. An intergovernmental paper on the implementation of the IPF proposals in 1999 concluded that it was "difficult to single out the impacts of IPF from those induced by macroeconomic changes and other policy processes."[67]

The issues on which states expressed the strongest disagreement were those involving potential international agreements: financial assistance, trade and sustainable forest management, and a global forest convention. Although major new international initiatives were proposed on each of these issues, the IPF was unable to reach agreement on any of them.

Financial Aid and Technology Transfer. The IPF recognized that existing levels of financing were insufficient for "management, conservation and sustainable development of all types of forests" and that greater investment was needed from "all sources." The G-77 and China noted that private sector capital flows were increasing faster than public funding, and that these investments were often not motivated by environmental considerations. They supported the establishment of an international forest management fund. But some donor countries favored a proposal to invite UNDP and the Bretton Woods institutions, as well as other relevant intergovernmental organizations, to come up with innovative ways to generate additional public and private financial resources to support forest objectives. The Panel discussed various options for an international forest management fund but did not reach an agreement.

Certification and Ecolabeling for Wood Products. One of the issues on which the greatest differences and the most political maneuvering occurred was certification and ecolabeling schemes for wood products. Certification and labeling became international issues after the establishment in 1994 of the Forest Stewardship Council (FSC), an independent, nongovernmental organization that created the world's first third-party ecolabeling scheme for wood products. By 1995 FSC had begun to set standards for sustainable forest management and criteria for potential certifiers to meet and had released a label that could be used to show that a produce is certified by FSC standards. FSC's governing body is comprised of its more than 200 member organizations and individuals equally divided among environmental, social, and economic voting "chambers." FSC hoped to create a market for certified forest products among consumers and to use that market to leverage more sustainable forest management. And "buyers groups" comprised of major retailers had been formed in the UK, accounting for a significant share of the market for wood-based products in that country, pledging to purchase only timber from FSC-certified sources.[68]

Timber industries in a number of major forest countries were disturbed by the prospect of certification of wood products according to a scheme run by an NGO with strong environmentalist influences. In Canada and New Zealand, industry associations created their own alternative certification schemes, based on the environmental management system approach to environmental certification adopted by the International Organization for Standardization (ISO). The ISO 14000 standard for certification of environmental management systems requires that a company have a management plan that is kept up to date, with long-term management objectives and targets; that it monitor the environmental impacts of its activities; and that it work continually to improve its environmental performance. It is possible for a forest company to be certified according to ISO 14000 standards while continuing to clear-cut natural forests and thus make a major contribution to deforestation, as happened in the case of one leading Indonesian pulp and paper company.[69]

Forestry industry associations in Canada, Australia, and New Zealand also lobbied their respective governments to work in favor of a global forest certification system, as a counterweight to the growing influence of the FSC. At the IPF, those three states raised the issue that certification and labeling schemes are "disguised protectionism" and that they may be "used in a discriminatory way." They also argued for the intervention by governments and international organizations to regulate private, voluntary certification and labeling schemes. The EU and NGOs proposed language to soften these proposals, and the United States seemed to be occupying a position somewhere in between, questioning whether the value of certification and labeling schemes for sustainable forest management could be assumed but not supporting proposals for new international regulation.

The final report reflected a careful balance between the Canada–New Zealand–Australia position and the EU position. In the narrative report, it leaned toward an anti-FSC position by saying, "International efforts should focus on ensuring that existing and new certification and labeling schemes are ... not used as a form of disguised protectionism, and are not in conflict with international obligations"—an obvious reference to WTO rules. This language suggested a strategy to get an international policy declaring that the FSC system of certification is a form of trade protectionism that is not GATT-consistent.

But in the "proposals for action," the report urged countries to "consider the potentially mutually supportive relationship between sustainable forest management, trade, and voluntary certification and labeling schemes operating in accordance with national legislation." The antitimber ecolabeling position was then repeated, but with some softening, as countries were urged to "ensure, as necessary, that such schemes are not used as a form of disguised protectionism, and to help to ensure, as necessary that they do not conflict with international obligations."[70]

After the IPF finished its work in 1997, the FSC continued to expand its influence worldwide. By early 1999, the FSC had certified a total of 15 million hectares of forests in 29 countries worldwide, and its close ally, the Worldwide Fund for Nature, had set a goal of reaching 25 million hectares certified by 2001. Nine buyers' groups were operating in Europe, North America, and Australia, and several more were being formed.[71]

The market impact of these developments had already registered with tropical timber exporters. Malaysia's Minister of Primary Industries complained in October 1998 that Malaysia had lost half of its markets for tropical timber products in Europe during the previous two years.[72] Some Malaysian timber exporters had begun to call on the government to make an accommodation with the FSC, and Indonesian exporters, increasingly dependent on European and American markets, were beginning to think about the need for certification acceptable to those markets.[73] Reflecting this new market power, FSC was able to negotiate agreements in 1998–1999 with key institutions in both Malaysia and Indonesia on collaboration on a certification system compatible with the FSC criteria.[74] The FSC was making major strides toward becoming a truly global system for certification and labeling of wood products.

Global Forest Convention. Although the issue of a global forest convention had sharply polarized the UNCED negotiations between North and South, by 1996 that polarization had been replaced by a new alignment of some key tropical forest countries (Malaysia and Indonesia) with Canada and the EU in support of such a convention. Russia also joined this odd coalition. And a number of developing countries supported it in the hope that it would generate new sources of development assistance for forests. But a new international coalition consisting of the United States, Japan, Brazil, Venezuela, Colombia, Peru, Australia, and New Zealand argued against a convention.

Both Malaysia and Canada apparently believed that a global agreement on sustainable forestry could be the basis for an officially sponsored international ecolabel for wood products, which their timber industries could use to fend off pressures for certification by the FSC. Former Canadian natural resources minister Anne McLellan, in a 1997 speech to the Canadian pulp and paper industry, said that Canada was leading a push for a forest convention to secure an internationally recognized ecolabel for wood-based products. She linked the project to the threat to Canada's forestry industry, the country's largest export sector, from environmental protests and boycotts over clear-cutting of old-growth forests.[75] The Canadian government revealed in a paper for the CSD a few weeks later that its proposal would authorize each country to establish its own standards and approaches for achieving sustainable forest management, thus giving the Canadian ISO-based standard an international patina.[76]

Malaysia's surprising turnabout on a global forest convention can similarly be explained in terms of trade-related aims. Malaysia no longer feared that internationally negotiated standards for forest management would threaten its freedom to exploit its forests. Instead it saw the possibility of eliminating through binding agreement the restrictions on its access to export markets in North America and Europe.

The European Union still officially supported negotiation of a binding treaty. Some of its key member states (Germany, France, and Italy) had long been the staunchest supporters of a global forest treaty. German chancellor Helmut Kohl had personally championed it since the issue first arose in 1990. But by 1996, some environmental groups and aid agencies in EU member states had begun to oppose a binding agreement, in part because they saw that no new money would be forthcoming to support it. Germany had started to view it as a potentially dangerous agreement, pushed by some of the very states that had opposed any meaningful norms of forest management at UNCED. And in 1997, the UK and Sweden broke openly with the EU position.[77]

The United States and New Zealand strongly opposed a convention. Forest industry trade associations in both countries opposed a binding treaty dealing with forestry management, regardless of the intentions of the Canadian and Malaysian governments, because they feared that environmentalists would have too much influence on the outcome.[78] Brazil's strong resistance to any binding treaty on forests reflected similar fears about environmental requirements finding their way into the agreement. The forest convention issue thus shows how different states—and the timber industry in different countries—can share the same political and economic interests (in this case freedom from third-party certification by a system that the industry didn't trust) but come out on opposite sides of the issue because of differing assessments of the situation.

NGOs in the United States and Europe, which had generally been enthusiastic about a forest convention in the early 1990s, strongly opposed it in the IPF. The fact that the main sponsors were major exporters of forest products led NGOs to fear that they wanted to use a convention to promote free trade in forest products.[79] At IPF-4 in February 1997, over 80 environmental organizations signed an International Citizens Declaration Against a Global Forest Convention.

In the end, the IPF was unable to agree on any recommendation on a global forest convention. The Panel proposed the following three options to the CSD: to continue the policy dialogue within existing forums; to continue the dialogue through another intergovernmental forum under the Commission for Sustainable Development; or to establish under the authority of the UN General Assembly an intergovernmental negotiating committee on a legally binding instrument. The Commission declined to take a decision and passed it to the UN General Assembly Special Session to review implementation of Agenda 21, which in June 1997 agreed to establish an Intergovernmental Forum on Forests under the auspices of the CSD.[80] In other words, governments supported the need for dialogue but could advance matters no further than the status quo.

Canada did not given up its aim of getting agreement on a global forest convention. It pursued the issue in the institutional successor to the IPF, the Intergovernmental Forum on Forests, beginning in 1998. And during 1999, it organized a series of six "expert meetings" and "regional consultations" that focused mainly on the case for a forest convention. But the existence of a coalition of industrialized and developing states inflexibly opposed to negotiating on a forest treaty doomed the Canadian effort.

Intergovernmental Forum on Forests. The Intergovernmental Forum on Forests (IFF), which held its first meeting in October 1997 and concluded its work in February 2000, was charged with promoting and facilitating implementation of the IPF's proposals for action; reviewing, monitoring, and reporting on progress in the management, conservation, and sustainable development of all types of forests; and considering matters left pending by the Panel, in particular trade, finance and technology transfer, and a possible forest convention.

The same issues that stymied the IPF continued to prove difficult for the IFF to resolve. Trade and sustainable forest management issues continued to provide some of the most intense debates, along the same lines as the IPF. Long-held differences between developed and developing countries on the financial resources and the provision of new technology also remained unresolved.

Although the IFF did succeed in producing conclusions and proposals for action on all of the issues under its mandate, delegates failed to reach a consensus on many key issues left pending from the IPF. For example on finance, the Forum could not agree on any of the three options advocated by some participating states: a new financial mechanism, creation of an international forest fund, or exploring expansion of the GEF's scope to include a wider range of sustainable forest management activities. The Forum spent long hours discussing voluntary certification and/or labeling schemes and agreed that such schemes should not lead to unjustifiable obstacles to market access, but it disagreed on what the role of the WTO should be in this regard. The Forum was also unable to reach agreement on an action proposal linking intellectual property rights and traditional forest-related knowledge in the development of mechanisms to realize benefits of such knowledge.

On the question of a forest convention, the debate proceeded along the same lines as the IPF had three years earlier. After round-the-clock negotiations, delegates agreed to recommend to the CSD that the UN establish an intergovernmental body called the UN Forum on Forests and, within five years, "consider with a view to recommending the parameters of a mandate for developing a legal framework on all types of forests." The language is sufficiently obscure that both proconvention and anticonvention coalitions felt they had achieved a successful outcome to the negotiations. A new "permanent" forum will be established, but the question of a future convention has not been ruled out. As one delegate confided after the negotiations, "In five years time, a vast array of lawyers will spend large amounts of public money trying to interpret what the negotiators meant."[81]

Other Initiatives in Support of Sustainable Forest Management. While negotiations continue under the auspices of the IFF, a number of other initiatives are under way to try to bridge the North-South gap and promote sustainable forest management. For example, more than 150 countries are currently participating in international processes aimed at the development and implementation of national-level criteria and indicators for sustainable forest management. Criteria and indicators are tools for assessing national trends in forest conditions and forest management. Whereas "criteria" define the essential components of sustainable forest management, "indicators" are ways to measure or describe a criterion. Together they provide a common framework for describing, monitoring, and evaluating progress toward sustainable forest management.[82]

Current efforts are grouped into seven regional and ecoregional initiatives.[83] These initiatives differ somewhat in content and/or structure, including the number of national-level criteria, the level of assessment considered (national level versus forest level and/or regional or global level), and the number and array of indicators. Nevertheless, they are similar in objectives and approach. They all incorporate, in some fashion, the following elements of criteria for sustainable forest management: extent of forest resources; biological diversity; forest health and vitality; productive functions of forests; protective functions of forests; socioeconomic benefits and needs; and legal, policy, and institutional framework.[84]

The initiatives to establish criteria and indicators by which progress toward sustainable forest management could be measured represent potential bases for international mechanisms that could hold governments accountable for such progress. But thus far there have been no commitments either to reporting data on the criteria and indicators or to meeting targets for any of the indicators. So it is not clear if these exercises will have any impact on actual forest management.

Is a Global Forest Regime Possible?

The experience of the past decade in international discussions and negotiations on forests suggests that it may not be possible to create a regime for conserving and sustainably managing the world's forests. The international negotiations have been dominated by states whose interests have been to avoid any international norms, whether binding or nonbinding, that could restrict the freedom of their timber industries to exploit forests or the freedom of their agroindustries to convert forests for commercial crops. Some of these states, who vetoed even the mildest expression of a global interest in sustainable forest management during the UNCED negotiations, have been on the offensive, pushing their own free trade agenda since 1995.

Indeed, with the emergence of an independent system of forest certification and labeling, the most contentious issues have been provoked by initiatives taken by these states to remove private, nongovernmental potential restrictions on their markets. And instead of pressing the international community for more ambitious actions in support of forest conservation, potential lead states have become more cautious and timid. The EU has been unable to get beyond the issue of a convention, and the

United States has trimmed its sails to avoid major actions that would offend its forestry industry.

It can be argued that the initiative on global forest protection has passed from states to nonstate actors—that the FSC and the sustainable wood buyers' groups that have sprung up in OECD countries, along with cities as purchasing agents, have had a greater impact on the issue of sustainable forestry than the IPF and the IFF combined. They have forced recalcitrant forestry companies to recognize reluctantly that at least some of their markets will increasingly be influenced by concerns about sustainable forest management. Whether this is sufficient to cause real changes in forestry management remains to be seen.

At a deeper level, the absence of proposals for a strong regime is related to the fact that a regime to protect the world's remaining forests would require a system to compensate some states for not converting large parts of their forests for short-term economic benefits. Despite expressions of international concern about forest loss over the years, the wealthy nations have never given serious consideration to the commitment of major financial resources to reverse deforestation in tropical countries such as Indonesia and Brazil. Nor have they been willing to allow the issue of conversion of forests to other uses to interfere with restoring normal trade flows, as was shown in the case of the IMF–World Bank handling of Indonesia's financial crisis in 1998–1999.

Before any meaningful regime for protecting the world's forests can be contemplated, therefore, the issue of the international community's valuation of forests and the economic value of the same forests to the states that have sovereignty over the resources would have to be confronted honestly. The cost of getting an agreement to protect large areas of "frontier forest" in Brazil and Indonesia would be an order of magnitude greater than past bilateral and multilateral assistance for forest conservation and sustainable management. No new international forum on forests can do anything about the continuing hemorrhaging of frontier forests without a fundamental commitment by the world's wealthiest states to the aim of a new understanding about global compensatory arrangements. If that commitment is present, a regime for forests could be shaped either separately or under the umbrella of the existing biodiversity regime.

CONCLUSION: TOWARD EFFECTIVE
GLOBAL ENVIRONMENTAL REGIMES

The stakes in global environmental politics continue to increase as the costs of environmental degradation and of measures to reverse it grow and as global environmental regimes require greater changes in development strategies and production techniques to be effective. At the same time, however, as globalization of investment and liberalization of trade have accelerated, the effectiveness of global environmental policy is increasingly threatened by global *economic* forces and the policies that support them. Thus the ambitious agenda of sustainable development set by the world's leaders in Rio in 1992 is in danger of being overwhelmed by the economic forces that threaten the health of the planet.

In the context of these larger economic forces, is the international community on a path that will bring effective cooperation in reversing the main threats to the global environment? The case studies presented in this book show that, on some issues, states have been able to take collective actions that have stopped or significantly reduced specific environmental threats, such as the taking of endangered species of whales and the poaching of African elephants. In the Antarctic case, they have been able to act preventively on the threat of mineral exploitation. And in the case of the ozone layer, states have devised a regime that has been both innovative in its rule making and effective in phasing out products that were responsible for the damage.

But the successful regimes have in each case had favorable circumstances: a relatively small number of economic actors whose interests were involved and substitute technology that turned out to be cost-effective for the companies in the ozone case, the availability of whale species that were not endangered in the case of whaling, the ability of a few major countries to shut down the market for elephant ivory, and the absence of an urgent need to exploit Antarctic minerals.

In some cases, the international community has not yet been able to reach an effective agreement on global environmental issues involving major economic and social interests, notably forests. The lack of progress toward a forest regime has reflected the veto power wielded by key developing countries in which forests have been a cash cow both for the economies as a whole and for key officials. But potential lead actors have also failed to define the issue in a way that would have contributed to an effective regime, in large part because they are unwilling to do anything that would restrict the global trade in forest products. Nor have the world's major industrialized states been willing to consider compensating some states for not converting large parts of their forests for short-term economic benefits. Slowing the hemorrhaging of the world's forests will require that the wealthy countries consider what value the remaining tropical rain forests have to present and future generations worldwide.

This book has emphasized the importance of continuous international efforts to make environmental regimes effective once they are adopted.

We have shown how regimes can be strengthened by tightening the requirements for regulating activities that are causing the environmental disruption or resource depletion, by improving compliance with those requirements, or by broadening state participation in the regime. The regimes for climate change, biodiversity, and fisheries will need different kinds of strengthening in the next several years in order to become effective in reversing their respective threats. Each of these issues is at a different stage of development and has a unique combination of political and economic dynamics. But for each threat, it will take unprecedented political commitments by major states to create an effective regime.

The climate change regime must be strengthened in all three of these dimensions: It must increase significantly the stringency of commitments of industrialized countries to reducing greenhouse gas emissions, establish a compliance system that does not allow a state to avoid domestic changes in fossil fuel use by fulfilling its commitments through investments in developing countries, and broaden participation by getting U.S. ratification and by finding a way to induce developing countries to control the increases in their emissions.

The biodiversity regime must both tighten up the existing language of the Convention itself and negotiate new, more specific commitments on biodiversity conservation in different kinds of ecosystems (e.g., forests, oceans, mountains). But thus far, the Conference of the Parties to the Convention on Biological Diversity has shown little interest in doing anything to strengthen the regime. As a result the biodiversity regime has little promise of bringing about fundamental changes in land use policies and practices.

The fisheries regime needs strengthening primarily in the compliance system and in participation. The regime for global fisheries management is more complex than any of the others discussed in this book, consisting of both a legally binding regime governing management of straddling fish stocks and highly migratory fish stocks and the nonbinding FAO Code of Conduct for Responsible Fisheries and the FAO International Plan of Action on Managing Fishing Capacity, which apply to all fisheries under national sovereignty. The straddling stocks agreement lacks a conference of the parties, relying entirely on regional fisheries organizations to track compliance, and most of the major fishing states have failed to ratify it. The Code of Conduct, adopted in 1995, has strong and relatively concrete norms for sustainable fisheries management but has a weak system of accountability. The FAO is responsible for reporting on progress in implementing the norms in the agreement, but it has no mandate to monitor and report on the implementation of the norms by individual states, so states feel little or no pressure to conform to the norms. The FAO Plan of Action on Managing Fishing Capacity, which could be the most important part of the regime for overfishing, has the same problem.

But environmental regimes are not the only forces that influence the global environment. The world's global trade and financial institutions—the WTO, the IMF, and the World Bank—have often pursued policies that run counter to the needs of effective global environmental regimes. WTO dispute panels have rendered decisions against unilateral trade measures for environmental purposes that seemed to rule out such measures even in cases of endangered species, not because these measures were protectionist but because they would restrict trade. The WTO's most recent decision on the shrimp/turtle issue suggests the possibility of an accommodation between global trade rules and carefully crafted environmental trade measures, but the issue remains a potential conflict among states and between trade specialists and environmentalists. Also still unresolved is whether the WTO will accommodate the use of trade measures by multilateral environmental agreements.

The IMF and the World Bank have similarly been driven by economic interests that are often in conflict with global cooperation on environmental threats. The Indonesian structural adjustment episode of 1998–1999 demonstrates the unwillingness of those institutions to use their considerable financial power to curb even the most egregious national policies damaging to the global environment when the economy in question is of interest to the world's trade and finance systems. Similarly, the World Bank's refusal to consider phasing out financing traditional fossil fuel development projects reflects the predominance of the same interests in shaping the Bank's policies. These institutions cannot be expected to change their policies unless the finance ministries of the world's major industrialized countries are forced by domestic political pressures to do so.

Multilateral institutions have also helped create global environmental regimes by agenda setting (UNEP, CSD), bringing states together to negotiate (CSD, UNEP, FAO), by monitoring the state of the global environment (UNEP), or by providing financial support for environmental activities (GEF, World Bank, UNDP). But these institutions have generally lacked the resources and the mandate to promote strong regimes. The GEF has funding that can accomplish only a tiny fraction of what is needed to support effective international cooperation in biodiversity, climate, ozone protection, and international waters. UNEP and the CSD are both subject to the vetoes and weak political will of powerful states.

Some observers have argued that global environmental regimes will not be effective until the ability of individual states to veto action is finally overcome. They have proposed a new Global Environmental Organization, paralleling the World Trade Organization, that could impose binding decisions on all member states like a global legislature and even impose sanctions on those that fail to comply with global policies.[85] Such proposals appear to put the cart of effective global regimes ahead of the horse of adequate political will. Without the political will to make greater sacrifices to reverse global environmental degradation, it is clear that the world's major states will not agree to give up their power to choose which regimes to adopt. The real problem that must be addressed is how to raise consciousness of the importance of effective international cooperation on these issues to a significantly higher level in each society. That cannot be accomplished by establishing a new international organization.

The leadership of the highly industrialized countries, beginning with the United States, is a key to effective regimes. The United States is the one state actor without whose leadership any environmental regime is certain to be much weaker. When the United States has been actively engaged in trying to achieve consensus on stronger institutions or actions, it has often been able to overcome reluctance on the part of other industrialized countries, as in the negotiations on ozone depletion, African ele-

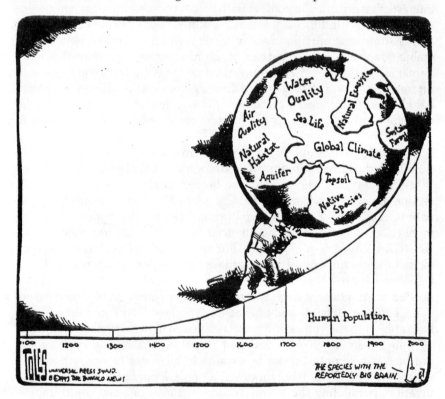

Tom Toles/The Buffalo News © 1993.

phants, whaling, and fish stocks. When the United States has been a veto state, as in the case of climate change and the hazardous waste trade, or has played a much lower-profile role, as in cases of desertification and biodiversity, the resulting regime is weaker because of that role. But the U.S. executive branch has wavered on these issues over the past decade, and Congress has remained a force for reducing U.S. leadership and enforcing a veto role, especially in the climate change negotiations. And the United States has consistently been a veto state on the issue of committing adequate funding to global environmental threats.

The Group of Eight industrialized countries must also give greater weight to the global environment in their foreign policies and global economic policies than in the past. Japan and Canada have been part of the veto coalition rather than helping to strengthen the climate regime, and the EU and Japan have not even ratified the UN straddling stocks agreement. Without leadership from the key industrialized states, there is little hope for effective global regimes for these key issues.

Developing-country governments, too, must move beyond simply demanding technology transfer and financial assistance and must participate fully in global environmental regimes, particularly those for biodiversity, forests, climate change, and fisheries. But it may be unrealistic. They need to take new initiatives for North-South bargains in which developing countries accept new commitments in each of the major areas in return for financial or other forms of compensation. In the case of the fisheries regime, for example, key developing-country fishing states might agree to ratify and implement the straddling stocks agreement in return for commitments by other distant-water fishing states to give them a larger share of the catch in regional fisheries organizations.

There is increasing awareness among business groups of the implications of both global environmental threats and global environmental regimes for their interests. As a result, more and more corporations and trade associations have been playing an active role in global environmental politics. With the realization that many environmental treaties could impose significant new costs on them or otherwise reduce expected profits, they have recognized that early involvement in the negotiating process will often bring long-term benefits once the regime is in place. This involvement can in some cases have a beneficial impact on the outcome. For example, during the Montreal Protocol negotiations, U.S. chemical companies that manufactured CFCs saw the writing on the wall and started to develop CFC alternatives. The chemical companies thus enabled the U.S. negotiators to take a stronger position and emerge as a lead state in the negotiations. On the opposite side, however, corporations and industry associations can also work to defeat strong international environmental measures. The Global Climate Information Project 1997 campaign against greenhouse gas emissions, for example, had a major impact on U.S. public and congressional support for the Kyoto Protocol.

In a political arena in which both regime negotiations and the policies of global economic institutions are determined by states, and especially their trade and finance ministries, domestic political support for new political commitments on global environmental issues will have to be built state by state. None of this will happen without environmental movements that can influence national opinion in those countries. The worldwide NGO movement continues to become more sophisticated in cooperating across national boundaries and regions, especially through use of electronic mail and the Internet. International NGO networks on biodiversity and desertification are mapping strategies for monitoring treaty implementation in every country and ensuring popular participation in national action programs and strategies. TRAFFIC continues to monitor the international trade in endangered species. The global climate network is continuing to develop its technical expertise in analyzing climate action plans. International NGOs such as Greenpeace and WWF are contributing substantial ideas for negotiations on land-based sources of marine pollution and fisheries. Nevertheless, the most important challenge to the NGO movement will be to build political pressure on reluctant states to support participation in or strengthening of global environmental regimes.

The fundamental paradigm shift and the profound social and political transformation needed for a sustainable planet may be under way, but they are still far from complete, and the most difficult political decisions still lie ahead. Underneath the fluctuations of electoral politics and economic cycles, an inexorable trend toward more effective cooperation on global environmental threats can already be seen. The question is whether that cooperation will develop rapidly enough to stave off and reverse those threats.

□ □ □

Discussion Questions

CHAPTER ONE

1. Discuss the ways in which population and environmental factors interact. What is the effect on forests? On energy? Why is per capita consumption an issue?

2. Why are global environmental trends an issue now? Why weren't they an issue before the 1970s? What has changed physically and in terms of consciousness?

3. What is a veto state? Why is it so important in global environmental politics?

4. How are global environmental politics different from security and global economic politics? How are they similar to human rights politics?

5. According to the different theoretical approaches described in this chapter, what factors make it easier or more difficult to achieve strong international agreement on a global environmental issue?

6. What is sustainable development? What are the differences in understanding of the concept? If pursued in the United States, how do you think it would change our economy and lifestyles? What are its implications for developing countries? For North-South relations?

CHAPTER TWO

1. How have industries affected international environmental issues in the past? In what ways, and why, is that role changing?

2. In what ways do the domestic politics of various states influence their policies toward global environmental issues?

3. Why may some states feel that there are "winners" and "losers" in a particular proposal for international cooperation on the environment, even though it may be in the interests of all states?

4. Why are multilateral banks, commercial banks, and bilateral development-assistance programs important to global environmental politics?

5. Why have environmental NGOs grown in importance in global environmental politics in the past decade?

6. What NGOs would you expect in a coalition on ozone depletion? The climate convention? The biodiversity convention? Why? What governments would they befriend or attack?

7. How does the role of particular U.S. industries affect the position of the U.S. government on international issues?

8. Make up a profile of any of the states frequently mentioned in this chapter—the OECD countries, China, India, Indonesia, Mexico, Brazil, Malaysia—and describe how active they are in lead or blocking roles. Could you do the same for the former Soviet Union? What other countries are conspicuously absent?

9. When might "soft law" take on the characteristics of an international agreement?

10. How has technology contributed to the growing influence and effectiveness of the environmental NGOs in the past decade?

CHAPTER THREE

1. On which global environmental issues has new scientific evidence altered the positions of government negotiators? On what other issues might it be relevant? To which has it been irrelevant? Why?

2. Consider the veto coalitions opposing strong action on the issues in this chapter. What are the primary motives of each individual member? What are the reasons for those coalitions' weakening?

3. Trace the role of specific environmental NGOs such as Friends of the Earth, Greenpeace, Environmental Defense Fund, or World Wildlife Fund through the regimes discussed in this chapter. Which appear to be most active on which issues?

4. Trace the role of a particular state on a variety of issues and try to assess the extent of its involvement in leadership or blocking roles.

5. What might be the effect of growing economic prosperity or recession in the United States or other countries on the specific global environmental issues discussed?

6. Discuss two framework conventions and the political, economic, and environmental factors that influenced their evolutions.

CHAPTER FOUR

1. What are some of the problems encountered with regard to submission and analysis of compliance data by parties to a convention? How might some of these problems be overcome?

2. What is the role of NGOs in monitoring compliance with an environmental convention? Give some specific examples.

3. What options for strengthening compliance with an agreement do you think may be the most effective in the short term? Why?

4. Why have ODA levels decreased since 1992? What effect does this trend have on compliance with international environmental agreements?

5. Why were developing countries dissatisfied with the original governing structure of the GEF? How were these concerns rectified?

6. What are some of the options available for generating additional financial support for the implementation of global environmental conventions? Which do

you think would generate the most funds? How would you overcome political resistance to this option?

CHAPTER FIVE

1. In what ways are the interests of developing countries and industrialized countries at odds over global environmental issues? In what sense are they compatible?

2. Explain how developing countries' concerns about economic growth and jobs might affect their position on ozone depletion or the climate treaty. Why would their position on the Basel Convention (to control international trade in toxic wastes) be different?

3. What is the relationship between consumption and production patterns and environmental degradation?

4. Explain how trade and environmental patterns affect each other. What are the main impacts of each on the other?

5. Compare the trade/environment issue with other global environmental issues of the regimes discussed in Chapter 3. Is the GATT an environmental regime in any sense? Why or why not?

6. How might previous trade experience with the United States sharpen European or developing-country concern about possible U.S. environmental trade measures?

7. What are some of the underlying causes of deforestation? Do you think that an international forest treaty could effectively address these issues?

8. What has been the difference between the UNCED and the post-UNCED international forest policy debate? What has influenced this change? Do you think it has made a difference in terms of fostering sustainable forest management at the local and national levels?

□ □ □

Notes

CHAPTER ONE

1. World Resources Institute (WRI), *World Resources 1998–99* (New York: Oxford University Press, 1998), p. 139.

2. The facts and figures in this paragraph are from A. Adriaanse et al., *Resource Flows: The Material Basis of Industrial Economies*, a joint publication of the World Resources Institute (WRI); the Wuppertal Institute; the Netherlands Ministry of Housing, Spatial Planning, and the Environment; and the National Institute for Environmental Studies (Washington, D.C.: WRI, 1997).

3. Nick Robins, *Sustainable Consumption: The Way Ahead*, presentation at the International Conference on Clean Technologies, February 12–13, 1999, New Delhi, India. [Internet: http://www.iied.org/scati/pub/cii-spee.htm]

4. UNDP, *Human Development Report 1998* (New York: UNDP, 1998).

5. United Nations Population Division, "World Population Nearing 6 Billion; Projected Close to 9 Billion by 2050" (New York: UN Population Division, 1998). [Internet: http://www.popin.org/pop1998/1.htm]

6. United Nations Commission on Sustainable Development, "Comprehensive Review of Changing Consumption and Production Patterns: Report of the Secretary-General," E/CN.17/1999/2, January 13, 1999, p. 7.

7. World Resources Institute, *World Resources 1998–99* (New York: Oxford University Press, 1998), p. 170.

8. International Energy Agency, *World Energy Outlook 1996* (Paris: IEA, 1996).

9. Douglas Southgate, "Tropical Deforestation and Agricultural Development in Latin America," World Bank, Environment Department, Divisional Working Paper no. 1991–20, March 1990.

10. Alex de Sherbinnin, *Population and Consumption Issues for Environmentalists* (Washington, D.C.: Population Reference Bureau for the Pew Charitable Trusts' Global Stewardship Initiative, October 1993), pp. 18–20.

11. National Science Board Task Force on Global Biodiversity, *Loss of Biological Diversity: A Global Crisis Requiring International Solutions* (Washington, D.C.: National Science Foundation, 1989), pp. 1, 3; interview with E. O. Wilson, "All Creatures, Great and Small," *Defenders*, September–October 1992, p. 10.

12. Richard Grainger and Serge Garcia, *Chronicles of Marine Fishery Landings (1950–1994): Trend Analysis and Fisheries Potential*, FAO Fisheries Technical Paper 359 (Rome: Food and Agriculture Organization, 1996), p. 31.

13. World Meteorological Organization, *Comprehensive Assessment of the Freshwater Resources of the World* (Geneva: WMO, 1997), p. 9.

14. Paul Raskin, "Water Futures: Assessment of Long-Range Patterns and Problems," background document to the *Comprehensive Assessment of the Freshwater Resources of the World* report (Geneva: WMO, 1997), p. 23.

15. Ibid., pp. 20–21.

16. United Nations Population Division, *World Urbanization Prospects: The 1996 Revision*, Annex Tables (New York: United Nations, 1997), pp. 44, 48.

17. World Resources Institute, *World Resources Report 1996–97* (New York: Oxford University Press, 1996), p. 3.

18. United Nations, *Fourth Review and Appraisal of the World Population Plan of Action* (A/CONF.17/PC/3), March 1, 1994, p. 19.

19. For an early effort to categorize the different types of international environmental problems, see Clifford S. Russell and Hans H. Landsberg, "International Environmental Problems—A Taxonomy," *Science* 172 (June 25, 1972), pp. 1307–1314.

20. Oran R. Young, *International Governance* (Ithaca: Cornell University Press, 1994), pp. 19–26.

21. Ibid., p. 23.

22. Ibid., p. 25.

23. Agreement on the Cartagena Protocol on Biosafety was reached in Montreal in January 2000. See Chapter 3.

24. See Susan Strange, "Cave! Hic Dragones: A Critique of Regime Analysis," *International Organization* 36 (Spring 1982), pp. 479–496.

25. This paragraph is adapted from I. William Zartman, *The 50% Solution* (New Haven: Yale University Press, 1983), pp. 9–10.

26. Oran Young, *International Cooperation* (Ithaca: Cornell University Press, 1989), pp. 13–14.

27. M'Gonigle and Zacher, *Pollution, Politics and International Law* (Berkeley: University of California Press, 1979), pp. 58–59, 84–85, 93–96; Jan Schneider, *World Public Order of the Environment: Toward an International Ecological Law and Organization* (Toronto: University of Toronto Press, 1979), pp. 33, 92–93.

28. For an analytical overview of theoretical approaches, see Stephan Haggard and Beth A. Simmons, "Theories of International Regimes," *International Organization* 41 (Summer 1987), pp. 491–517.

29. Robert O. Keohane and Joseph S. Nye, *Power and Interdependence* (Boston: Little, Brown, 1977), pp. 50–51.

30. For the former approach, see Robert Gilpin, *The Political Economy of International Relations* (Princeton: Princeton University Press, 1987); Joseph M. Grieco, "Anarchy and the Limits of Cooperation: A Realist Critique of the Newest Liberal Institutionalism," *International Organization* 42 (Summer 1988), pp. 485–508; and Strange, "Cave! Hic Dragones," pp. 337–343. Susan Strange, "The Persistent Myth of Lost Hegemony," *International Organization* 41 (Summer 1987), p. 570, argues that the erosion of international regimes has been caused by inconsistency in U.S. policy rather than the loss of U.S. global hegemony per se.

31. Oran R. Young, "The Politics of International Regime Formation: Managing Natural Resources and the Environment," *International Organization* 43 (Summer 1989), p. 355.

32. Fen Osler Hampson, "Climate Change: Building International Coalitions of the Like-Minded," *International Journal* 45 (Winter 1989–1990), pp. 36–74.

33. Robert O. Keohane, Peter M. Haas, and Marc A. Levy, "The Effectiveness of International Environmental Institutions," in Robert O. Keohane, Peter M. Haas, and Marc A. Levy, eds., *Institutions for the Earth* (Cambridge, Mass.: MIT Press, 1993), pp. 4–5.

34. See Peter M. Haas, "Do Regimes Matter? Epistemic Communities and Mediterranean Pollution Control," *International Organization* 43 (Summer 1989), pp. 378–403.

35. The issue of ocean dumping of radioactive wastes, in which scientific evidence was explicitly rejected as the primary basis for decisionmaking by antidumping states, is analyzed in Judith Spiller and Cynthia Hayden, "Radwaste at Sea: A New Era of Polarization or a New Basis for Consensus?" *Ocean Development and International Law* 19 (1988), pp. 345–366.

36. Robert Putnam, "Diplomacy and Domestic Politics: The Logic of Two-Level Games," *International Organization* 42, 3 (Summer 1988), pp. 427–460.

37. The description of paradigm shifts is not offered as a new theory to compete with existing theories of international regimes. Rather this is supposed to represent a new and supplementary set of lenses through which to discuss environmental issues.

38. Harold and Margaret Sprout, *The Ecological Perspective in Human Affairs* (Princeton: Princeton University Press, 1965); Kenneth Boulding, "The Economics of the Coming Spaceship Earth," in H. E. Jarrett, ed., *Environmental Quality in a Growing Economy* (Baltimore: Johns Hopkins University Press, 1966).

39. For an analysis of neoclassical economic assumptions as they bear on environmental management, see Daniel A. Underwood and Paul G. King, "On the Ideological Foundations of Environmental Policy," *Ecological Economics* 1 (1989), pp. 317–322.

40. See Michael E. Colby, *Environmental Management in Development: The Evolution of Paradigms* (Washington, D.C.: World Bank, 1990).

41. John McCormick, *Reclaiming Paradise: The Global Environmental Movement* (Bloomington: Indiana University Press, 1989), p. 67.

42. See Clem Tisdell, "Sustainable Development: Differing Perspectives of Ecologists and Economists, and Relevance to LDCs," *World Development* 16 (1988), pp. 377–378.

43. Donella H. Meadows et al., *The Limits to Growth* (New York: Universe Books, 1972); Global 2000 Study, *Global 2000 Report* (New York: Pergamon Press, 1980).

44. Julian Simon and Herman Kahn, eds., *The Resourceful Earth* (Oxford: Basil Blackwell, 1984).

45. For an account of the background of the sustainable development concept, see United Nations Center for Transnational Corporations, *Environmental Aspects of the Activities of Transnational Corporations: A Survey* (New York: United Nations, 1985).

46. See World Commission on Environment and Development, *Our Common Future* (Oxford: Oxford University Press, 1987).

47. See Jim MacNeill, "Sustainable Development, Economics and the Growth Imperative," paper presented at the conference "The Economics of Sustainable Development," Smithsonian Institution, Washington, D.C., January 23–26, 1990.

48. See Edith Brown Weiss, "In Fairness to Future Generations," *Environment* 32 (April 1990), pp. 7ff. See similar arguments made in *Our Own Agenda*, report of the Latin American and Caribbean Commission on Development and Environment (Washington, D.C., and New York: Inter-American Development Bank and United Nations Development Programme, 1990).

49. See Alan Durning, "How Much Is Enough?" *Worldwatch* 3 (November-December 1990), pp. 12–19.

50. See Yusuf J. Ahmad, Salah El Serafy, and Ernst Lutz, eds., *Environmental Accounting for Sustainable Development* (Washington, D.C.: World Bank, 1989). For a concrete example of how natural resources accounting would work, see Robert Repetto et al., *Accounts Overdue: Natural Resources Depreciation in Costa Rica* (Washington, D.C.: World Resources Institute, 1991).

51. See Partha Dasgupta and Karl Goran Maler, "The Environment and Emerging Development Issues," paper presented at the World Bank Conference on Development Economics, April 26–27, 1990, pp. 14–20; Herman E. Daly, "Toward a Measure of Sustainable Social Net National Product," in Ahmad, Serafy, and Lutz, eds., *Environmental Accounting for Sustainable Development*, pp. 8–9; and Herman E. Daly and John B. Cobb, Jr., *For the Common Good: Redirecting the Economy Toward Community, the Environment and a Sustainable Future* (Boston: Beacon Press, 1989), pp. 368–373, 401–455. A similar effort to rate the distributive effects of national policies is embodied in the United Nations Development Programme's human development indicators in its annual *Human Development Report*. [Internet: http://www.undp.org/hdro/]

52. See, for example, Dasgupta and Maler, "The Environment and Emerging Issues," p. 22.

53. See Robert Repetto, *Promoting Environmentally Sound Economic Progress: What the North Can Do* (Washington, D.C.: World Resources Institute, 1990); and Daly, "Toward a Measure of Sustainable Social Net National Product."

54. Economic *Policies for Sustainable Development*, ministerial brief, Conference on Environment and Development in Asia and the Pacific, October 10–16, 1990, Bangkok, Thailand (Manila: Asian Development Bank, October 1990); Latin American and Caribbean Commission on Development and Environment, *Our Own Agenda*; and Organization of American States, Permanent Council, *Status Report Submitted by the Chairman of the Special Working Group on the Environment* (Washington, D.C.: General Secretariat of the OAS, February 6, 1991).

55. Al Gore, *Earth in the Balance: Ecology and the Human Spirit* (Boston: Houghton Mifflin, 1992), as cited in Gary C. Bryner, *From Promises to Performance: Achieving Global Environmental Goals* (New York: W. W. Norton, 1997), p. 329.

56. *Agenda 21, Rio Declaration, and Forest Principles* (New York: UN, 1992), Chapters 23–32: the final text of agreements negotiated by governments at the UNCED, June 3–14, 1992, Rio de Janeiro, Brazil. "Major groups" include women, youth, indigenous peoples, NGOs, local authorities, unions, business, the science and technology community, and farmers.

57. Ibid. See especially Chapter 8 of Agenda 21.

58. See the text of "International Policies to Accelerate Sustainable Development in Developing Countries and Related Domestic Policies," based on negotiations on A/CONF.151/PC/100 Add.3 (no date), pp. 10–11. The final version of that section of Agenda 21 calls only for further negotiations between debtor countries and creditor banks but no action by governments. And it fails to use the usual "should" in regard to reducing bilateral debt. "Report of the United Nations Conference on Environment and Development," A/CONF.151/26 (vol. 1), August 12, 1992, Section 1, Chapter 2, pp. 26–27.

59. Cf. "International Policies," pp. 2–4; and "Report of the United Nations Conference," p. 20.

60. *Earth Summit Update*, no. 8 (April 1992), p. 8.

61. United Nations Development Programme, "UNDP Commits to Follow-up Activities to Assist Small Island Developing States," *Update* 7, no. 10 (May 23, 1994), p. 2; "Summary of the UN Global Conference on the Sustainable Development of Small Island Developing States, 25 April–6 May 1994," *Earth Negotiations Bulletin* 8, no. 28 (May 9, 1994); *Environment Australia's International Agenda* (Washington, D.C.: Embassy of Australia, January 1994); and *Earth Negotiations Bulletin* 8, no. 31 (October 1, 1999).

62. For a range of assessments of the outcomes of the Rio conference, see Michael Grubb et al., *The Earth Summit Agreements: A Guide and Assessment* (London: Royal Institute of International Affairs and Earthscan, 1993); Pratap Chatterjee and Matthias Finger, *The Earth Brokers* (London and New York: Routledge, 1994), pp. 39–60; Peter M. Haas, Marc A. Levy, and Edward A. Parson, "Appraising the Earth Summit," *Environment*, October 1992, pp. 7–11, 26–33; Marc Pallemaerts, "International Law from Stockholm to Rio: Back to the Future?" and Ileana Porras, "The Rio Declaration: A New Basis for International Cooperation," in Philippe Sands, ed., *Greening International Law* (London: Earthscan, 1993), pp. 1–34; and Ken Conca and Geoffrey D. Dabelko, "The Earth Summit," in Ken Conca and Geoffrey D. Dabelko, eds., *Green Planet Blues*, 2nd edition (Boulder, Colo.: Westview, 1998), pp. 161–167.

63. Tariq Banuri, "The Landscape of Diplomatic Conflicts," in Wolfgang Sachs, ed., *Global Ecology: A New Arena of Political Conflict* (London: Zed Books, 1993), p. 63.

64. J. Baird Callicott and Fernando J. R. da Rocha, eds., *Earth Summit Ethics: Toward a Reconstructive Postmodern Philosophy of Environmental Education* (Albany: SUNY Press, 1996), pp. 3–4.

65. Tommy Koh, "Five After Rio and Fifteen Years After Montego Bay: Some Personal Reflections," *Environmental Policy and Law* 27, no. 4 (1997), p. 242.

66. Reg Green, "Priorities for the Future," in *Earth Summit '92: The United Nations Conference on Environment and Development* (London: Regency Press, 1992), p. 35.

67. Ken Conca and Geoffrey D. Dabelko, eds., *Green Planet Blues*, 2nd edition (Boulder, Colo.: Westview, 1998), pp. 136–137.

CHAPTER TWO

1. It has been argued by some, on the basis of game-theoretic approaches, that a unilateral move to regulate an activity by a state would have the effect of discour-

aging other states from joining a collective effort to regulate the problem because it invites free-riding. However, this logic fails to take into account the effect of domestic and international public pressures on states to act on global commons issues and the value of leading by example to such efforts.

2. David Day, *The Whale War* (Vancouver and Toronto: Douglas and MacIntyre, 1987), pp. 103–107.

3. Michael M'Gonigle and Mark W. Zacher, *Pollution, Politics and International Law: Tankers at Sea* (Berkeley: University of California Press, 1979).

4. See Peter Dauvergne, *Shadows in the Forest* (Cambridge, Mass.: MIT Press, 1997), pp. 59–98; David W. Brown, *Addicted to Rent: Corporate and Spatial Distribution of Forest Resources in Indonesia* (Jakarta: Indonesia-UK Tropical Forest Management Programme, 1999).

5. Richard Benedick, *Ozone Diplomacy* (Cambridge, Mass.: Harvard University Press, 1991), p. 59.

6. John McCormick, *Acid Earth: The Global Threat of Acid Pollution* (London: Earthscan, 1985), pp. 88–90.

7. The German Green Party lost all of its parliamentary members in the first all-German elections since 1932 because it opposed reunification, but it had begun to rebound by mid-1991, when polls showed it had the support of 6 percent of the voters—above the 5 percent needed to achieve representation in the parliament. The Green Party won 34 seats in the German Parliament in 1998 and made history by becoming part of a coalition government with the Social Democratic Party.

8. Denmark has the highest ratio of environmental organization membership in the entire world: The combined memberships of its environmental organizations are greater than the total population of the country. Brian Wynne, "Implementation of Greenhouse Gas Reductions in the European Community: Institutional and Cultural Factors," *Global Environmental Change Report*, March 1993, pp. 113, 122.

9. *UNEP News*, September–October 1987, p. 12. Since Prime Minister John Howard was elected in 1996, there has been a major shift in Australia's environmental policy.

10. *Earth Summit Update*, no. 7 (March 1992), p. 3.

11. Carolyn Thomas, *The Environment in International Relations* (London: Royal Institute of International Affairs, 1992), p. 228.

12. On EU ambitions for global leadership on the environment, see Wynne, "Implementation of Greenhouse Gas Reductions," p. 102; Paleokrassas is quoted in *Energy, Economics and Climate Change*, July 1994, p. 14.

13. *Washington Post*, June 9, 1992.

14. Press release, City of Portland, Oregon, November 10, 1993; *Worldwatch*, March–April 1994, p. 7.

15. *Environmental News from the Netherlands*, no. 2 (1992), pp. 7–8.

16. Personal communication from Jaime Lerner, Mayor, Curitiba, Brazil, May 8, 1993. As a follow-up to UNCED, the mayor of Manchester, England, hosted a world conference, "Cities and Sustainable Development," in October 1993.

17. For a discussion of California's international interests, see James O. Goldsborough, "California's Foreign Policy," *Foreign Affairs*, Spring 1993, pp. 88–96.

18. Eric Rodenburg, *Eyeless in Gaia: The State of Global Environmental Monitoring* (Washington, D.C.: World Resources Institute, 1991); "Tropical Deforestation: Not Just a Problem in Amazonia," *Science* 259 (March 5, 1993), p. 1390.

19. Remarks by UNEP Executive Director Elizabeth Dowdeswell, Washington, D.C., October 14, 1994.

20. Richard Elliott Benedick, "The Ozone Protocol: A New Global Diplomacy," *Conservation Foundation Letter*, no. 4 (1989), pp. 6–7; and *Ozone Diplomacy* (Cambridge: Harvard University Press, 1991), pp. 109–110.

21. "Discussion of Major UNEP Priority Activities with Executive Director," n.d.

22. For more details on the challenges that UNEP faced in the latter half of the 1990s, see David L. Downie and Marc A. Levy, "The United Nations Environment Programme at a Turning Point: Options for Change," in Pamela S. Chasek, ed., *The Global Environment in the 21st Century: Prospects for International Cooperation* (Tokyo: UNU Press, 2000).

23. For more information on the CSD, see Pamela Chasek, "The United Nations Commission on Sustainable Development: The First Five Years," in Pamela S. Chasek, ed., *The Global Environment in the 21st Century: Prospects for International Cooperation* (Tokyo: UNU Press, 2000).

24. Peter H. Sand has described these soft-law alternatives to treaties in *Lessons Learned in Global Environmental Governance* (Washington, D.C.: World Resources Institute, 1990), pp. 16–17.

25. See Khalil Sesmou, "The Food and Agriculture Organization of the United–Nations: An Insider's View," *Ecologist* 21 (March–April 1991), pp. 47–56, and other critical analyses in this special issue on the FAO.

26. For FAO's vision of the TFAP, see Committee on Forest Development in the Tropics, Seventh Session, "Draft Proposals for Action Programmes in Tropical Forestry," FAO: FDT/85/3, April 1985. For other assessments of TFAP and FAO's role, see Robert Winterbottom, *Taking Stock: The Tropical Forestry Action Plan After Five Years* (Washington, D.C.: World Resources Institute, 1990); Charles J. Lankester, principal technical adviser, UNDP, "The Earth's Green Mantle," address to World Forestry Charter Gathering, London, December 1989.

27. *International Environment Reporter*, October 10, 1990, p. 427.

28. See "Researchers Score Victory over Pesticides—and Pests—in Asia," *Science* 256 (May 29, 1992), pp. 1272–1273.

29. Michael Hansen, *Sustainable Agriculture and Rural Development: FAO at the Crossroads* (Yonkers, N.Y.: Consumers Union of the United States, 1993), pp. 16–18.

30. United Nations Association of the United States of America, *A Global Agenda: Issues Before the 53rd General Assembly of the United Nations* (New York: Rowman and Littlefield, 1998), p. 127.

31. UNDP, "Implementing the Rio Agreements: A Guide to UNDP's Sustainable Energy and Environment Division" (New York: UNDP, 1997), p. 8. [Internet: http://www.undp.org/seed/guide/intro.htm]

32. See Gareth Porter, Raymond Clémençon, Waafas Ofosu-Amaah, and Michael Philips, *Study of GEF's Overall Performance* (Washington, D.C.: GEF, 1998), pp. 47–51.

33. Documentation and Statistics Office, Bureau for Programme Policy and Evaluation, United Nations Development Programme, *Compendium of Ongoing Projects*, UNDP/Series A/Nos. 22–27, 1992–1996.

34. UNDP, *Compendium of Ongoing Projects as of 31 December 1996*, Series A/no. 27, p. 43.

35. Gareth Porter et al., *Study of GEF's Overall Performance*, p. 49.

36. This formulation is used in the context of a different conceptualization of the role of IOs in global environmental policymaking in Marc A. Levy, Robert O. Keohane, and Peter M. Haas, "Improving the Effectiveness of International Environmental Institutions," in Peter M. Haas, Robert O. Keohane, and Marc A. Levy, eds., *Institutions for the Earth: Sources of Effective International Environmental Protection* (Cambridge, Mass., and London: MIT Press, 1993), p. 400.

37. India, whose high level of defense spending was criticized in the 1994 *Human Development Report*, complained publicly that UNDP's pressure on countries to conform to its norm for allocation of resources was in contradiction to national sovereignty. See Jack Freeman, "Development Report: Southern Nations Attack an Emerging Premise of U.N. Policy," and "What India Told the G-77 About the Report," *Earth Times*, October 15, 1994, pp. 6–7.

38. For a critical analysis of the environmental impacts of various multilateral development bank loans, see Bruce Rich, *Mortgaging the Earth: The World Bank, Environmental Impoverishment, and the Crisis of Development* (Boston: Beacon Press, 1994).

39. Jim Douglas, "World Bank Involvement in Sector Adjustment for Forests in Indonesia: The Issues," unpublished paper, 1998.

40. Gareth Porter et al., *Study of the GEF's Overall Performance*, p. 44.

41. Ibid., pp. 38–43. Note that it takes two to three years for a project to go from initial development to final approval by the Executive Board, so 1994 is the first effective year for comparing Bank lending after its new commitments to the GEF.

42. World Bank Group, "Mainstreaming the Global Environment in World Bank Group Operations," GEF/C/12/6, October 1, 1998, p. 30.

43. Loan totals are from Hagler Baily, Stockholm Environment Institute, and IIEC, *The Effect of a Shadow Price on Carbon Emissions in the Energy Portfolio of the Bank: A Backcasting Exercise*. Final Report to the Global Climate Change Unit, Global Environment Division, World Bank, June 13, 1997, p. I–1; impact on emissions from the Institute for Policy Studies and the International Trade Information Service, *The World Bank and the G-7: Changing the Earth's Climate for Business, 1992–1997* (Washington, D.C.: IPS, 1997). [Internet: http://www.seen.org/wbreport1/index.html]

44. See World Bank, Environment Department, Land, Water and Natural Habitats Division, *The Impact of Environmental Assistance: The World Bank's Experience* (Washington, D.C.: World Bank, 1996), p. xv.

45. Gareth Porter et al. *Study of the GEF's Overall Performance*, p. 45.

46. Ibid., pp. 38–43.

47. World Bank Group, "Mainstreaming the Global Environment in World Bank Group Operations," p. 21.

48. For a defense of the IMF's macroeconomic policy prescriptions in environmental terms, see Ved. P. Gandhi, "The IMF and the Environment" (Washington, D.C.: IMF, 1998).

49. David Reed, ed., *Structural Adjustment and the Environment* (Boulder, Colo.: Westview Press, 1992), esp. pp. 161–178.

50. "IMF Reviews Its Approach to Environmental Issues," *IMF Survey*, April 15, 1991, p. 124.

51. "Seminar Explores Links Between Macro Policy and the Environment," *IMF Survey*, June 14, 1993, p. 192.

52. For more information about the HIPC initiative, see Anthony R. Boote and Kamau Thugge, *Debt Relief for Low-Income Countries; the HIPC Initiative*, Pamphlet Series No. 51 (Washington, D.C.: IMF, 1999), or http://www.imf.org/external/np/hipc/hipc.htm.

53. Ved P. Gandhi, "The IMF and the Environment" (Washington, D.C.: IMF, 1998).

54. See *Jakarta Post*, October 4, 1997.

55. This account of the adjustment loans to Indonesia in 1998–1999 is based on interviews by one of the authors (Gareth Porter) in Jakarta in April 1999.

56. APEC, "APEC Economic Leaders' Declaration," Kuala Lumpur, Malaysia, November 18, 1998. [Internet: http://www.apec.org/leaders_declaration.htm]

57. For more information about SPREP, see the organization's WWW site. [Internet: http://www.sprep.org.ws/]

58. Personal communication with Jorge Cabrera, coordinator of CCAD's small secretariat, March 24, 1994. The treaty, the Regional Convention for the Management and Conservation of Forest Natural Ecosystems and the Development of Forestry Plantations, was signed in Guatemala City by Panama, Costa Rica, Honduras, Guatemala, Nicaragua, and El Salvador in October 1993.

59. For additional information about CCAD, see its WWW site: [Internet: http://www.ccad.org.gt/].

60. See Thomas Weiss and Leon Gordenker, eds., *NGOs, the UN and Global Governance* (Boulder, Colo.: Lynne Rienner, 1996); Paul Wapner, "Politics Beyond the State: Environmental Actions and World Civic Politics," *World Politics* 47, no. 3 (April 1995), pp. 311–340; Thomas Princen and Matthias Finger, eds., *Environmental NGOs in World Politics* (London and New York: Routledge, 1994); and Barbara Bramble and Gareth Porter, "Non-Governmental Organizations and the Making of US International Environmental Policy," in Andrew Hurrell and Benedict Kingsbury, eds., *The International Politics of the Environment* (Oxford: Clarendon Press, 1992).

61. For the official UN definition, see Jens Martens, "NGOs in the U.N. System: The Participation of Non-Governmental Organizations in Environment and Development Institutions of the United Nations," Projectstelle UNCED, DNR/BUND, Bonn, September 1992, p. 4.

62. Greenpeace, *Annual Report 1998* (Amsterdam: Greenpeace, 1999).

63. Transatlantic Environment Dialogue, "Message to the EU-U.S. Summit," Bonn, June 21, 1999.

64. See Julie Fisher, *The Road from Rio: Sustainable Development and the Nongovernmental Movement in the Third World* (Westport, Conn.: Praeger, 1993), pp. 123–128; Nonita Yap, "NGOs and Sustainable Development," *International Journal* 45 (Winter 1989–1990), pp. 75–105.

65. Interview with Barbara Bramble, National Wildlife Federation, March 1990; Stephen Schwartzman, "Deforestation and Popular Resistance in Acre: From Local Movement to Global Network," paper presented to Eighty-eighth Annual Meeting of the American Anthropological Association, Washington, D.C., November 15–19, 1989.

66. David Malin Roodman, "Building a Sustainable Society," in Lester R. Brown, Christopher Flavin, and Hilary French, eds. *State of the World 1999* (New York: W. W. Norton, 1999), p. 183.

67. Working with Merck and Genentech, the World Resources Institute, the World Wildlife Fund, and the Environmental and Energy Study Institute drafted an interpretive statement and persuaded President Clinton to sign the treaty with such a statement attached.

68. Statement by Craig Van Note before the Subcommittee on Human Rights and International Organizations, Committee on Foreign Affairs, U.S. House of Representatives, September 28, 1989.

69. Conversation with Jim Barnes, director, International Program, Friends of the Earth U.S., February 14, 1994.

70. Robert Boardman, *International Organization and the Conservation of Nature* (Bloomington: Indiana University Press, 1981), pp. 88–94.

71. Patricia Birnie, "The Role of International Law in Solving Certain Environmental Conflicts," in John E. Carroll, ed., *International Environmental Diplomacy: The Management and Resolution of Transfrontier Environmental Problems* (Cambridge: Cambridge University Press, 1988), pp. 107–108.

72. Personal communication from a member of the U.S. delegation to the biodiversity negotiations, February 1994.

73. Kal Raustiala, "States, NGOs and International Environmental Institutions," *International Studies Quarterly* 41 (1997), p. 728.

74. The *Earth Negotiations Bulletin* was initially published as the *Earth Summit Bulletin* and was created by Johannah Bernstein, Pamela Chasek, and Langston James Goree VI. For more information, go to: [Internet: http://www.iisd.ca/linkages/].

75. Kal Raustiala, "States, NGOs and International Environmental Institutions," p. 730.

76. Laura H. Kosloff and Mark C. Trexler, "The Convention on International Trade in Endangered Species: No Carrot, But Where's the Stick?" *Environmental Law Reporter* 17 (July 1987), pp. 10225–10226.

77. Paul Lewis, "Rich Nations Plan $2 Billion for Environment," *New York Times*, March 17, 1994. Also, see Zoe Young, "NGOs and the Global Environmental Facility: Friendly Foes?" *Environmental Politics* 8, no. 1 (1999), pp. 243–267. For an additional discussion of the GEF, see Chapter 4.

78. This discussion is based on Barbara J. Bramble and Gareth Porter, "Non-Governmental Organizations and the Making of U.S. International Environmental Policy," in Andrew Hurrell and Benedict Kingsbury, eds., *The International Politics of the Environment* (Oxford, UK: Clarendon Press, 1992), pp. 325–346.

79. P. J. Simmons, "Learning to Live with NGOs," *Foreign Policy*, Fall 1998, p. 86.

80. A. Enders. "Openness and the WTO." IISD Working Paper (Winnipeg: IISD, 1996); Dan Esty, *Why the WTO Needs Environmental NGOs* (Geneva: International Centre for Trade and Sustainable Development, 1997).

81. Marc Williams and Lucy Ford, "The World Trade Organisation, Social Movements and Global Environmental Management," *Environmental Politics* 8, no. 1 (1999), p. 281.

82. Center for Applied Studies in International Negotiations, Issues and Non-Governmental Organizations Program, Report on the Participation of Non-Governmental Organizations in the Preparatory Process of the United Nations Conference on Environment and Development (Vienna, August 1992), p. 5; UN Non-Governmental Liaison Service, E and D File 1992: Briefings for NGOs on UNCED, no. 25 (April 1992), p. 1, and no. 30 (July 1992), p. 1.

83. WEDO, "United Nations-Related Advocacy," n.d. [Internet: http://www.wedo.org/advocacy/united.htm]

84. Peter Mucke, "Non-Governmental Organizations" in Felix Dodds, ed., *The Way Forward: Beyond Agenda 21* (London: Earthscan, 1997), pp. 97–98.

85. "Joint Statement of the Business Environmental Leadership Council," at the Pew Center's WWW site: [Internet: http://www.pewclimate.org/belc/statement.html].

86. See Gareth Porter, *The United States and the Biodiversity Convention: The Case for Participation* (Washington, D.C.: Environmental and Energy Study Institute, 1992).

87. *International Environment Reporter*, June 2, 1993, p. 416.

88. Julian E. Salt, "Kyoto and the Insurance Industry: An Insider's Perspective," *Environmental Politics* 7, no. 2 (Summer 1998), p. 164.

89. M'Gonigle and Zacher, *Pollution, Politics and International Law*, pp. 58–62.

90. For more information, see the Global Climate Coalition web site: [Internet: http://www.globalclimate.org/sign.htm].

91. Interview with Jim Barnes, March 22, 1994.

92. David Day, *The Whale War* (Vancouver and Toronto: Douglas and MacIntyre, 1987), pp. 103–107.

93. Interview with William Nitze, Alliance to Save Energy, June 20, 1994.

94. Alan S. Miller and Durwood Zaelke, "The NGO Perspective," *Climate Alert* 7, no. 3 (May–June 1994), p. 3.

95. *Daily Environment Reporter*, August 27, 1992, p. B–2.

96. *Global Environmental Change Report*, November 20, 1992.

97. BP Amoco, "Where BP Amoco Stands on Climate Change," 1999. [Internet: http://www.bpamoco.com/_nav/hse/index_climate.htm]

98. Robert L. Paarlberg, "Managing Pesticide Use in Developing Countries," in Peter M. Haas, Robert O. Keohane, and Marc A. Levy, eds., *Institutions for the Earth: Sources of Effective International Environmental Protection* (Cambridge, Mass., and London: MIT Press, 1993), p. 319.

99. For additional information on the persistent organic pollutants (POPs) negotiations, see UNEP's WWW site: [Internet: http://irptc.unep.ch/pops/] or the *Earth Negotiations Bulletin:* [Internet: http://www.iisd.ca/linkages/chemical/index.html].

100. François Nectoux and Yoichi Kuroda, *Timber from the South Seas: An Analysis of Japan's Tropical Timber Trade and Its Environmental Impact* (Gland, Switzerland: World Wildlife Fund, 1989), p. 94; David Swinbanks, "Sarawak's Tropical Rain-Forests Exploited by Japan," *Nature* 238 (July 30, 1987), p. 373.

101. Peter Dauvergne, "Globalisation and Deforestation in the Asia-Pacific," *Environmental Politics* 7, no. 4 (Winter 1998), p. 128.

102. See Stephen Schmidheiny, with the Business Council for Sustainable Development, *Changing Course: A Global Business Perspective on Development and the Environment* (Cambridge, Mass.: MIT Press, 1992). Another publication reflecting a new corporate environmental consciousness is Paul Hawken, *The Ecology of Commerce: Doing Good Business* (New York: Harper Business Publications, 1993).

103. World Business Council for Sustainable Development, "An Overview of Our Work," 1998. [Internet: http://www.wbcsd.ch/aboutus.htm]

CHAPTER THREE

1. For a more detailed discussion on this dilemma, see Richard Elliot Benedick, "Perspectives of a Negotiation Practitioner," in Gunnar Sjöstedt, ed. *International Environmental Negotiations* (Beverly Hills, Calif.: Sage, 1993), pp. 240–243.

2. This discussion of decisionmaking procedures in global environmental regimes is based on Glenn Wiser and Stephen Porter, "Effective Decision-Making: A Review of Options for Making Decisions to Conserve and Manage Pacific Fish Stocks," Prepared by the Center for International Environmental Law for the World Wildlife Fund-US, January 1999.

3. Lars Bjorkbom, "Resolution of Environmental Problems: The Use of Diplomacy," in John E. Carroll, ed., *International Environmental Diplomacy: The Management and Resolution of Transfrontier Environmental Problems* (Cambridge: Cambridge University Press, 1988), p. 128; Harold Dovland, "Monitoring European Transboundary Air Pollution," *Environment* 29 (December 1987), p. 12.

4. Lothar Gundling, "Multilateral Cooperation of States Under the ECE Convention on Long-Range Transboundary Air Pollution," in C. Flinterman et al., eds., *Transboundary Air Pollution* (Dordrecht, Netherlands: Martinus Nijhoff, 1987), pp. 19–30.

5. Sten Nelson and Peter Druinker, "The Extent of Forest Decline in Europe," *Environment* 29, no. 9 (1987), pp. 7–8.

6. Seven states pledged to reduce their emissions by 40 or 50 percent by various dates. See John McCormick, *Acid Earth: The Global Threat of Acid Pollution* (Washington, D.C.: Earthscan and International Institute for Environment and Development, 1985), especially Figure 1, p. 11.

7. Swedish NGO Secretariat on Acid Rain, "The LRTAP Convention" (environmental fact-sheet), October 1998. [Internet: http://www.acidrain.org/clrtap.html]

8. Peter H. Sand, "Air Pollution in Europe: International Policy Responses," *Environment*, December 1987, p. 18.

9. See Marc A. Levy, "European Acid Rain: The Power of Tote-Board Diplomacy," in Peter M. Haas, Robert O. Keohane, and Marc A. Levy, eds., *Institutions for the Earth* (Cambridge, Mass.: MIT Press, 1993), pp. 99–100.

10. Noelle Eckley, "Drawing Lessons About Science-Policy Institutions: Persistent Organic Pollutants (POPs) under the LRTAP Convention," *ENRP Discussion Paper E-99-11*, Kennedy School of Government, Harvard University, October 1999.

11. Swedish NGO Secretariat on Acid Rain, "The LRTAP Convention."

12. See Iwona Rummel-Bulska, "The Protection of the Ozone Layer Under the Global Framework Convention," in Flinterman et al., *Transboundary Air Pollution*, pp. 281–296.

13. Richard Elliot Benedick, *Ozone Diplomacy* (Cambridge: Harvard University Press, 1991), p. 33.

14. Yasuko Kawashima, "Policy Making Processes for Global Environmental Problems," p. 4, English translation of a paper submitted to *Jukaku Gyosei* in 1994.

15. "An Analysis of the Montreal Protocol on Substances That Deplete the Ozone Layer," staff paper prepared by the Oceans and Environment Program, Office of Technology Assessment, U.S. Congress, December 10, 1987, Table 1, p. 9.

16. Benedick, *Ozone Diplomacy*, p. 43.

17. Alan S. Miller, "Incentives for CFC Substitutes: Lessons for Other Greenhouse Gases," in *Proceedings of the First North American Conference on Preparing for Global Climate Change: A Cooperative Approach, October 27–29, 1987* (Washington, D.C.: Government Institutes, n.d.).

18. Benedick, *Ozone Diplomacy*, pp. 4–7; David D. Doniger, "Politics of the Ozone Layer," *Issues in Science and Technology* 4 (Spring 1988), p. 87; David A. Wirth and Daniel A. Lashof, "Beyond Vienna and Montreal: Multilateral Agreements on Greenhouse Gases," *Ambio* 19 (October 1990), pp. 305–310.

19. Secretariat for the Multilateral Fund for the Implementation of the Montreal Protocol, "General Information." [Internet: http://www.unmfs.org/general.htm]

20. Rudy Abramson, "Ninety Nations Agree on Three Steps to Protect Ozone Layer," *Los Angeles Times*, November 26, 1992.

21. *Into the Sunlight: Exposing Methyl Bromide's Threat to the Ozone Layer*, a report by eight U.S. NGOs (Washington, D.C.: Friends of the Earth, November 1992).

22. "Declaration on Methyl Bromide," UNEP/OzL.Pro. 5/12, Annex VII, Bangkok, November 17–19, 1993, p. 62. The parties declared their "firm determination" to reduce the use of methyl bromide 25 percent by 2000 and to phase it out completely "as soon as technically possible."

23. s.a.f.e. (Sustainable Agriculture, Food and Environment) Alliance press release, London, December 3, 1993.

24. *Financial Times*, September 9, 1994; *International Environmental Reporter*, November 2, 1994, p. 884.

25. UNEP, "Report of the Ninth Meeting of the Parties to the Montreal Protocol on Substances That Deplete the Ozone Layer," UNEP/Oz.L.Pro.9/12, September 25, 1997.

26. Ozone Secretariat, "Press Backgrounder," August 16, 1998. [Internet: http://www.unep.org/ozone/oz_press_back.htm]

27. This analysis is based primarily on David Day, *Whale War* (Vancouver and Toronto: Douglas and MacIntyre, 1987); Patricia Birnie, "The Role of Developing Countries in Nudging the International Whaling Commission from Regulating Whaling to Encouraging Non-Consumptive Uses of Whales," *Ecology Law Quar-*

terly 12, no. 4 (1985), pp. 938–968; interview with Patricia Forkan, Humane Society of the United States, Washington, D.C., June 15, 1990.

28. A revised version of the Endangered Species Conservation Act passed in 1973 banned whaling in U.S. waters or by U.S. citizens, outlawed the import of whale products, and required that the United States initiate bilateral and multilateral negotiations on an agreement to protect and conserve whales.

29. The effort to build an IWC majority to ban whaling was stymied in the latter half of the 1970s because otherwise antiwhaling states such as Canada, Mexico, and other Latin American states were primarily concerned about protecting rights to regulate economic activities within their own 200-mile (320-kilometer) economic zones and opposed the jurisdiction of an international body over whaling.

30. Statement by Craig Van Note, Monitor Consortium, before the Subcommittee on Human Rights and International Organizations, Committee on Foreign Affairs, U.S. House of Representatives, September 28, 1989.

31. "Whaling: Soviet Kills Could Affect Sanctuary Decision," *Greenwire*, February 22, 1994.

32. Teresa Watanabe, "Japan Is Set for a Whale of a Fight," *Los Angeles Times*, April 20, 1993.

33. Paul Brown, "Playing Football with the Whales," *London Guardian*, May 1, 1993. The Caribbean states cooperating with Japan are Grenada, St. Lucia, St. Kitts–Nevis, Antigua and Barbuda, Dominica, and St. Vincent.

34. Greenpeace, "During Clinton's Watch Global Whaling Triples," news release, May 20, 1997. [Internet: http://www.greenpeace.org/~oceans/]

35. Greenpeace, "Greenpeace Locates Burning Japanese Whaling Ship—First Year Without Antarctic Whale Hunting Since 1904?" news release, November 25, 1998. [Internet: http://www.greenpeace.org/~oceans/]

36. Kieran Mulvaney, "The Whaling Effect" (Washington, D.C.: World Wildlife Fund, 1999). [Internet: http://panda.org/resources/publications/species/iwc_whales/effect1.html]

37. Whale and Dolphin Conservation Society, "IWC—The IWC to Enter the New Millennium with a New Focus," press release, May 27, 1999. [Internet: http:// www.wdcs.org]

38. *Greenwire*, May 28, 1999; WWF, "IWC Steps Back from the Brink," press release, May 28, 1999.

39. Kieran Mulvaney, "The Whaling Effect."

40. WWF, "Report from the Third Day of the 51st IWC Meeting—26 May 1999" [Internet: http://panda.org/iwc/update3.html]; UNEP, "CITES Maintains Trade Bans on High-Profile Species," UNEP News Release 2000/48, April 20, 2000.

41. TRAFFIC, *Annual Report 1997–98* (London: TRAFFIC, 1998), p. 1.

42. See Sarah Fitzgerald, *Whose Business Is It?* (Washington, D.C.: World Wildlife Fund, 1989), pp. 3–8, 13–14.

43. World Resources Institute, *World Resources 1990–1991* (New York: Oxford University Press, 1990), p. 135.

44. Fitzgerald, *Whose Business Is It?* p. 67.

45. *TRAFFIC (USA)* 9 (June 1989), p. 2.

46. Chris Huxley, "Lies, Damned Lies and Population Figures," *Independent* (London), June 30, 1990, p. 13.

47. David Harland, "Jumping on the 'Ban' Wagon: Efforts to Save the African Elephant," *Fletcher Forum on World Affairs* 14 (Summer 1990), pp. 284–300.

48. "CITES 1989: The African Elephant and More," *TRAFFIC (USA)* 9 (December 1989), pp. 1–3.

49. *New York Times*, June 5, 1990, p. C2; Raymond Bonner, *At the Hand of Man: Peril and Hope for Africa's Wildlife* (New York: Vintage Books, 1994), p. 157.

50. World Wildlife Fund, "The Challenge of African Elephant Conservation," *Conservation Issues*, April 1997. [Internet: http://www.wwf.org/new/issues/apr_97/trade.htm]

51. Chris Chinaka, "Global Ban in Ivory Trade for African States," Reuters, June 19, 1997. [Internet: http://forests.org]

52. "CITES and the African Elephants: The Decisions and the Next Steps Explained," *TRAFFIC Dispatches*, April 1998, pp. 5–6.

53. CITES, "Verification of Compliance with the Precautionary Undertakings for the Sale and Shipment of Raw Ivory," Doc. SC.42.10.2.1, Forty-second meeting of the Standing Committee, Lisbon (Portugal), September 28–October 1, 1999.

54. For a theoretical discussion of the value of bans in global environmental policymaking, see Thomas Princen, "The Zero Option and Ecological Rationality in International Environmental Politics," *International Environmental Affairs* 8 (Spring 1996), pp. 147–176.

55. Katharine Kummer, *International Management of Hazardous Wastes: The Basel Convention and Related Legal Rules* (Oxford: Clarendon Press, 1995), p. 5.

56. Jonathan Krueger, *International Trade and the Basel Convention* (London: Earthscan, 1999), p. 14.

57. "Report of the Ad Hoc Working Group on the Work of Its Fourth Session," UNEP/WG.190/4, February 13, 1989, p. 3.

58. Carol Annette Petsonk, "The Role of the United Nations Environment Programme (UNEP) in the Development of International Environmental Law," *American University Journal of International Law and Policy* 5 (Winter 1990), pp. 374–377; *International Environment Reporter*, April 1989, pp. 159–161.

59. See David P. Hackett, "An Assessment of the Basel Convention on the Control of Transboundary Movements of Hazardous Wastes and Their Disposal," *American University Journal of International Law and Policy* 5 (Winter 1990), pp. 313–322; Mark A. Montgomery, "Travelling Toxic Trash: An Analysis of the 1989 Basel Convention," *Fletcher Forum of World Affairs* 14 (Summer 1990), pp. 313–326.

60. *International Environment Reporter*, April 1989, pp. 159–160.

61. *Greenpeace Waste Trade Update* 2 (July 15, 1989, and December 1989).

62. *International Environment Reporter*, May 6, 1992, p. 275.

63. Only the republics of the former Soviet Union, desperate for foreign exchange and willing to disregard the health and environmental consequences, appeared willing to accept significant shipments of hazardous wastes. See Steven Coll, "Free Market Intensifies Waste Problem," *Washington Post*, March 23, 1994; Tamara Robinson, "Dirty Deals: Hazardous Waste Imports into Russia and

Ukraine," *CIS Environmental Watch* (Monterey Institute of International Studies), no. 5 (Fall 1993).

64. Greenpeace, *The International Trade in Wastes: A Greenpeace Inventory*, 5th ed. (Washington, D.C.: Greenpeace, 1990); *Toxic Trade Update*, no. 6.2 (1993), pp. 6, 7, 12–26; "Chemicals: Shipment to South Africa Draws Enviro Protests," *Greenwire*, February 18, 1994; and "Deadly Trade in Toxics," *U.S. News and World Report*, March 7, 1994, pp. 64–67.

65. John H. Cushman Jr., "Clinton Seeks Ban on Export of Most Hazardous Waste," *New York Times*, March 1, 1994; "Basel Convention Partners Consider Ban on Exports of Hazardous Wastes," *International Environment Reporter*, March 22, 1994, p. A9

66. Charles P. Wallace, *Los Angeles Times*, March 23, 1994, cited in *Greenwire*, March 23, 1994. For a detailed account of the Geneva meeting, see Jim Puckett and Cathy Fogel, "A Victory for Environment and Justice: The Basel Ban and How It Happened," Greenpeace International Toxic Trade Campaign, Washington, D.C., September 1994.

67. Jim Vallette and Heather Spalding, *The International Trade in Wastes: A Greenpeace Inventory, International Waste Trade Schemes and Related International Policies*, 5th ed. (Washington, D.C.: Greenpeace 1990).

68. *Database of Known Hazardous Waste Exports from OECD to non-OECD Countries: 1989–March 1994*, prepared for the Second Conference of Parties to the Basel Convention (Washington, D.C.: Greenpeace, 1994).

69. Jim Puckett, "The Basel Ban: A Triumph over Business-as-Usual" (Amsterdam: Basel Action Network [Greenpeace]), October 1997. [Internet: http://www.ban.org/about_basel_ban/jims_article.html]

70. "Basel Treaty Partners Agree to Ban Waste Exports to Nations Outside OECD," *International Environment Reporter*, March 28, 1994, p. AA1.

71. Jonathan Krueger, "The Basel Convention and Transboundary Movements of Hazardous Wastes," Briefing Paper no. 45 (London: Royal Institute of International Affairs Energy and Environment Programme, May 1998). The Working Group was expected to report to COP-5 in December 1999. For updated information, go to the Basel Convention's WWW site: [Internet: http://www.unep.ch/basel/].

72. Another issue that emerged at COP-4 was the expansion of the list of countries included in Annex VII to include non-OECD countries. This would, in effect, circumvent the ban amendment because countries in Annex VII could export hazardous wastes to each other. For more information on this issue, see Basel Action Network, *Basel Ban Victory at COP-4: A Report on the Negotiations and Results of the Fourth Conference of Parties to the Basel Convention Held in Kuching, Malaysia, 23–27 February 1998* (Amsterdam: Greenpeace/Basel Action Network, 1998). [Internet: http://www.ban.org/issues_for_cop4/what_happened.html]

73. Given the economic and technological barriers to onshore mining, it is generally believed that only oil and gas exploration would be practical. See Barbara Mitchell, *Frozen Stakes: The Future of Antarctic Minerals* (London and Washington, D.C.: International Institute for Environment and Development, 1983), pp. 7–21.

74. Barbara Mitchell, "Undermining Antarctica," *Technology Review*, February–March 1988, p. 56.

75. Ibid., pp. 50–51, 68–69.

76. These meetings were closed to the public and press as well as to nontreaty nations, and the documents being considered were not released to the public. *The Future of the Antarctic: Background for a Third UN Debate* (East Sussex, UK: Greenpeace International, 1985), p. 15.

77. *Christian Science Monitor,* June 7, 1988.

78. For description and analysis of CRAMRA and its environmental provisions, see R. Tucker Scully and Lee A. Kimball, "Antarctica: Is There Life After Minerals?" *Marine Policy,* April 1989, pp. 87–98; Lee A. Kimball, *Southern Exposure: Deciding Antarctica's Future* (Washington, D.C.: World Resources Institute, 1990), pp. 16–18; Antarctic and Southern Oceans Coalition, "Analysis of the Convention on the Regulation of Antarctic Mineral Resource Activities," ASOC Information Paper 1988–4, October 29, 1988.

79. *Christian Science Monitor,* June 7, 1988.

80. *International Environment Reporter,* June 19, 1991, p. 331; Embassy of Australia, *Australian Report* (Washington, D.C.: Embassy of Australia, July 15, 1991).

81. See Wirth and Lashof, "Beyond Vienna and Montreal," pp. 305–310.

82. For a brief summary of the state of the science of global warming, see WRI, *World Resources 1998–99* (New York: Oxford University Press, 1998), pp. 173–174.

83. On the importance of perceptions of cost to early climate policies and absence of accurate cost estimates for the Netherlands, Germany, Japan, and the United States, see Yasuko Kawashima, "A Comparative Analysis of the Decision-making Processes of Developed Countries Toward CO_2 Emissions Reduction Targets," *International Environmental Affairs* 9 (Spring 1997), pp. 95–126.

84. See Matthew Paterson, *Global Warming and Global Politics* (London: Routledge, 1996), pp. 77–82.

85. Richard A. Houghton and George M. Woodwell, "Global Climatic Change," *Scientific American* 260 (April 1989), pp. 42–43.

86. Lamont C. Hempel and Matthias Kaelberer, "The Changing Climate in Greenhouse Policy: Obstacles to International Cooperation in Agenda Setting and Policy Formulation," unpublished paper, April 1990, p. 6; and Daniel Bodansky, "The United Nations Framework Convention on Climate Change: A Commentary," *Yale Journal of International Law* 18, no. 2 (Summer 1993), p. 461.

87. Genn Frankel, "U.S. Moves to Block Pact on Emissions," *Washington Post,* November 7, 1989, pp. A1, 21; *Washington Post,* July 10, 1990; *New York Times,* July 10, 1990.

88. Japan subsequently backtracked by proposing a process of "pledge and review" in place of binding commitments. Individual countries, it suggested, would set for themselves appropriate targets that would be publicly reviewed. Most EC member states and NGOs were cool to the idea. Bodansky, "The United Nations Framework Convention on Climate Change," p. 486.

89. Intergovernmental Panel on Climate Change, *The Formulation of Response Strategies: Report by Working Group III, Policymakers' Summary,* June 1990, p. 11, Table 2. For country contributions and rankings at the time of the negotiations, see World Resources Institute, *World Resources, 1992–1993* (New York: Oxford University Press, 1992), pp. 205–213, 345–355. For a good discussion of different methods

of greenhouse-gas accounting, see Peter M. Morrisette and Andrew J. Plantinga, "The Global Warming Issue: Viewpoints of Different Countries," *Resources* (Washington, D.C.: Resources for the Future), no. 103 (Spring 1991), pp. 2–6.

90. *Earth Summit Update*, no. 9 (May 1992), p. 1; *Wall Street Journal*, May 22, 1992, p. 1.

91. As of October 1999, 180 countries had ratified the Convention. UN Framework Convention on Climate Change, "Status of Ratification," September 29, 1999. [Internet: http://www.unfccc.de/]

92. For a complete summary and analysis of the Kyoto Protocol, see Herman E. Ott, "The Kyoto Protocol: Unfinished Business," *Environment* 40, no. 6 (1998), p. 16ff.; Clare Breidenrich, Daniel Magraw, Anne Rowley, and James W. Rubin, "The Kyoto Protocol to the United Nations Framework Convention on Climate Change," *American Journal of International Law* 92, no. 2 (1998), p. 315.

93. Subsequently, the White House revealed that the United States planned to achieve up to 75 percent of the U.S. reduction requirement by purchasing allowances from the Russian Federation and Ukraine. See Christopher Flavin, "Last Tango in Buenos Aires," *WorldWatch*, November-December 1998, p. 13.

94. See Martin Parry et al., "Adapting to the Inevitable," *Nature*, October 22, 1998, p. 741; T. M. L. Wigley, "The Kyoto Protocol: CO_2, CH4 and Climate Implications," *Geophysical Research Letters* 25 (1998), pp. 2285–2288.

95. Chris Mitchell, "Science, Kyoto and Climate Change," CSIRO Climate change page: [http://www.csiro.au/news/issues/cm97.htm].

96. Kelly Sims, "International Negotiations on Climate Change Meeting Summary and State of the Process," Ozone Action. [http://www.ozone.org/COP4.html]

97. Kenton R. Miller et al., "Issues on the Preservation of Biological Diversity," in Robert Repetto, ed., *The Global Possible: Resources, Development and the New Century* (New Haven and London: Yale University Press, 1985), pp. 341–342; IUCN, "Explanatory Notes to Draft Articles Prepared by IUCN for Inclusion in a Proposed Convention on the Conservation of Biological Diversity and the Establishment of a Fund for That Purpose," Part 1: General Comments, p. 1.

98. The main interest of the Reagan administration in making that proposal was to save money by bringing the multiplicity of species-specific or region-specific conservation conventions already in existence under one convention, so that there could be a single secretariat instead of several secretariats. Personal communication from E. U. Curtis Bohlen, former assistant secretary of state for oceans, environment, and science, Washington, D.C., February 2, 1994.

99. "Report of the Ad Hoc Working Group on the Work of Its Second Session in Preparation for a Legal Instrument on Biological Diversity of the Planet," UNEP/Bio.Div2/3, February 23, 1990, p. 7.

100. Personal communication from a member of the U.S. delegation to the biodiversity convention negotiations, April 12, 1994.

101. For contrasting analyses of the text of the convention regarding intellectual property rights, see Melinda Chandler, "The Biodiversity Convention: Selected Issues of Interest to the International Lawyer," *Colorado Journal of International Environmental Law and Policy* 4, no. 1 (Winter 1993), pp. 161–165; and Gareth Porter, *The*

United States and the Biodiversity Convention: The Case for Participation (Washington, D.C.: Environmental and Energy Study Institute, 1992), pp. 13–21.

102. Personal communication from a member of the U.S. delegation to the biodiversity convention negotiations, October 21, 1994. See also Fiona McConnell, *The Biodiversity Convention: A Negotiating History* (London: Kluwer Law International, 1996).

103. A coalition of NGOs with major interests in biodiversity got together with several companies to pressure the Clinton administration to sign the treaty. The Clinton administration dealt with the objections to the text that had been raised by the Bush administration by announcing that it would issue a statement asserting that it interpreted the treaty's provisions on intellectual property rights and the financial mechanism to be compatible with U.S. interests. See U.S. Congress, Senate, *Convention on Biological Diversity: Message from the President of the United States*, November 20, 1993, Treaty Document 103-20 (Washington, D.C.: U.S. Government Printing Office, 1993).

104. For a summary of the negotiations and a synopsis of the Protocol, see *Earth Negotiations Bulletin* 9, no. 137 (January 31, 2000). [Internet: http://www.iisd.ca/biodiv/excop/]

105. "Synthesis of Information Contained in National Reports on the Implementation of the Convention," Revised Note by the Executive Secretary, Conference of the Parties to the Convention on Biological Diversity, Fourth Meeting, Bratislava, May 4–15, 1998. The national reports of four Asian countries (China, Vietnam, Malaysia, and Indonesia) indicate that only China adopted measurable targets for conservation and sustainable use, and that none of the four adopted detailed indicators of success.

106. United Nations Environment Programme, *Desertification: The Problem That Won't Go Away* (Nairobi: UNEP, 1992); Ridley Nelson, "Dryland Management: The 'Desertification' Problem," World Bank Policy Planning and Research Staff, Environment Department Working Paper no. 8, September 1988, p. 2.

107. *Crosscurrents*, no. 1 (March 2, 1992), p. 5. For a more detailed later report on these findings, see William K. Stevens, "Threat of Encroaching Deserts May Be More Myth Than Fact," *New York Times*, January 18, 1994, pp. C1, 10.

108. UN Governmental Liaison Service, "Second Session of Desertification Negotiations, Geneva, 13–24 September 1993," *E and D File* 2, no. 13 (October 1993).

109. "A Convention for Africans," *Impact* (Nairobi), no. 6 (September 1992), p. 3.

110. United Nations Environment Programme, *Desertification Control Bulletin* (Nairobi), no. 20 (1991); Dr. Mostafa K. Tolba, "Desertification and the Economics of Survival," statement to the International Conference on the Economics of Dryland Degradation and Rehabilitation, Canberra, Australia, March 10–11, 1986.

111. *World Bank News*, May 27, 1993, p. 4; *Crosscurrents*, no. 5 (March 16, 1992), p. 13

112. E. U. Curtis Bohlen, deputy chief of the U.S. delegation, recalls that he made the decision personally without consulting with any higher U.S. officials. Private communication from Bohlen, August 15, 1994. On the earlier suggestion by African countries of a possible bargain linking African support for a forest convention with U.S. support for a desertification convention, see *Crosscurrents*, no. 5 (March 16, 1992), p. 13.

113. *Earth Summit Bulletin* 2, no. 13 (June 16, 1992), p. 3.

114. "Summary of the First Session of the INC for the Elaboration of an International Convention to Combat Desertification, 24 May–3 June 1993," *Earth Negotiations Bulletin* 4, no. 11 (June 11, 1993), pp. 2–6.

115. "Summary of the Fifth Session of the INC for the Elaboration of an International Convention to Combat Desertification, 6–17 June 1994," *Earth Negotiations Bulletin* 4, no. 55 (June 20, 1994), pp. 7–8.

116. "Summary of the Second Session of the INC for the Elaboration of an International Convention to Combat Desertification, 13–24 September 1993," *Earth Negotiations Bulletin* 4, no. 22 (September 30, 1993), p. 11.

117. "Summary of the Fifth Session," pp. 9–10.

118. For more information on the challenges faced by the Convention, see "Summary of the Second Conference of the Parties to the Convention to Combat Desertification, 30 November–11 December 1998," *Earth Negotiations Bulletin* 4, no. 127 (December 14, 1998).

119. FAO, *The State of World Fisheries and Aquaculture* (Rome: FAO, 1995), p. 8.

120. On serial overfishing, see FAO, *The State of World Fisheries and Aquaculture 1996* (Rome: FAO, 1997), Figure 22, p. 37; U.S. Department of Commerce, National Oceanic and Atmospheric Administration, National Marine Fisheries Service, *Our Living Oceans: The Economic Status of US Fisheries 1996* (Silver Spring, Md.: NOAA, 1996), p. 15. On global catch figures, see *The State of World Fisheries 1998* (Rome: FAO, 1999), Figure 2, p. 5.

121. See Gareth Porter, *Estimating Overcapacity in the Global Fishing Fleet* (Washington, D.C.: World Wildlife Fund, 1998).

122. FAO, *The State of World's Fisheries and Aquaculture 1998*, Table 12, p. 102; FAOSTAT Fisheries Data.

123. See, for example, Commission of the European Communities, "Fishing on the High Seas: A Community Approach," Communication from the Commission to the Council and the European Parliament, SEC (92) 565, April 2, 1992, p. 5.

124. On Canadian mismanagement, see Raymond Rogers, *The Oceans Are Emptying* (Montreal: Black Rose Books, 1995), pp. 96–147; on EU allocations and Spanish and Portuguese catch see background document by Bruce Atkinson, Canadian Department of Fisheries and Oceans, Northwest Atlantic Fisheries, Centre, St. Johns, Newfoundland.

125. "Canada Hits EU's Atlantic Overfishing," *Washington Times*, February 19, 1995, p. A11.

126. Marvin Soroos, "The Turbot War: Resolution of an International Fishery Dispute," in Nils Petter Gleditsch, ed., *Conflict and the Environment* (Dordrecht, Netherlands: Kluwer Academic Publishers, 1997), p. 248.

127. *Earth Negotiations Bulletin* 7, no. 54 (August 7, 1995).

128. See Gareth Porter, *Too Much Fishing Fleet, Too Few Fish: A Proposal for Eliminating Global Fishing Overcapacity* (Washington, D.C.: World Wildlife Fund, 1998); FAO Fisheries Department, "The International Plan of Action for the Management of Fishing Capacity." [Internet: http:"fao.org/waicent/faoinfo/fishery/ipa/capace.htm]

CHAPTER FOUR

1. This number is derived from a comprehensive collection of legal instruments that includes agreements with important provisions relating to the environment. The commonly cited figure of about 150 multilateral environmental agreements is taken from UNEP data and includes only multilateral agreements totally directed to environmental issues. See Harold K. Jacobson and Edith Brown Weiss, "A Framework for Analysis," in Edith Brown Weiss and Harold K. Jacobson, eds., *Engaging Countries: Strengthening Compliance with International Environmental Accords"* (Cambridge, Mass.: MIT Press, 1998), pp. 1, 18.

2. Ibid., p. 1.

3. Ibid., p. 4.

4. Abram Chayes and Antonia H. Chayes, "Compliance Without Enforcement: State Behavior Under Regulatory Treaties," *Negotiation Journal* 7 (1991), pp. 311–330.

5. William J. Broad, "Russians Describe Extensive Dumping of Nuclear Waste," *New York Times*, April 27, 1993; and Peter James Spielman, AP/*Philadelphia Inquirer*, February 21, 1994, cited on *Greenwire*, February 22, 1994.

6. Edith Brown Weiss, Daniel B. Magraw, and Paul C. Szasz, *International Environmental Law: Basic Instruments and References* (Dobbs Ferry, N.Y.: Transnational, 1992), p. 696; Peter H. Sand, ed., *The Effectiveness of International Environmental Law* (Cambridge: Grotius Publications, 1992).

7. Edith Brown Weiss, "The Five International Treaties: A Living History," in Edith Brown Weiss and Harold K. Jacobson, *Engaging Countries: Strengthening Compliance with International Environmental Accords* (Cambridge, Mass.: MIT Press, 1998), p. 112.

8. Juan Carlos di Primio, "Data Quality and Compliance Control," in David G. Victor et al., eds., *The Implementation and Effectiveness of International Environmental Commitments: Theory and Practice* (Cambridge, Mass.: MIT Press, 1998), pp. 283–299.

9. Staff and budget information was gathered from the most recent reports of the Conferences of the Parties to the five conventions.

10. U.S. Government Accounting Office, "International Agreements Are Not Well Monitored," GAO/RCED-92-3, January 1992, pp. 28–33.

11. See, for example, Ronald B. Mitchell, *Intentional Oil Pollution at Sea* (Cambridge, Mass.: MIT Press, 1994); Edith Brown Weiss and Harold K. Jacobson, *Engaging Countries: Strengthening Compliance with International Environmental Accords* (Cambridge, Mass.: MIT Press, 1998); David G. Victor et al., eds., *The Implementation and Effectiveness of International Environmental Commitments: Theory and Practice* (Cambridge, Mass.: MIT Press, 1998); Michael J. Kelly, "Overcoming Obstacles to the Effective Implementation of International Environmental Agreements," *Georgetown International Environmental Law Review* 9, no. 2 (1997).

12. Peter H. Sand, ed., *The Effectiveness of International Environmental Agreements* (Cambridge: Grotius, 1992), p. 82.

13. Michael J. Kelly, "Overcoming Obstacles," pp. 462–463.

14. David Vogel and Timothy Kessler, "How Compliance Happens and Doesn't Happen Domestically," in Edith Brown Weiss and Harold K. Jacobson, *Engaging Countries: Strengthening Compliance with International Environmental Accords* (Cambridge, Mass.: MIT Press, 1998), p. 23.

15. Kelly, "Overcoming Obstacles," p. 464.

16. Andrew J. Heimert, "How the Elephant Lost His Tusks," *Yale Law Journal* 104 (1995), p. 1473, as cited in Kelly, "Overcoming Obstacles," p. 465.

17. Environmental Investigation Agency and Telepak, *The Final Cut: Illegal Logging in Indonesia's Orangutan Parks* (London: 1999); David W. Brown, *Addicted to Rent: Corporate and Spatial Distribution of Forest Resources in Indonesia: Implications for Forest Sustainability and Government Policy* (Jakarta: Indonesia-UK Tropical Forest Management Programme, 1999).

18. Vogel and Kessler, "How Compliance Happens," p. 35.

19. Ibid., p. 24.

20. For additional information, see the TRAFFIC WWW site: [Internet: http://www.traffic.org].

21. Statement by Dr. Mostafa K. Tolba, executive director, UN Environment Programme, to the Eighth Meeting of the Parties to CITES, Kyoto, Japan, March 1992, p. 5.

22. David Mulenex, "Improving Compliance Provisions in International Environmental Agreements," in Lawrence E. Susskind, Eric Jay Dolin, and J. William Breslin, *International Environmental Treaty-Making* (Cambridge: Program on Negotiation at Harvard Law School, 1992), p. 174.

23. Bill Padgett, "The African Elephant, Africa and CITES: The Next Step," *Indiana Journal of Global Legal Studies* 2 (1995), pp. 529, 538–540, as cited in Kelly, "Overcoming Obstacles," pp. 469–470.

24. Ronald B. Mitchell, *Intentional Oil Pollution at Sea*, p. 42.

25. Edith Brown Weiss, "The Five International Treaties," p. 162.

26. Ibid., p. 162.

27. Comment from the U.S. Department of State in "International Agreements Are Not Well Monitored," p. 54.

28. Edith Brown Weiss, "The Five International Treaties," pp. 162–163.

29. Ibid., pp. 115–116.

30. Ronald B. Mitchell, *Intentional Oil Pollution at Sea*, pp. 47–48.

31. See, for example, Lawrence E. Susskind, *Environmental Diplomacy: Negotiating More Effective Global Agreements* (New York: Oxford University Press, 1994), pp. 113–117.

32. Harold K. Jacobson and Edith Brown Weiss, "Assessing the Record and Designing Strategies to Engage Countries," in Edith Brown Weiss and Harold K. Jacobson, *Engaging Countries: Strengthening Compliance with International Environmental Accords* (Cambridge, Mass.: MIT Press, 1998), p. 527.

33. UN Department of Economic and Social Affairs and UN Conference on Trade and Development, *World Economic Situation and Prospects for 1999* (New York/Geneva: United Nations, 1998), p. 1.

34. Jens Martens and James A. Paul, "The Coffers Are Not Empty: Financing for Sustainable Development and the Role of the United Nations," Global Policy Forum paper, July 1998. [Internet: http://www.igc.org/globalpolicy/socecon/global/paul.htm]

35. Jubilee 2000 Coalition, "Who We Are." [Internet: http://www. jubilee 2000uk.org/about.html]

36. OECD/DAC Statistical Reporting Systems, "Total ODA Flows," February 8, 1999 [Internet: http://www.oecd.org/dac/htm/oda5097.HTM], and OECD, "Aid and Private Flows Fell in 1997," OECD News Release, June 18, 1998.

37. The ODA levels for Australia, Denmark, Ireland, Luxembourg, the Netherlands, New Zealand, Norway, and the United Kingdom increased slightly between 1992 and 1997. OECD/DAC Statistical Reporting Systems, "Total ODA Flows," February 8, 1999.

38. OECD, "Aid and Private Flows Fell in 1997," OECD news release, June 18, 1998.

39. "Report of the Fourth Expert Group Meeting on Financial Issues of Agenda 21," Santiago, Chile, January 8–10, 1997. UN document E/CN.17/1997/18.

40. United Nations Commission on Sustainable Development, "Financial Flow Statistics," Background Paper no. 17, Sixth Session, 1998 [Internet: http://www.un.org/esa/sustdev/finsd4.html]. Although these are figures reported by the OECD Development Assistance Committee (DAC) to the UN Commission on Sustainable Development, it is generally known that DAC statistics can be unreliable because they rely on voluntary reporting by donor country agencies, which does not always occur or is incomplete. When it does occur, the reporting is not reviewed for its accuracy or definitional consistency.

41. The draft by the EC, the Nordics, and Japan offered only a commitment by industrial countries "in a position to do so" (a formula allowing the United States to refuse) to reach the target of 0.7 percent of GNP going to ODA and gave no time frame for achieving it.

42. "Financial Negotiations End in Deadlock," Earth Summit Update, no. 8 (April 1992), p. 6.

43. The Netherlands, Denmark, and France supported the target of 0.7 percent of GNP by the year 2000; the United Kingdom and Germany did not. Earth Summit Bulletin, June 17, 1992, p. 17.

44. The head of the U.S. delegation, E. U. Curtis Bohlen, indicated that he was concerned about that possibility at a U.S. delegation meeting at PrepCom III.

45. Author's interview with a member of the U.S. delegation, Rio, June 9, 1992.

46. For more information on the Montreal Protocol Fund, see Elisabeth R. DeSombre and Joanne Kauffman, "The Montreal Protocol Multilateral Fund: Partial Success Story," in Robert O. Keohane and Marc A. Levy, eds., Institutions for Environmental Aid: Pitfalls and Promises (Cambridge, Mass.: MIT Press, 1996), pp. 89–126.

47. Secretariat for the Multilateral Fund for the Implementation of the Montreal Protocol, "General Information." [Internet: http://www.unmfs.org/general.htm]

48. Richard N. Mott, "Financial Transfers Under the Conventions on Climate Change and Biodiversity," International Environmental Affairs 7, no. 1 (Winter

1995), p. 71; "Third World Suspicious of 'Green Fund' in World Bank," UNCED PrepCom III Daily Press Bulletin (Inter Press Service) 15/1, August 30, 1991.

49. For the final text of the agreement, see Global Environment Facility, "Instrument for the Establishment of the Restructured Global Environment Facility," report of the GEF participants meeting, Geneva, Switzerland, March 14–16, 1994, and March 31, 1994.

50. During the Operational Phase (GEF 1), 60 percent of the funding for biodiversity went to the top 25 countries in concentration of biodiversity, 16 percent to the next 25, and 24 percent to countries that were not among the top 50. See Gareth Porter et al., *Study of GEF's Overall Performance*, pp. 78–79.

51. Ibid., p. 81.

52. Ibid., pp. 4–5.

53. In half of the projects in the sample studied for the GEF's Overall Performance Study in 1997, it was found that cofinancing that was claimed as leveraging for the global environment was actually funding for national development that presumably would have been spent in any case. See Porter et al., *Study of GEF's Overall Performance*, pp. 8–11.

54. OECD/DAC, "Table 19: Aid by Major Purposes, 1996," *1998 Development Co-operation Report: Efforts and Policies of the Members of the Development Assistance Committee* (Paris: OECD, 1998).

55. David Parker and Eva Jespersen, "20/20: Mobilizing Resources for Children in the 1990s," UNICEF Staff Working Paper no. 12, January 1994; and UNDP and UNICEF, "Country Experiences in Assessing Public Spending on 20/20," paper prepared for the Hanoi Meeting on 20/20, October 1998.

56. *Earth Negotiations Bulletin* 10, no. 31 (January 21, 1995).

57. Eva Jespersen, "Why 20/20?" paper prepared for meeting, "Estimating Resource Needs for Population Activities," Harvard Center for Population and Development Studies, June 28, 1994; "Report of the World Summit for Social Development: 6–12 March 1995," *Earth Negotiations Bulletin* 10, no. 4 (March 15, 1995). China was one of the few to oppose the concept.

58. UN Commission on Sustainable Development, "Financial Resources and Mechanisms for Sustainable Development: Overview of Current Issues and Developments," Report of the Secretary-General E/CN.17/ISWG.II/1994/2 (February 22, 1994), p. 24.

59. The original proposal, by Nobel Prize–winning economist James Tobin, was for a 0.5 percent tax on speculative currency transactions that would raise $1.5 *trillion* annually and was aimed at deterring such transactions. The UNDP proposed reducing the tax to 10 percent of the original level. See UNDP, *Human Development Report 1994* (New York: Oxford University Press, 1994), pp. 69–70.

60. Martin Walker, "Global Taxation: Paying for Peace," *World Policy Journal* 10, no. 2 (Summer 1993), pp. 7–12.

61. International Institute for Sustainable Development, "Financing Climate Change: Global Environmental Tax?" *Developing Ideas*, no. 15 (September–October 1998).

62. For more information on the HIPC initiative, see the World Bank's HIPC WWW site: [Internet: http://www.worldbank.org/hipc/].

63. Joseph Hanlon, *HIPC Heresies and the Flat Earth Response* (London: Jubilee 2000, 1998). [Internet: http://www.jubilee2000uk.org/hipc_heres.html]

64. A. De Moor and P. Calamai, *Subsidizing Unsustainable Development: Undermining the Earth with Public Funds* (San Jose, Costa Rica: Earth Council, 1997); V. P. Gadhi, D. Gray, and R. McMorran, "A Comprehensive Approach to Domestic Resources for Sustainable Development," in *Finance for Sustainable Development: The Road Ahead* (New York: United Nations, 1997).

65. World Bank, *Expanding the Measure of Wealth: Indicators of Environmentally Sustainable Development* (Washington, D.C.: World Bank, 1997).

66. World Trade Organization, Committee on Trade and Environment, "Environmental Benefits of Removing Trade Restrictions and Distortions: Note by the Secretariat" (Geneva: WTO, 1997); FAO Subcommittee on Fish Trade, Committee on Fisheries, "Issues of International Trade, Environment and Sustainable Fisheries Development: Fisheries Management, Subsidies and International Fish Trade" (Rome: FAO, 1998).

67. A. P. G. de Moor, "Key Issues in Subsidy Policies and Strategies for Reform," paper prepared for the UN Fourth Expert Group Meeting on Financial Issues of Agenda 21, Santiago, Chile, January 8–10, 1997.

CHAPTER FIVE

1. See Karl P. Sauvant and Hajo Hasenpflug, eds., *The New International Economic Order: Confrontation or Cooperation Between North and South?* (Boulder, Colo.: Westview Press, 1977).

2. This was part of a longer-term decline in the real prices of primary products in the world market, caused by slow growth in demand, the development of cheaper substitutes, and overproduction. See United Nations Development Programme, *Human Development Report 1992* (New York: UNDP, 1992), p. 59.

3. UNDP, "Financial Inflows and Outflows," *Human Development Report 1998* (New York: Oxford University Press, 1998). The term *least developed countries* (LDCs) was originally used at the UN in 1971 to describe the "poorest and most economically weak of the developing countries, with formidable economic, institutional and human resources problems, which are often compounded by geographical handicaps and natural and man-made disasters." There are currently 50 LDCs.

4. World Bank, *Global Economic Prospects and the Developing Countries* (Washington, D.C.: World Bank, 1992), p. 13.

5. WTO Committee on Trade and Development, "Participation of Developing Countries in World Trade: Overview of Major Trends and Underlying Factors," WT/COMTD/W/15, August 16, 1996. [Internet: http://www.wto.org/wto/develop/w15.htm]

6. International Centre for Trade and Sustainable Development, "Developing Countries Wary over Agriculture," *Bridges Weekly Trade News Digest*," June 7, 1999. [Internet: http://www.ictsd.org/html/story3.07–06–99.htm]

7. UNDP, *Human Development Report 1992*, p. 34; World Bank, "1997 GDP" *1999 World Development Indicators* CD-Rom [http://www.worldbank.org/data/data-

bytopic/GDP97.pdf]. The 20 richest countries are the United States, Japan, Germany, France, United Kingdom, Italy, China, Brazil, Canada, Spain, Russian Federation, Republic of Korea, Mexico, Australia, India, Netherlands, Argentina, Switzerland, Belgium, and Sweden.

8. For the example of the Philippines, see Gareth Porter, with Delfin Ganapin, Jr., *Population, Resources and the Philippines' Future* (Washington, D.C.: World Resources Institute, 1988); Robin Broad, with John Cavanagh, *Plundering Paradise: The Struggle for Environment in the Philippines* (Berkeley and Los Angeles: University of California Press, 1993); Peter Dauvergne, *Shadows in the Forest: Japan and Politics of Timber in Southeast Asia* (Cambridge, Mass.: MIT Press, 1997).

9. "The Price of the Environment," *Environmental News from the Netherlands*, no. 1 (1992).

10. Mark Fritz, "Imports Hurting African Farmers," *Sacramento Bee*, December 20, 1993, p. A18.

11. For more information on subsidies, see OECD, *Subsidies and Environment: Exploring the Linkages* (Paris: OECD, 1996); David Malin Roodman, "Paying the Piper: Subsidies, Politics and the Environment," Worldwatch paper no. 23 (Washington, D.C.: Worldwatch, December 1996); Matteo Milazzo, "Subsidies in World Fisheries," World Bank Technical Paper no. 406 (Washington, D.C.: World Bank, 1998); Gareth Porter, "Fisheries Subsidies, Overfishing and Trade," UNEP Environment and Trade Series no. 16 (Geneva: UNEP, 1998); World Trade Organization, Committee on Trade and Environment, "Environmental Benefits of Removing Trade Restrictions and Distortions" (Geneva: WTO, 1997); A.P.G. de Moor, *Perverse Incentives: Subsidies and Sustainable Development* (San Jose, Costa Rica: Earth Council, 1997).

12. Statement by H. E. Datuk Amar Stephen K. T. Yong, leader of the Malaysian delegation, at the second meeting of the parties to the Montreal Protocol, London, June 27–29, 1990.

13. Talk by Mohammed El-Ashry, then vice-president of World Resources Institute, at the Egyptian Embassy, Washington, D.C., March 9, 1990.

14. "Final Document of the XIIth Summit of the Non-Aligned Movement," September 2–3, 1998, Durban, South Africa. [http://nam.gov.za/finaldocument. html]

15. UNDP, *Human Development Report 1998* (New York: Oxford University Press, 1998). For details and illustrations of the developing-country point of view, see also Anil Agarwal, Sunita Narain, and Anju Sharma, eds. *Green Politics: Global Negotiations*, Vol. 1 (New Delhi: Center for Science and Environment, 1999).

16. Friends of the Earth Netherlands developed the environmental space concept as part of its 1992 Sustainable Netherlands Action Plan. Environmental space is the total amount of pollution, nonrenewable resources, agricultural land, and forests that can be used globally without impinging on access by future generations to the same resources. For additional information, see the report of the Oslo Ministerial Roundtable on Sustainable Production and Consumption, February 6–10, 1995. [Internet: http://www.iisd.ca/linkages/consume/oslo000.html]

17. See *Outreach 1997* 1, no. 24 (April 22, 1997).

18. "Proposed Elements of a Protocol to the United Nations Framework Convention on Climate Change, Presented by Brazil in Response to the Berlin Man-

date," Ad Hoc Group on the Berlin Mandate, seventh session, Bonn, July 31– 7 August 7, 1997, p. 22.

19. Steve Charnovitz, "Environmentalism Confronts GATT Rules," *Journal of World Trade* 28 (January 1993), p. 37; Daniel C. Esty, "Economic Integration and the Environment," p. 192.

20. John J. Audley, *Green Politics and Global Trade: NAFTA and the Future of Environmental Politics* (Washington, D.C.: Georgetown University Press, 1997).

21. "Agreement Establishing the World Trade Organization (WTO)," GATT/WTO, Preamble, 1994.

22. Ibid.

23. The full report of the CTE to the 1996 WTO Ministerial Conference can be found on-line: [Internet: http://iisd1.iisd.ca/trade/wto/ctereport.htm].

24. The description of the trade provisions is excerpted from Community Nutrition Institute, "Multilateral Environmental Agreements and the GATT/WTO Regime," paper presented at the Joint Policy Dialogue on Environment and Trade, January 1996.

25. This analysis is based on WTO Committee on Trade and Environment, "Report of the Committee on Trade and Environment," WT/CTE/1, November 14, 1996, especially paragraphs 5–31. [Internet: http://iisd.ca/trade/wto/ ctereport.htm]

26. The term *environmental trade measures* is used in Steve Charnowitz, "The Environment vs. Trade Rules: Defogging the Debate," *Environmental Law* (Northwestern School of Law of Lewis and Clark College) 23 (1993), p. 490. Charnowitz lists all of these forms of ETMs except mandatory ecolabeling.

27. Sang Don Lee, "The Effect of Environmental Regulations on Trade: Cases of Korea's New Environmental Laws," *Georgetown International Environmental Law Review,* Summer 1993, p. 659.

28. "Principles on General Rights and Obligations," Principle 14 of the Rio Declaration, p. 5; unclassified Department of State telegram, June 14, 1992. The U.S. interpretive statement is nowhere mentioned in the official UN version of the Rio Declaration.

29. One example of a small country threatening retaliatory trade measures is when Ecuador, in November 1999, said it would seek WTO approval for retaliatory sanctions against the EU for the EU's failure to comply with the WTO ruling on its banana import regime, which discriminated against a number of South and Central American banana-exporting countries. As a developing country and a relatively small importer of EU goods, to impose punitive tariffs on EU imports would have little impact on the EU but would have a devastating effect on Ecuador's consumers. Instead, Ecuador said it would be likely to target intellectual property rights and services for retaliation. See ICTSD, "Ecuador, U.S. Reject EU Banana Proposal; Ecuador to Cross-Retaliate," *Bridges Weekly Trade News Digest* 3, no. 45 (November 15, 1999).

30. It was widely believed among NGOs that more such disputes over unilateral actions in the future would ultimately force the negotiation of new GATT rules on the issue. See Bruce Stokes, "The Road from Rio," *National Journal*, May 30, 1992, p. 1288.

31. Esty, *Greening the GATT*, p. 188. In an ironic twist, research undertaken by the Inter-American Tropical Tuna Commission found that "dolphin-safe" tuna fishing results in catching tuna at least 35 times more immature (since young tuna do not school beneath groups of dolphins as mature tuna do) and thus threatens to deplete tuna fisheries. See Richard Parker, "The Use and Abuse of Trade Leverage to Protect the Global Commons: What We Can Learn from the Tuna-Dolphin Conflict," *Georgetown International Environmental Law Review* 12, 1 (1999), pp. 37–38.

32. For environmental critiques of the decision, see Steve Charnovitz, "GATT and the Environment: Examining the Issues," *International Environmental Affairs* 4, no. 3 (Summer 1992), pp. 203–233; Robert Repetto, "Trade and Environment Policies: Achieving Complementarities and Avoiding Conflict," *WRI Issues and Ideas*, July 1993, pp. 6–10. For an alternative view of the decision, see John H. Jackson, "World Trade Rules and Environmental Policies: Congruence or Conflict?" *Washington and Lee Law Review* 49 (Fall 1992), pp. 1242–1243.

33. For an excellent summary, see Donald M. Goldberg, "GATT Tuna-Dolphin II: Environmental Protection Continues to Clash with Free Trade," CIEL Brief no. 2 (June 1994).

34. The panel's conclusions were released in GATT, "United States Taxes on Automobiles: Report of the Panel," restricted, DS31/R, September 29, 1994.

35. Ibid.

36. Janet Welsh Brown, "Trade and the Environment," *Encyclopedia of Violence, Peace and Conflict*, Vol. 3 (San Diego: Academic Press, 1999), p. T12–4.

37. The Appellate Body noted that the United States had failed to sign the Convention on Migratory Species or the United Nations Convention on the Law of the Sea and had not ratified the Convention on Biological Diversity, nor had it raised the issue of sea turtles during recent CITES conferences. These inconsistencies in the U.S. record on protection of endangered species do not prove, of course, that the U.S. intention in Shrimp/Turtle case was not protecting endangered sea turtles.

38. See "Revised Guidelines for the Implementation of Section 609 of Public Law 101-162 Relating to the Protection of Sea Turtles in Shrimp Trawl Fishing Operations," Public Notice 3086, *Federal Register,* July 1999.

39. "Trade, Environment and Development: Lessons from Empirical Studies: The Case of Brazil," synthesis report by the UNCTAD secretariat, Trade and Development Board, Ad Hoc Working Group on Trade, Environment and Development, Third Session, Geneva, November 6, 1995, p. 13.

40. WTO, "Background Document," WTO High Level Symposium on Trade and Environment, Geneva, March 15–16, 1999, p. 16.

41. World Trade Organization, "WTO Trade and Environment Committee Discusses Proposals on Trade Measures in Multilateral Environmental Agreements and on Eco-Labelling," *Trade and Environment*, no. 8 (April 29, 1996), pp. 8–11.

42. World Wide Fund for Nature, "The WTO Committee on Trade and Environment—Is It Serious?" December 1996. [Internet: http://www.panda.org/resources/publications/sustainability/wto/intro.htm]

43. Seung Wha Chang, "GATTing a Green Trade Barrier: Eco-Labelling and the WTO Agreement on Technical Barriers to Trade," *Journal of World Trade* 31 (1997), pp. 137–159.

44. See World Trade Organization, Committee on Trade and Environment, *Environmental Benefits of Removing Trade Restrictions and Distortions: Note by the Secretariat* (Geneva: WTO, 1997); Gareth Porter, *Fisheries Subsidies, Overfishing and Trade* (Geneva: United Nations Environment Programme, 1998).

45. The Cairns Group's members are Canada, Australia, New Zealand, Thailand, Indonesia, Malaysia, the Philippines, Argentina, Brazil, Colombia, Chile, Uruguay, Fiji, and Hungary.

46. Stephen J. Kobrin, "The MAI and the Clash of Globalizations," *Foreign Policy*, Fall 1998, p. 100. For a summary of the provisions of the MAI, see Stephen J. Kobrin, "The MAI and the Clash of Globalizations," p. 101; and Preamble Center, "The Multilateral Agreement on Investment: Basic Facts," briefing sheet, October 1998. [Internet: http://www.preamble.org/MAI/maifact.html]

47. Preamble Center, "The Multilateral Agreement on Investment: Basic Facts."

48. Ibid.; Mark Vallianatos, with Andrea Durbin, *License to Loot: The MAI and How to Stop It* (Washington, D.C.: Friends of the Earth, 1998); Stephen J. Kobrin, "The MAI and the Clash of Globalizations," p. 98.

49. Ibid.

50. Dirk Bryant, Daniel Nielsen, and Laura Targley, *The Last Frontier Forests: Ecosystems and Economics on the Edge* (Washington, D.C.: World Resources Institute, 1997), p. 1.

51. WRI, *World Resources 1998–99* (New York: Oxford University Press, 1998), p. 185.

52. FAO, *State of the World's Forests 1999* (Rome: FAO, 1999), p. 1.

53. FAO, *The Challenge of Sustainable Forest Management* (Rome: FAO, 1993), p. 9.

54. Eric Wakker, "Lipstick Traces in the Rainforest: Palm Oil, Crisis and Forest Loss in Indonesia: The Role of Germany" (Frankfurt, Germany: WWF Germany, 1998).

55. Bryant et al., *The Last Frontier Forests*, p. 15; Peter Dauvergne, "Globalisation and Deforestation in the Asia-Pacific," *Environmental Politics* 7, no 4 (Winter 1998), pp. 120–121; Duncan Poore, *No Timber Without Trees* (London: Earthscan, 1989); Malcolm Gillis, "The Logging Industry in Tropical Asia," in Julie Sloan Denslow and Christine Paddoch, eds., *People of the Tropical Rainforest* (Berkeley: University of California Press, 1988); K. Brown and D. W. Pearce, eds., *The Causes of Tropical Deforestation: The Economic and Statistical Analysis of Factors Giving Rise to the Loss of Tropical Forests* (London: University College Press, 1994).

56. Peter Dauvergne, "Globalisation and Deforestation in the Asia-Pacific," p. 122.

57. Ibid.

58. Ibid.

59. Malaysia demanded that industrialized countries (most of whom had long since reduced their forest cover to a small fraction of the preindustrial level) draw up national forestry action plans aimed at substantially increasing that forest cover. Intervention by Malaysian delegate to Working Group 1, PrepCom II, March 20, 1991.

60. See U.S. delegation reporting cable, "UNCED PREPCOM III: Report of Second Week," August 26, 1991.

61. David Humphreys, "The UNCED Process and International Responses to Deforestation," paper presented to the Inaugural Pan-European Conference on International Studies, Heidelberg, Germany, September 16–20, 1992, pp. 34–35.

62. Malaysia openly charged that industrialized countries were using the issue of conserving tropical forests to prevent rapidly industrializing countries from achieving developed-country status. Claude Smadja, "Malaysia: Objective 2020," *World Link* (Geneva), no. 3 (1991), pp. 26–29.

63. *Earth Summit Update*, no. 8 (April 1992), p. 7.

64. Jag Maini, "Introduction," in A. J. Grayson and W. B. Maynard, *The World's Forests—Rio+5: International Initiatives Towards Sustainable Management* (Oxford: Commonwealth Forestry Association, 1997), p. ix. Also see David Humphreys, "The Global Politics of Forest Conservation Since the UNCED," *Environmental Politics* 5, no. 2 (Summer 1996), pp. 231–256.

65. For a summary of the international initiatives in support of the IPF process, see A. J. Grayson and W. B. Maynard, *The World's Forests—Rio+5: International Initiatives Towards Sustainable Management* (Oxford: Commonwealth Forestry Association, 1997), pp. 29–46.

66. The IPF's report to the Commission on Sustainable Development (E/CN.17/1997/12) can be found on-line: [Internet: http://www.un.org/documents/ecosoc/cn17/1997/ecn171997-12.htm].

67. *Practitioner's Guide to the Implementation of the IPF Proposals for Action*, prepared by the Six Country Initiative in Support of the UN *Ad Hoc* Intergovernmental Forum on Forests, 2nd rev. ed., May 1999.

68. Cheri Sugal, "Labeling Wood: How Timber Certification May Reduce Deforestation," *World Watch*, September–October 1996, p. 34.

69. See the Asia Pulp and Paper WWW site: [Internet: http://www.asiapulppaper.com/environ.htm].

70. "Final Report of the Intergovernmental Panel on Forests on Its Fourth Session," E/CN.17/1997/12, March 20, 1997. [Available on-line: http://www.un.org/esa/documents/esc/cn17/ipf/session4/ecn17ipf1997-12.htm]

71. "Forest Certification Hits 15 Million Hectares Worldwide," Environment News Service, January 27, 1999.

72. "Eco-Worries Undercut Tropical Timber Market," Environment News Service, November 2, 1999.

73. Bruce Gilley, "Westerners' Calls for Labelling of Forest-Friendly Wood Imports Are Putting Pressure on Asian Timber Producers," *Far Eastern Economic Review*, January 14, 1999.

74. "Agreement for Collaboration on Forestry Standards and Certification in Malaysia," March 13, 1999. [Internet: http://www.fscoax.org/not/noteng/not8.htm]

75. See "Americans, Canadians at Odds over 'Sustainable Forestry' Plan," *Ottawa Citizen*, February 1, 1997.

76. "The Sustainable Management of Forests," prepared in connection with Canada's participation at the meeting of the United Nations Commission on Sustainable Development, April 1997, p. 9. The same point is included in the Cana-

dian pulp and paper industry's list of elements of a forest convention: "Sustaining the Earth's Forests: A Canadian Pulp and Paper Association Statement to IPF-III," no date.

77. NGO briefings on developments in IPF and the convention on biodiversity at BIONET, January 26, 1996, and December 5, 1996.

78. See Henson Moore, President of the American Forest and Paper Association, quoted in the *Ottawa Citizen*, February 1, 1997.

79. Scott Paul, "Forest Convention Withers at Earth Summit II." Amsterdam: Friends of the Earth International, 1997.

80. "Summary of the Nineteenth United Nations General Assembly Special Session to Review Implementation of Agenda 21: 23–27 June 1997," *Earth Negotiations Bulletin* 5, no. 88 (June 30, 1997), pp. 5–6; David Humphreys, "The Report of the Intergovernmental Panel on Forests," pp. 219–220.

81. "Summary of the Fourth Session of the Intergovernmental Forum on Forests: 31 January–11 February 2000," *Earth Negotiations Bulletin* 13, no. 66 (February 14, 2000). See also the Report of the Fourth Session of the Intergovernmental Forum on Forests, E/CN.17/IFF/2000/L.1 and Add.1–7.

82. This definition of "criteria and indicators" is taken from FAO, *State of the World's Forests 1999*, p. 86.

83. These seven initiatives include the International Tropical Timber Organization (ITTO), covering the 28 tropical timber producing members of ITTO; the Helsinki Process, covering temperate, boreal, and Mediterranean forests of 37 European countries (including the Russian Federation) and the European Union; the Montreal Process, covering temperate and boreal forests in 12 non-European countries; the Tarapoto Proposal, covering tropical forests in the eight member countries of the Amazon Cooperation Treaty; the Dry-Zone Africa Process, for dry-zone forests in 28 sub-Saharan countries; the Near East Process, for dry-zone forests in 30 Near East countries; and the Central American Process of Lepaterique, covering all types of forests in the seven member countries of the Central American Commission on Environment and Development and Cuba. For more information about these processes, see A. J. Grayson and W. B. Maynard, *The World's Forests*, pp. 51–81.

84. FAO, *State of the World's Forests 1999*, p. 87.

85. See, for example, Daniel C. Esty, "The Case for a Global Environmental Organization," in Peter B. Kenen (ed.), *Managing the World Economy: Fifty Years After Bretton Woods* (Washington, D.C.: Institute for International Economics, 1994).

□ □ □

Suggested Readings

Agarwal, Anil, Sunita Narain, and Anju Sharma (eds.). *Green Politics: Global Negotiations*, Vol. 1. New Delhi: Center for Science and Environment, 1999.

Barnes, James N., Ellen Grosman, and Walter V. Reid. *Bankrolling Successes: A Portfolio of Sustainable Development Projects*. Washington, D.C.: Friends of the Earth and the National Wildlife Federation, 1995.

Benedick, Richard Elliott. *Ozone Diplomacy*. Cambridge: Harvard University Press, 1991.

Birnie, Patricia W., and Alan E. Boyle. *International Law and the Environment*. New York: Oxford University Press, 1992.

Bodansky, Daniel. "The United Nations Framework Convention on Climate Change: A Commentary." *Yale Journal of International Law* 18, no. 2 (Summer 1993): 451–558.

Brack, Duncan. *International Trade and the Montreal Protocol*. London: Earthscan, 1996.

Bramble, Barbara, J., and Gareth Porter. "Non-Governmental Organizations and the Making of U.S. International Environmental Policy," in Andrew Murrell and Benedict Kinsbury (eds.), *The International Politics of the Environment: Actors, Interests and Institutions*. New York: Oxford University Press, 1992.

Brown, Lester R., et al. *State of the World 1999: A Worldwatch Institute Report on Progress Toward a Sustainable Society*. New York: W. W. Norton, 1999. (Published annually since 1984.)

Bryner, Gary C. *From Promises to Performance: Achieving Global Environmental Goals*. New York: W. W. Norton, 1997.

Caldwell, Lynton Keith. *International Environmental Policy: From the 20th Century to the 21st Century*. Durham, N.C.: Duke University Press, 1996.

Caldwell, Lynton Keith, and Robert V. Bartlett. *Environmental Policy: Transnational Issues and National Trends*. Westport, Conn.: Quorum Books, 1997.

Carroll, John E. (ed.). *International Environmental Diplomacy: The Management and Resolution of Transfrontier Environmental Problems*. Cambridge: Cambridge University Press, 1988.

Carson, Rachel. *Silent Spring*. Boston: Houghton Mifflin, 1987.

Chasek, Pamela S. "The Convention to Combat Desertification: Lessons Learned for Sustainable Development." *Journal of Environment and Development* 6, No. 2 (June 1997).

_____. "A Comparative Analysis of Multilateral Environmental Negotiations." *Group Decision and Negotiation* 6, No. 5 (September 1997).

255

Chasek, Pamela S. (ed.). *The Global Environment in the 21st Century: Prospects for International Cooperation*. Tokyo: UNU Press, 2000.

Chatterjee, Pratap, and Matthias Singer. *The Earth Brokers*. London and New York: Routledge, 1994.

Choucri, Nazli (ed.). *Global Accord: Environmental Challenges and International Responses*. Cambridge, Mass.: MIT Press, 1993.

Colby, Michael E. *The Evolution of Paradigms of Environmental Management in Development*. Washington, D.C.: Policy Planning and Research Staff, World Bank, 1989.

Conca, Ken, and Geoffrey D. Dabelko (eds.). *Green Planet Blues: Environmental Politics from Stockholm to Kyoto*, 2nd edition. Boulder, Colo.: Westview Press: 1998.

Cruz, Wilfrido, and Robert Repetto. *The Environmental Effects of Stabilization and Structural Adjustment Programs: The Philippines Case*. Washington, D.C.: World Resources Institute, 1992.

Daly, Herman E., and John B. Cobb. *For the Common Good: Redirecting the Economy Toward Community, the Environment and a Sustainable Future*. Boston: Beacon Press, 1989.

Dauvergne, Peter. *Shadows in the Forest : Japan and the Politics of Timber in Southeast Asia*. Cambridge, Mass.: MIT Press, 1997.

_____. "Globalisation and Deforestation in the Asia-Pacific." *Environmental Politics* 7, no. 4 (Winter 1998): 114–135.

Depledge, Joanna. "Coming of Age at Buenos Aires: The Climate Change Regime After Kyoto." *Environment* 41, no. 7 (September 1999): 15–20.

Dodds, Felix (ed.). *The Way Forward: Beyond Agenda 21*. London: Earthscan, 1997.

Ehrlich, Paul R., and Anne H. Ehrlich. *The Population Explosion*. New York: Simon and Schuster, 1990.

Esty, Daniel. *Greening the GATT*. Washington, D.C.: Institute for International Economics, 1994.

Fisher, Julie. *The Road from Rio: Sustainable Development and the Non-Governmental Movement in the Third World*. Westport, Conn., and London: Praeger, 1993.

Flavin, Christopher, and Nicholas Lanssen. *Power Surge: Guide to the Coming Energy Revolution*. New York: W. W. Norton, 1994.

French, Hilary F. "Making Environmental Treaties Work." *Scientific American*, December 1994, pp. 62–65.

_____. *Partnership for the Planet: An Environmental Agenda for the United Nation*, Worldwatch Paper No. 126. Washington, D.C.: Worldwatch, 1995.

Gleick, Peter H. (ed.). *Water in Crises: A Guide to the World's Freshwater Resources*. New York: Oxford University Press, 1993.

Glowka, Lyle, Françoise Burhenne-Guilmin, and Hugh Synge. *A Guide to the Convention on Biological Diversity*. Gland, Switzerland: IUCN, 1994.

Gore, Al. *Earth in the Balance: Ecology and the Human Spirit*. Boston: Houghton Mifflin, 1992.

Grubb, Michael, et al. *The "Earth Summit" Agreements: A Guide and Assessment*. London: Earthscan, 1993.

Gupta, Joyeeta. *The Climate Change Convention and Developing Countries: From Conflict to Consensus?* Boston: Kluwer Academic, 1997.

Haas, Ernst. *When Knowledge Is Power*. Berkeley: University of California Press, 1990.

Haas, Peter M. *Saving the Mediterranean: The Politics of International Environmental Cooperation*. New York: Columbia University Press, 1990.

Haas, Peter M., Robert O. Keohane, and Marc A. Levy (eds.). *Institutions for the Earth*. Cambridge, Mass.: MIT Press, 1993.

Hampson, Fen Osler. "Climate Change: Building International Coalitions of the Like-Minded." *International Journal* 45, no. 1 (Winter 1989–1990):36–74.

Hampson, Fen Osler, and Michael Hart. *Multilateral Negotiations: Lessons from Arms Control, Trade and the Environment*. Baltimore: Johns Hopkins University Press, 1995.

Hempel, Lamont C. *Environmental Governance: The Global Challenge*. Washington, D.C.: Island Press, 1996.

Homer-Dixon, Thomas, J. Boutwell, and G. W. Rathgens. "Environmental Change and Violent Conflict." *Scientific American*, February 1993, pp. 38–45.

Houghton, Richard A., and George M. Woodwell. "Global Climatic Change." *Scientific American*, April 1989, pp. 36–44.

Humphreys, David. "The Global Politics of Forest Conservation Since the UNCED." *Environmental Politics* 5, no. 2 (Summer 1996): 231–256.

Hurrell, Andrew, and Benedict Kingsbury (eds.). *The International Politics of the Environment: Actors, Interests and Institutions*. New York: Oxford University Press, 1992.

Imber, Mark F. *Environmental Security and UN Reform*. New York: St. Martin's Press, 1994.

Kelly, Michael J. "Overcoming Obstacles to the Effective Implementation of International Environmental Agreements." *Georgetown International Environmental Law Review* 9, no. 2 (1997): 447–488.

Keohane, Robert O., and Marc A. Levy (eds.). *Institutions for Environmental Aid*. Cambridge, Mass.: MIT Press, 1996.

Kimball, Lee A. *Forging International Agreements: Strengthening Intergovernmental Institutions for Environment and Development*. Washington, D.C.: World Resources Institute, 1992.

Klare, Michael T., and Yogesh Chandrani (eds.). *World Security: Trends and Challenges for a New Century*. New York: St. Martin's Press, 1998.

Krueger, Jonathan. *International Trade and the Basel Convention*. London: Earthscan, 1999.

Latin American and Caribbean Commission on Development and Environment. *Our Own Agenda*. Washington, D.C., and New York: Inter-American Development Bank and United Nations Development Programme, 1990.

MacNeill, Jim, Peter Winsemius, and Taizo Yakushiji. *Beyond Interdependence: Meshing of the World's Economy and the Earth's Ecology*. New York: Oxford University Press, 1991.

Mathews, Jessica Tuchman. "Redefining Security." *Foreign Affairs* 68 (Spring 1989): 162–177.

McConnell, Fiona. *The Biodiversity Convention: A Negotiating History*. London: Kluwer Law International, 1996.

Meadows, Donella H., et al. *The Limits to Growth*. New York: Universe Books, 1972.

Miller, Marian A. L. *The Third World in Global Environmental Politics*. Boulder, Colo.: Lynne Rienner, 1995.

Mintzer, Irving M., and J. A. Leonard (eds.). *Negotiating Climate Change: The Inside Story of the Rio Convention*. Cambridge: Cambridge University Press, 1994.

Mitchell, Ronald B. *Intentional Oil Pollution at Sea: Environmental Policy and Treaty Compliance*. Cambridge, Mass.: MIT Press, 1994.

Muñoz, Heraldo, and Robin Rosenberg (eds.). *Difficult Liaison: Trade and the Environment in the Americas*. New Brunswick, N.J.: Transaction Books, 1993.

Orr, David W., and Marvin S. Soroos. *The Global Predicament: Ecological Perspectives on World Order*. Chapel Hill: University of North Carolina Press, 1979.

Ostrom, Elinor. *Governing the Commons: The Evolution of Institutions for Collective Action*. New York: Cambridge University Press, 1990.

Parker, Richard. "The Use and Abuse of Trade Leverage to Protect the Global Commons: What We Can Learn from the Tuna-Dolphin Conflict." *Georgetown Environmental Law Review* 12 (1999): 1–123.

Paterson, Matthew. *Global Warming and Global Politics*. London and New York: Routledge, 1996.

Porter, Gareth. *Fishing Subsidies, Overfishing and Trade*. Geneva: UNEP, 1998.

Postel, Sandra. *Pillar of Sand: Can the Irrigation Miracle Last?* New York: W. W. Norton, 1999.

Princen, Thomas, and Matthias Finger. *Environmental NGOs in World Politics: Linking the Local and the Global*. New York: Routledge, 1994.

Raustiala, Kal. "States, NGOs and International Environmental Institutions." *International Studies Quarterly* 41 (1997), pp. 719–740.

Repetto, Robert. *Trade and Sustainable Development*. Geneva: United Nations Environment Programme, 1994.

Repetto, Robert, et al. *Accounts Overdue: Natural Resources Depreciation in Costa Rica*. Washington, D.C.: World Resources Institute, 1991.

_____. *Mortgaging the Earth: The World Bank, Environmental Impoverishment, and the Crisis of Development*. Boston: Beacon Press, 1994.

Runge, C. Ford, with Francois Ortalo-Magne and Philip Vande Kamp. *Freer Trade, Protected Environment*. New York: Council on Foreign Relations Press, 1994.

Sand, Peter H. *Lessons Learned in Global Environmental Governance*. Washington, D.C.: World Resources Institute, 1990.

Sandbrook, Richard. "UNGASS Has Run Out of Steam." *International Affairs* 73, no. 4 (1997): 641–654.

Sands, Phillippe (ed.). *Greening International Laws*. London: Earthscan, 1993.

Schmidheiny, Stephan, with the Business Council for Sustainable Development. *Changing Course: A Global Business Perspective on Development and the Environment*. Cambridge, Mass.: MIT Press, 1992.

Shabecoff, Philip. *A New Name for Peace: International Environmentalism, Sustainable Development and Democracy*. Hanover, N.H.: University Press of New England, 1996.

Simmons, P. J. "Learning to Live with NGOs." *Foreign Policy*, Fall 1998, pp. 82–96.

Sjostedt, Gunnar (ed.). *International Environmental Negotiation*. Newbury Park, Calif.: Sage, 1993.

Sjostedt, Gunnar, et al. (eds.). *Negotiating International Regimes: Lessons Learned from the United Nations Conference on Environment and Development*. London: Graham and Trotman, 1994.

Srinivasan, T. N. *Developing Countries and the Multilateral Trading System: From the GATT to the Uruguay Round and the Future*. Boulder, Colo.: Westview Press, 1998.

Susskind, Lawrence E. *Environmental Diplomacy: Negotiating More Effective Global Agreements*. New York: Oxford University Press, 1994.

Susskind, Lawrence E., Eric Jay Dolin, and J. William Breslin. *International Environmental Treaty-Making*. Cambridge: Harvard Law School Program on Negotiation, 1992.

Swanson, Timothy. *Global Action for Biodiversity*. London: Earthscan, 1997.

Thomas, Caroline. *The Environment in International Relations*. London: Royal Institute of International Affairs, 1992.

Tolba, Mostafa K. *Global Environmental Diplomacy: Negotiating Environmental Agreements for the World, 1973–1992*. Cambridge, Mass.: MIT Press, 1998.

United Nations Development Programme. *Human Development Report 1999*. New York: Oxford University Press, 1999 (Published annually.)

United Nations Environment Programme. *Register of International Treaties and Other Agreements in the Field of the Environment*. Nairobi: UNEP, 1991.

_____. *UNEP's New Way Forward: Environmental Law and Sustainable Development*. Nairobi: UNEP, 1995.

UNFPA. *The State of World Population, 1998*. New York: United Nations Population Fund, 1998. (Published annually since 1978.)

Victor, David G., Kal Raustiala, and Eugene B. Skolnikoff (eds.). *The Implementation and Effectiveness of International Environmental Commitments*. Cambridge, Mass.: MIT Press, 1998.

Vig, Norman J., and Regina S. Axelrod (eds.). *The Global Environment: Institutions, Law and Policy*. Washington, D.C.: Congressional Quarterly Press, 1999.

Vogler, John, and Mark F. Imber (eds.). *The Environment and International Relations*. New York: Routledge, 1996.

Weiss, Edith Brown, and Harold K. Jacobson. "Getting Countries to Comply with International Agreements." *Environment*, 41, no. 6 (July–August 1999): 16–20, 37–45.

Weiss, Edith Brown, and Harold K. Jacobson (eds.). *Engaging Countries: Strengthening Compliance with International Environmental Accords*. Cambridge, Mass.: MIT Press, 1998.

Weiss, Edith Brown, Daniel B. Magraw, and Paul C. Szasz. *International Environmental Law: Basic Instruments and References*. Dobbs Ferry, N.Y.: Transnational, 1992.

Werksman, Jacob (ed.). *Greening International Institutions*. London: Earthscan, 1996.

Williams, Marc, and Lucy Ford. "The World Trade Organisation, Social Movements and Global Environmental Management." *Environmental Politics* 8, no. 1: 268–289.

Wilson, E. O. (ed.). *Biodiversity*. Washington, D.C.: National Academy of Sciences Press, 1988.

World Commission on Environment and Development. *Our Common Future*. New York: Oxford University Press, 1987.

World Resources Institute. *World Resources, 1998–99,* New York: Oxford University Press, 1998. (Published biennially since 1990.)

Young, Oran R. *International Cooperation: Building Regimes for Natural Resources and the Environment.* Ithaca: Cornell University Press, 1989.

_____. *International Governance: Protecting the Environment in a Stateless Society.* Ithaca: Cornell University Press, 1994.

Young, Oran R., and Gail Osherenko (eds.). *Polar Politics: Creating International Environmental Regimes.* Ithaca: Cornell University Press, 1993.

List of Internet Resources

The following list of Internet resources does not represent a comprehensive list of all resources related to global environmental politics. Instead, the list below consists of organizations mentioned in this book and their Internet addresses that are in use as of the date of publication. All Internet addresses are subject to change at any time.

Antarctic and Southern Ocean Coalition:

http://www.asoc.org/

Asia-Pacific Economic Cooperation:

http://www.apec.org

Asian Development Bank:

http://www.adb.org/

Bank Watch:

http://www.bankwatch.org/

**Basel Convention on the Control of
Transboundary Movements of Hazardous
Wastes and Their Disposal:**

http://www.basel.int/

**Central American Commission
on Environment and Development:**

http://www.sicanet.org.sv/ccad/

Climate Action Network:

http://www.climatenetwork.org

COICA:

http://www.satnet.net/coica/

Commission for the Conservation of Antarctic Living Marine Resources:

http://www.ccamlr.org/

Conservation International:

http://www.conservation.org/

Convention on Migratory Species:

http://www.wcmc.org.uk/cms/

Convention on Biological Diversity:

http://www.biodiv.org

Convention on Long-Range Transboundary Air Pollution:

http://www.unece.org/env/rtap/

Convention on Trade in Endangered Species:

http://www.cites.org

Convention to Combat Desertification:

http://www.unccd.de

Environmental Defense:

http://www.edf.org/

Environmental Treaties and Resource Indicators:

http://sedac.ciesin.org/pidb/pidb-home.html

European Environment Bureau:

http://www.eeb.org/

Food and Agriculture Organization:

http://www.fao.org

**Framework Convention
on Climate Change:**

http://www.unfccc.de

Friends of the Earth (UK):

http://www.foe.co.uk/

Friends of the Earth (U.S.):

http://www.foe.org

**Friends of the Earth
International:**

http://www.foei.org

Global Climate Coalition:

http://www.globalclimate.org/

Global Environment Facility:

http://www.gefweb.org/

Greenpeace International:

http://www.greenpeace.org

**INC for a Convention on
Persistent Organic Pollutants:**

http://irptc.unep.ch/pops/

Inter-American Development Bank:

http://www.iadb.org/

Intergovernmental Panel on Climate Change:

http://www.ipcc.ch/

International Chamber of Commerce:

http://www.iccwbo.org/

**International Institute for
Environment and Development:**

http://www.iied.org/

**International Institute for
Sustainable Development:**

http://iisd.ca/

International Marine Forum:

http://www.ocimf.com/

**International Maritime
Organization:**

http://www.imo.org/

International Monetary Fund:

http://www.imf.org/

**International Tropical
Timber Organization:**

http://www.itto.or.jp/

**International Union for
the Conservation of Nature:**

http://www.iucn.org

International Whaling Commission:

http://ourworld.compuserve.com/homepages/iwcoffice/

Linkages/Earth Negotiations Bulletin (IISD):

http://www.iisd.ca/linkages/

Montreal Protocol:

http://www.unep.ch/ozone/

**Multilateral Fund for the Implementation
of the Montreal Protocol:**

http://www.unmfs.org/

National Audubon Society:

http://www.audubon.org/

National Wildlife Federation:

http://www.nwf.org

Natural Resources Defense Council:

http://www.nrdc.org

**NGO Steering Committee for
the Commission on Sustainable Development:**

http://www.igc.org/csdngo/

**Organization for Economic
Cooperation and Development:**

http://www.oecd.org

Organization of African Unity:

http://www.oau-oua.org/

**Ramsar Convention on Wetlands
of International Importance:**

http://www.ramsar.org

Sierra Club:

http://www.sierraclub.org/

**South Pacific Regional
Environment Programme:**

http://www.sprep.org.ws/

Stockholm Environment Institute:

http://www.sei.se/

TRAFFIC:

http://www.traffic.org/

United Nations:

http://www.un.org

United Nations Commission on Sustainable Development (CSD):

http://www.un.org/esa/sustdev/csd.htm

United Nations Development Programme (UNDP):

http://www.undp.org

United Nations Development Programme Sustainable Energy and Environment Division:

http://www.undp.org/seed/

United Nations Division for Ocean Affairs and the Law of the Sea:

http://www.un.org/Depts/los/index.htm

United Nations Environment Programme (UNEP):

http://www.unep.org

United Nations Environment Programme (UNEP)— Geneva Executive Center:

http://www.unep.ch

Women's Environment and Development Organization:

http://www.wedo.org

World Bank:

http://www.worldbank.org

World Business Council for

Sustainable Development:

http://www.wbcsd.ch/

World Health Organization:

http://www.who.org

World Heritage Convention:

http://www.unesco.org/whc/

World Resources Institute:

http://www.wri.org

World Trade Organization:

http://www.wto.org

Worldwide Fund for Nature International:

http://www.panda.org/

World Wildife Fund (U.S.):

http://www.worldwildlife.org/

Glossary

Acid rain is precipitation that deposits nitric or sulfuric acids on the earth, buildings, and vegetation.

Biodiversity (or **biological diversity**) is the variety of organisms, including species of plants and animals, genetic variation within individual species, and diversity of ecosystems.

Biosafety refers to a set of precautionary practices to ensure the safe transfer, handling, use, and disposal of living modified organisms derived from modern biotechnology.

Biosphere refers to the earth's land, water, atmosphere, and living things, or to a particular zone of the whole.

Biotechnology is the branch of molecular biology that studies the use of microorganisms to perform specific industrial processes.

A **blocking** or **veto state** is one that by virtue of its importance on a particular environmental issue is able to block or weaken international agreement.

Boreal forests are those lying between arctic tundra to the north and warmer temperate forests to the south.

Bretton Woods institutions are the international financial institutions, such as the World Bank, the International Monetary Fund, and the International Finance Corporation, named after the New Hampshire resort at which they were negotiated.

CAFE standards are the Corporate Average Fuel Economy standards, a measure of fuel efficiency, imposed on U.S. auto manufacturers and importers of cars since 1975.

Certification and Labeling is the process of inspecting particular forests or woodlands to see if they are being managed according to an agreed-on set of principles and criteria, and labeling them as such.

Civil society refers to an array of private-sector institutions such as trade unions, business associations, environmental and development organizations, women's and youth groups, cooperatives, and religious groups having an interest in public policy issues and decisions.

Climate change refers to the likelihood of increased change in the average weather over a period of time (usually 30 or more years) from natural causes (e.g., ice ages brought on by changes in the earth's orbit around the sun) or as the result of human intervention (e.g., through the release of carbon dioxide and other greenhouse gases).

The **commons** are the natural resources and vital life support services that belong to all humankind rather than to any one country.

A **convention** is a multilateral legal agreement and the most common form of legal instrument used in agreements on international environmental issues.

Desertification is the deterioration of the biological potential of land from a combination of adverse climate and excessive human exploitation, leading ultimately to desertlike conditions.

Environmental accounting involves various methods of figuring national income accounts that assign value to resources such as soil, water, forests, and minerals and therefore reflect more accurately in the accounting system the depletion of natural resources and the degradation of natural systems.

Environmental services are the conserving or restorative functions of nature, for example, the ability of plants to convert carbon dioxide to oxygen, the ability of marshlands to cleanse polluted waters, or the capacity of a vegetation-covered floodplain to dissipate the destructive power of a river in flood.

The **exclusionist paradigm** (also known as *frontier economics*) is the dominant social paradigm in contemporary societies and holds that humans are not subject to natural laws in their use of natural resources and systems for economic purposes.

Exclusive economic zones (EEZs) are the 200-mile-wide (320-kilometer-wide) territorial waters under the jurisdiction of individual nations.

A **framework convention** is a multilateral agreement that establishes common principles but does not include binding commitments to specific actions.

The **General Agreement on Tariffs and Trade** (GATT) is the multilateral agreement governing the world trading system.

Global commons are the natural resources and vital life-support services, such as the earth's climate system, ozone layer, and oceans and seas, that belong to all humankind rather than to any one country or private enterprise.

Global warming refers to the apparent trend of increasing temperatures on the world's surface and in the lower atmosphere, believed to be caused by the entrapment of heat due to the buildup of certain gases (see **greenhouse effect**).

The **greenhouse effect** occurs when certain gases—mainly carbon dioxide, ground-level ozone, chlorofluorocarbons (CFCs), and halons, methane, and nitrous oxide—build up in the atmosphere.

Green taxes include a variety of measures that would penalize practices that pollute or degrade the environment or encourage excessive use or waste of a valuable natural resource or service.

Gross world product is the value of the total goods and services produced in the world annually.

The **Group of Eight** (or **G-8**) industrialized nations includes the United States, Canada, the United Kingdom, Japan, Germany, France, Italy, and Russia.

The **Group of Seven** (or **G-7**) includes the seven industrialized democracies: the United States, Canada, Japan, the United Kingdom, France, Germany, and Italy.

The **Group of 77** is a coalition of developing countries (numbering more than 130) that has pressed for reform of North-South economic structures since the mid-1970s.

A **hegemonic power** is a state that is able to set the primary rules of an international system, usually through a combination of military and economic power.

Intellectual property rights (IPR) are the rights of businesses, individuals, or states to legal protection of their discoveries and inventions.

Intergenerational equity is a norm of state behavior that calls for giving adequate consideration to the interests of future generations in the enjoyment of a healthy environment and natural resources.

International financial institutions are international organizations such as the World Bank, the regional development banks, the International Monetary Fund, and the International Finance Corporation, which are also known as the **Bretton Woods institutions.**

An **international regime** is a set of norms or rules of behavior, usually based on an international agreement, governing particular issues in world politics.

Joint implementation (JI) refers to a provision of the climate convention that allows parties to implement their commitments jointly with another state—the expectation being that an industrialized country would provide a developing country with financial or technical assistance.

The **Law of the Sea** was adopted in December 1982 by the Third United Nations Conference on the Law of the Sea. The Convention comprises 320 articles and nine annexes, governing all aspects of ocean space, such as delimitation, environmental control, marine scientific research, economic and commercial activities, transfer of technology, and the settlement of disputes relating to ocean matters. The Convention entered into force on November 16, 1994.

A **lead state** is one that sponsors and asserts leadership on behalf of the most advanced proposal for international regulation on an environmental issue.

Neoclassical economics is a school of economic theory maintaining that free markets will always allocate resources so as to satisfy the greatest number of people.

The **New International Economic Order** is the list of demands made in the 1970s by the Group of 77 developing nations for changes in the structure of North-South economic relations. The list is still in effect.

Nontariff barriers are trade barriers, other than tariffs, erected by a government to discourage imports, for example, quotas (both formal and "voluntary"), outright prohibition of specific imports (such as the Japanese refusal to import rice), discriminatory restrictions, or licensing requirements.

The **ozone layer** is the concentration of ozone in the stratosphere, between 15 and 50 kilometers (9.3 and 31 miles) above the earth's surface, depending on latitude, season, and other factors.

Paradigm refers to a set of assumptions about reality that define and often limit the scope of inquiry in any field of knowledge.

A **protocol** is a multilateral agreement providing detailed, specific commitments attached to a convention.

Soft law refers to nonbinding documents drawn up by international bodies that establish norms; these documents can take on the force of law through customary practice.

The **Stockholm Conference** (the United Nations Conference on the Human Environment, 1972) was the first worldwide conference of nations devoted to environmental problems.

A **supporting state** is one that is willing to publicly support and work for the most far-reaching proposal for international regulation on an environmental issue.

Sustainable development is a perspective on environmental management that emphasizes the need to reconcile present and future economic needs through environmental conservation.

Sustainable forest management is a process, rather than a prescribed system of forest management. Elements may include participatory and equitable approaches to decisionmaking geared toward maintaining ecosystem and landscape functions while also meeting economic, social, and cultural needs.

A **swing state** is one that attempts to bargain for major concessions in return for acceding to a global environmental agreement.

Technology transfer is the transfer, usually from highly industrialized to less industrialized developing countries, of the means of producing scientifically or technically advanced goods in the form of patents, machinery and equipment, or the necessary scientific-technical knowledge.

Transboundary air pollution is the emission of pollutants, especially nitric and sulfuric acids, across national boundaries.

A **unitary actor model** is an explanatory concept based on the assumption that state actors can be treated as though they are a single entity with a single, internally consistent set of values and attitudes.

The **Uruguay Round** is the negotiations under the auspices of the General Agreement on Tariffs and Trade on liberalization of world trade that began in 1985 in Uruguay and ended in 1994.

A **veto coalition** is a group of veto states that forms around a given issue.

A **veto** or **blocking state** is one that by virtue of its importance on a particular environmental issue is able to block or weaken international agreement.

Chronology

1940   The Convention on Nature Protection and Wildlife Preservation in the Western Hemisphere is signed.

1946   The International Convention for the Regulation of Whaling is signed.

1954   The International Convention for the Prevention of Pollution of the Sea by Oil is signed.

1959   Antarctic Treaty is signed.

1962   Publication of Rachel Carson's *Silent Spring*.

1969   National Environmental Policy Act of 1969 (NEPA) is passed by U.S. Congress.

1972   *The Limits to Growth* report for the Club of Rome is published.

1972   The United Nations Conference on the Human Environment is convened in Stockholm.

1972   Creation of the United Nations Environment Programme (UNEP).

1972   The Convention on the Prevention of Marine Pollution by Dumping of Wastes and Other Matter (or London Convention) is signed.

1972   Convention Concerning the Protection of the World Cultural and Natural Heritage is signed.

1972   Convention for the Conservation of Antarctic Seals is signed.

1973   The International Convention for the Prevention of Pollution from Ships (MARPOL) is signed.

1973   The Convention on International Trade in Endangered Species (CITES) is signed.

1973   U.S. Endangered Species Conservation Act banning whaling and whale imports becomes law.

1974   Declaration on the Establishment of a New International Economic Order (NIEO) is issued by the Sixth Special Session of the United Nations General Assembly.

1977   Ad Hoc Conference of Experts convened by UNEP approves the World Plan of Action on the Ozone Layer.

1979   The Convention on Long-Range Transboundary Air Pollution
        (LRTAP) is signed.
1979   First World Climate Conference in Geneva warns of danger of
        global warming.
1980   World Conservation Strategy launched by IUCN and UNEP.
1980   *Global 2000 Report to the President* is published.
1980   Convention on the Conservation of Antarctic Marine Living
        Resources (CCAMLR) is signed.
1982   Negotiations sponsored by UNEP begin on protection of the
        ozone layer.
1982   The United Nations Convention on the Law of the Sea
        (UNCLOS) is signed.
1982   Phase-out of commercial whaling over a three-year period is
        passed by the International Whaling Commission (IWC).
1984   International Tropical Timber Agreement (ITTA) is signed.
1985   The Helsinki Protocol to the LRTAP is signed, committing the
        signatories to reduce sulfur dioxide emissions.
1985   The Vienna Convention for the Protection of the Ozone Layer is
        signed.
1985   London Convention meeting of the parties votes to ban all
        further dumping of low-level radioactive wastes in oceans until
        it is proven safe.
1985   Conference of climate experts in Villach, Austria, produces
        consensus on serious possibility of global warming.
1985   Tropical Forestry Action Plan (TFAP) is approved by donor
        countries at a conference in The Hague.
1985   Montreal Guidelines for the Protection of the Marine
        Environment from Land-Based Sources are signed.
1986   Major explosion at the Soviet nuclear plant in Chernobyl spreads
        radioactive cloud across Western Europe and Japan.
1987   International Tropical Timber Organization (ITTO) holds first
        meeting in Yokohama, Japan.
1987   The Montreal Protocol on Substances That Deplete the Ozone
        Layer is signed.
1987   The Report of the World Commission on Environment and
        Development (the Brundtland Report) is published as *Our
        Common Future.*
1988   British scientists issue report on dramatic decrease in ozone layer
        over Antarctica; Ozone Trends Panel report documents ozone-
        layer decreases in Northern Hemisphere.
1988   The Sofia Protocol to the LRTAP is signed, committing the
        signatories to reduce nitrogen oxide emissions.

1988   Convention on the Regulation of Antarctic Mineral Resources Activities (CRAMRA) is signed in Wellington, New Zealand.

1988   Intergovernmental Panel on Climate Change (IPCC) is established by WMO and UNEP.

1989   Communiqué of the Group of Seven (G-7) heads of industrial democracies focuses on global environment.

1989   Twenty-four nations issue The Hague Declaration on the Environment.

1989   The Basel Convention on the Control of Transboundary Movements of Hazardous Wastes and Their Disposal is signed; the European Community reaches agreement with ACP (Africa, the Caribbean, and the Pacific) states to ban hazardous waste exports to countries without the capacity to dispose of them safely.

1989   Ministerial Conference on Atmospheric Pollution and Climate Change issues the Noordwijk Declaration, in the Netherlands, calling for stabilization of carbon dioxide emissions by 2000.

1989   Seventh CITES conference votes to ban trade in African elephant ivory products.

1990   Second meeting of the parties to the Montreal Protocol convenes in London to strengthen the Montreal Protocol.

1990   Communiqué of G-7 heads of state summit meeting in Houston calls for negotiation of an international agreement on the world's forests.

1990   Bergen Ministerial Declaration on Sustainable Development in the Economic Commission for Europe (ECE) calls stabilization of carbon dioxide emissions the first step.

1990   Meeting of Antarctic Treaty Consultative Parties (ATCPs) in Santiago, Chile, agrees to begin negotiations on a convention for environmental protection of Antarctica.

1990   Ban on whaling extended by the International Whaling Commission.

1991   Protocol on Environmental Protection to the Antarctic Treaty is signed.

1992   United Nations Conference on Environment and Development is convened in Rio de Janeiro.

1992   Convention on Climate Change is signed at Rio de Janeiro.

1992   Convention on Biological Diversity is signed at Rio de Janeiro.

1993   Central American Forest Treaty is signed.

1993   United Nations Conference on Straddling and Highly Migratory Fish Stocks is convened.

1994   International Convention to Combat Desertification is signed.

1994   United Nations Convention on the Law of the Sea enters into force.

1994   GATT Uruguay Round concludes negotiations in Marrakesh, Morocco.

1995   Agreement on the Conservation and Management of Straddling Fish Stocks and Highly Migratory Fish Stocks is signed.

1995   World Trade Organization is established.

1996   International Convention to Combat Desertification enters into force.

1997   Montreal Amendment to the Montreal Protocol signed on the tenth anniversary of the Protocol.

1997   UN General Assembly Special Session convenes in New York to review the implementation of Agenda 21.

1997   Tenth CITES conference votes to reopen the ivory trade in Botswana, Namibia, and Zimbabwe.

1997   Kyoto Protocol to the Framework Convention on Climate Change is signed.

1998   Protocols on Heavy Metals and Persistent Organic Pollutants to the Long-Range Transboundary Air Pollution Convention are signed.

1998   Convention on the Prior Informed Consent Procedure for Certain Hazardous Chemicals and Pesticides in International Trade is signed.

1998   Negotiations begin on a Legally Binding Instrument for Implementing International Action on Certain Persistent Organic Pollutants.

1999   First legal sale of ivory in a decade takes place in Windhoek, Namibia.

1999   Delegates postpone adoption of a Biosafety Protocol at an extraordinary session of the Conference of the Parties to the Convention on Biological Diversity.

1999   Protocol on Liability and Compensation to the Basel Convention on the Control of Transboundary Movements and Hazardous Wastes and Their Disposal is adopted.

1999   Protocol to Abate Acidification, Eutrophication and Ground-Level Ozone to the Long-Range Transboundary Air Pollution Convention is adopted.

2000   Cartagena Protocol on Biosafety is adopted by the Conference of the Parties to the Convention on Biological Diversity after an 11-month delay.

Index